at speed

My life in the fast lane

mark
cavendish

EBURY
PRESS

3 5 7 9 10 8 6 4 2

Published in 2013 by Ebury Press, an imprint of Ebury Publishing
A Random House Group company

The Random House Group Limited Reg. No. 954009

Addresses for companies within the Random House Group can be found at
www.randomhouse.co.uk

A CIP catalogue record for this book is available from the British Library

The Random House Group Limited supports the Forest Stewardship
Council® (FSC®), the leading international forest certification organisation.
Our books carrying the FSC label are printed on FSC® certified paper. FSC is
the only forest-certification scheme supported by the leading environmental
organisations, including Greenpeace. Our paper procurement policy can be
found at www.randomhouse.co.uk/environment

Designed and set by seagulls.net

Printed and bound in Great Britain by Clays Ltd, St Ives PLC

ISBN 9780091933401 (HB)
ISBN 9780091957629 (TPB)

To buy books by your favourite authors and register for offers visit
www.randomhouse.co.uk

at speed

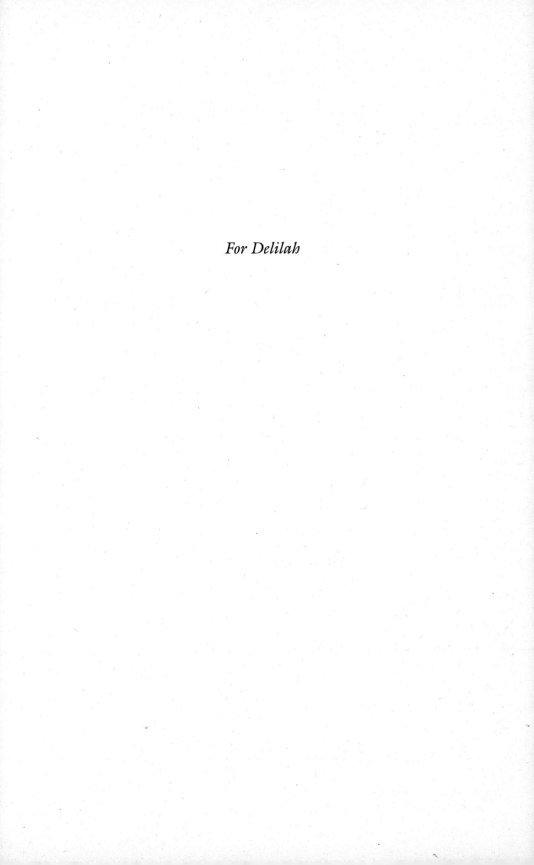

For Delilah

prologue

prologue

'Dave, I'm going to win the Worlds tomorrow.'

Dave was Dave Millar and I was, well, already the world champion in my own imagination. It was mid-afternoon on Saturday 24 September 2011, and we'd just watched the Italian, Giorgia Bronzini, win the women's world championship road race on a TV in our hotel room. Before Bronzini, the previous day, a twenty-year-old Frenchman named Arnaud Démare had taken the men's Under 23 race, and before Démare, Lucy Garner of Great Britain had been the first of the junior women to cross the line. Rod Ellingworth, my coach and the British team's that week, had stuck his head out of the car window and broken the good news about Lucy while we, the senior men, were on a tough final training ride. When Garner had got back to the hotel where the whole GB squad was staying, I'd been with an old teammate, the Swede Thomas Löfkvist, tinkering with my bike, but stopped to applaud Lucy as she walked in. As I clapped, my eyes had wandered towards the rainbow stripes of her new world champion's jersey –

then I'd quickly averted them out of superstition. That jersey – maybe the most sought-after in professional cycling, more than even the Tour de France's *maillot jaune* – was one thing that Bronzini's race, Démare's and Garner's all had in common. Another was a course circling a leafy suburb to the north of Copenhagen. And another was the way that the races had all ended: in a sprint. Twice could be coincidence, but three times was a pattern. I turned in my single bed to face Dave. 'Dude, I'm going to fucking win this. We can't lose.' Dave later told me that this was the moment when he knew as well. No sooner had I said it than I was already diving between gaps on a finishing straight tarmacked across my mind's eye, already ducking for the line and feeling the elation of victory hit me like an ocean wave. I'd been complacent about winning races before in my career but I'd also, gradually, learned the difference between healthy and unhealthy confidence: one energised and sharpened your instincts, your muscles, even your eyesight in the race; the other dulled, muffled and slowed everything. This was definitely the first kind.

Almost a year earlier, I'd gone with my old mate and HTC-Highroad *directeur sportif*, Brian Holm, to take a first look at the course. Brian is just about the best-connected man in Denmark and also the fourth-best dressed according to *GQ* magazine (though I'm not so sure). We'd done a lot beside ride our bikes on that trip, but the time we spent doing loops of the circuit with donors to Brian's cancer charity convinced me that this wouldn't be another Melbourne.

The Australian city had been the venue for the 2010 Worlds, which had taken place a few weeks before my visit to Copenhagen. Melbourne had not gone well. I was coming off a successful 2010 Vuelta a España, having won three stages and the points jersey, and was flying. Therein lay the problem and the excuse I gave myself for pushing too hard in pre-race training sessions that were intended to put the icing and a cherry on my form. I thought I could win it, but my over-zealousness in training jeopardised my chances in the race proper. Dave, one of only three British riders who had qualified for the race, knew I was overdoing it, as did the rest of team and the staff, but it took that mistake and the resulting, massively disappointing performance to teach me what proved to be an absolutely vital lesson.

All week in the run up to the Copenhagen race the atmosphere in the British camp had been fantastic. Everyone was rallied around the same cause, namely, making sure that the peloton was bunched together as we came into the last 200 metres of the 266 kilometres, whereupon it'd be over to me. It was a measure of my confidence not only in the nature of the course, but also in the guys, that I could only foresee one outcome.

The evening before the race Brian Holm came to our team hotel. I was getting my massage when he arrived, so Brian chatted to Dave and Brad Wiggins while he waited.

'I saw the races today … you're going to win this, aren't you?' Brian said when I finally appeared.

'Yeah, I am. I'm gonna win,' I told him.

Brian paused. 'Shit, I'm nervous.'

Nervous, I think, was the wrong word. I think he meant that he was excited. Brian always says that when I'm sure I'm unbeatable, like I was that day. It's been the same ever since we met at the Tour of Britain in 2006, when I was a mouthy, twenty-one-year-old *stagiaire* – cycling speak for work-experience boy – and he called me 'a fat fuck' for disobeying his orders to get to the front midway through the very first stage.

Over the years Brian had became a kind of father, brother and mentor. I was lucky to be rooming with another one of those that week in Dave. There are some riders, like Brad, who will always room alone given the choice, but it drives me absolutely crazy. If a roommate goes home early from a race or training camp, I'm climbing the walls within hours, pestering the management to be put with someone else.

Dave and I woke to sunshine the morning of the race. We ate breakfast, got ready, then climbed into the bus. I was quiet – quieter than usual. I rarely get nervous because I keep my mind too busy. Sudoku, logic puzzles, visualisation. All full gas. Every pro bike rider trains his legs but very few train their mind, the only muscle they use to make decisions in races. It mystifies me: the more you keep your brain active, the more it's whirring away and the less likely it is to get sabotaged by the kind of anxiety that can cause mistakes and compromise a performance.

Winning the Worlds, and before that ensuring it finished in a sprint, was also a logic puzzle that needed to be solved. To help us, in the days leading up to the race, we'd spoken to other teams who also had strong sprinters and might therefore want the same kind of finale – the Americans, the Australians and the Germans. They said they'd give us a hand but we all knew that the main responsibility would fall to the team with the fastest sprinter, unanimously acknowledged – namely me. For that reason it was better that we were prepared to lead the race for all 266 km, something that for any other team would be an impossible task, but which this one was going to relish. It took a special group of guys to achieve that: there would be no personal glory for my teammates, only sacrifice for the benefit of a rider who, for most of them, was an opponent in every other race of the season. That was the inherent contradiction of the Worlds: for one day, arguably the most important of the cycling season, allegiances to trade teams – companies to whom riders owed their livelihoods – were set aside in the name of patriotism. This was why a lot of national federations, though not British Cycling, put up a sizeable bonus to be shared among the riders in case of victory: it was compensation for what those guys would have given up.

Before we'd got off the bus, I'd said it one more time: 'If we do everything 100 per cent right, we'll win this.'

It was the kind of thing that's said in every team bus by every team leader or *directeur sportif* before every race. What we did over the next six hours would determine whether it was cliché or prophecy.

The World Championship road race generally follows a familiar pattern: a relatively large break of unfancied riders goes up the road early, the speed in the main group settles and the major cycling nations – Italy, Holland, Spain, Belgium and so on – share the pacemaking to ensure that the breakaway's advantage doesn't become irretrievable. When it's brought back – which it usually is with between 20 and 50 kilometres to go – the serious, potentially race-winning attacks begin. It may seem a counterintuitive way to operate but no team can control a race from start to finish, and certainly not a World Championship road race. Or so everyone had thought.

For the first 28 kilometres from Copenhagen to the circuit in Rudersdal – where we'll then complete seventeen laps of a 14.3 km loop – we don't lead. We're also happy to let the usual, we hope harmless, move clip off the front, shortly after reaching Rudersdal and the start of the circuits. By then, though, we're in complete command, with Ian Stannard and Geraint Thomas pouncing on any break that's too strong or too big and could pose a threat to our plan. When we're finally happy with the group that has formed, our red and blue jerseys mass to the front and Britannia rules. And rules for the next five hours.

The experts have been saying ever since it was unveiled more than a year ago that the Copenhagen course is a simple one, but subtlety and simplicity shouldn't be confused. There's no such thing as a bike race whose secrets and nuances I won't try to understand and master. Here, for instance, every time we approach the biggest hill on the circuit on the first nine laps, I'll start at the front with my minder for the day, a 37-year-old veteran called Jez Hunt. I'll drop my chain into the small ring and we'll drift back into the belly of the bunch as we tap up the slope: that way, I can afford to climb more slowly than everyone else in the bunch, in an easier gear, yet still find myself in the middle of the peloton at the top, when we start the only real headwind section on the circuit. I'll then move back up and reposition myself, with Jez, behind the puddle of blue and red British jerseys on the front.

For 60 kilometres the gap to the seven out front keeps rising but it's rising on our terms, only as much as we'll allow. At Melbourne a year ago I knew within a few kilometres of the start that I didn't have the legs to finish the race, let alone win the jersey. Today, however, I'm floating. I see riders steal a glance at my thighs, humming over the top tube, and I imagine alarm spreading through the peloton: *Cavendish is on one of those days.* Two riders who for the rest of the year are teammates, Lars Bak and Kanstantsin Sivtsov, ride alongside me, look down, and repeat what I have been saying for the last 24 hours, what Brian said and Dave had thought but kept to himself: 'Cav, you're going to win today. You're going to be world champion.'

The laps tick by. Steve Cummings and Chris Froome are on the front, behind them are Dave, Gee, Brad, Stannard and Jez Hunt, my babysitter. Radio contact with our team cars isn't allowed at the Worlds, so information about time-gaps is relayed to us on blackboards twice every lap. Our team staff can communicate with us the same way from the 'pits' where we can also pick up drinks and food. At one point the blackboard tells me that I'm too far forward and need to move back. I ignore it. If I'm supposed to be my team's leader, I'm staying with them.

Eight laps to go. Seven. The gap to the early break is shrinking now: Froomey and Steve are slowly reeling them in, two Trojans. Counter-moves are starting to develop but they're quickly extinguished, asphyxiated and stifled by our pacemaking. Six laps to go and we get our first big scare; the French rider Blel Kadri crashes, others pile into him and the peloton suddenly splits. This is why you ride at the front, because pretty much everyone behind the bodies, including the defending champion Thor Hushovd, has to stop. On a fast course like this one, with us driving, they won't see the front of the race again. Gee – Geraint Thomas – is our only rider caught in the mess but manages to untangle himself and miraculously rejoins our train. Like I said, it's a scare, a warning, and perhaps a sign that today our luck is in.

With five laps to go a counter-attack joins the seven who went away early on, so now they're eleven with a two-minute gap. It's a big group, under normal circumstances a dangerously big group, but we're still playing this race like a computer game and we've got everyone right where we want them. Froomey and Steve have done their work and will pull off in a minute and then it'll be Jez's turn on the front. Dave will come after Jez and Brad will come after Dave. On the last lap, Brad will then hand over to Stannard, who'll come before Gee, whose job it is to position and launch me in the sprint.

The attacks are coming in flurries now but we're irresistible, inescapable. On the climbs especially, my heart is pounding the inside of my ribcage and I'm clenching my teeth so hard that I'll break one of them and need dental surgery in two days. It's all bearable, though, because I'm being whipped along on a magic current created by my teammates. It's the perfect microcosm of my life as it stands in September 2011: the ups and downs that I've endured over the past two years, more criticism than some riders face in an entire career, some of it deserved; arguments with my team and my manager, personal problems, health problems, historic successes and intermittent but devastating failures. A lot of it I've kept to myself. I've ridden the bumps in the same way that I'm surviving this course today, thanks in equal parts to my resilience, or rather my bloody-mindedness, and the support of some exceptional people. If anything is in danger of overwhelming me today, it's pride.

The same emotion swells when I see Jez pull off and Dave take over with two laps to go. Then just as we catch the remnants of the early break, the French rider Thomas Voeckler counter-attacks and is soon joined by the Dane Nikki Sorensen and the Belgian Klaas Lodewijk in probably the most dangerous move of the day so far. Dave drapes his hands over the middle of his bars and clicks into time trial mode to keep us within striking distance. Voeckler is a top rider but this is desperate stuff now. Back in the peloton, resignation spreads like gangrene: this race will end in a sprint, just like we said and wanted, and Mark Cavendish is going to win.

One lap to go.

Voeckler and his group are still away but Brad's taken over and he's gunning now, gunning like I've never seen. We go through the finish line, take the bell, and Brad's dropping the peloton. He's five metres ahead, ten metres.

'Brad!'

One of the lads shouts to him above the crowd noise to slow down. I've zoned out from everything – or rather zoned in. Brad has this race by the scruff of the neck, and he's dragging around this circuit; yanking it every which way, bullying it, brutalising it. I knew already Brad was committed to this, and that when he's committed there's no one like him, but I *really* knew the previous day, in our last big meeting on the bus before race-day, when we started discussing contingency plans if, say, I had a mechanical problem near the end of the race. After a few minutes of ideas pinging back and forth, I finally said, 'Look, guys, if I puncture with three K to go, Gee, you sprint for yourse—'

Brad, who generally keeps his thoughts to himself in this kind of meeting, and had barely opened his mouth so far in this one, didn't let me finish.

'Listen,' he said, 'if Cav punctures 50 kilometres from the end, we're waiting for him. If Cav punctures three kilometres from the end, we're waiting for him. And if Cav punctures 700 metres from the line, we're fucking waiting for him then, as well …'

To this, no one said a word. Eyes just darted around the bus, from rider to rider, in silent recognition not of what had been said, but of who had said it, what it meant in the present context. Hearing Brad speak, I felt a cold tingle up my spine. Over the previous couple of years, certainly in the days before and even more so during the race, there were endless little moments when you could say, with hindsight, that the Worlds was won. This was without doubt one of them.

Of course Brad and I had had our problems. Neither of us is what you'd call an 'easy' character. Together we'd had the best of times – like in the Madison at the 2008 track Worlds – and we'd had the worst of them too. At the Beijing Olympics I simply didn't feel that his mind was fully in the velodrome after his gold medals in the individual and team pursuits, and our Madison race was an unmitigated, well-documented disaster. That night I called Rod Ellingworth and the British Cycling performance director Dave Brailsford into my room in the Olympic Village. I told them that I was disgusted with how I'd effectively been forced to leave the Tour de France to get ready for the Olympics, disgusted with Brad's attitude in the race, and that their apologies were coming 'too late'. For two months after we'd ridden off the track in Beijing, in different directions, Brad and I didn't speak. Then he sent me a conciliatory text – 'Hi, do you remember me?' – and the ice was broken.

Three years on, my biggest worry for a while hadn't been my relationship with Brad but Dave Millar's. That had soured pretty badly when Brad left Garmin for Sky at the end of 2009. For a long time I feared that the tension between them would either keep one of them, probably Brad, from even riding in Denmark, or undermine whatever harmony we were trying to create in the team. The fact was that I needed both of them to win: I needed Dave because not only is he a fantastic natural athlete and hugely experienced but also because he is one of the best in-race communicators in the peloton. Dave's character is also a kaleidoscope of eccentricities totally at odds with my own ticks and quirks, yet which somehow complements me perfectly. Dave and I have roomed together a few times at races and training camps, and we almost invariably find ourselves staying up most of the night, just talking shit that to us at the time seems like the final word on modern civilisation.

The reason I needed Brad was even more straightforward: on the bike, he's an absolute beast. If any doubt about that remained, even after his third place in the 2009 Tour and third in the 2011 Vuelta, he was banishing – obliterating – it now. Just a few weeks earlier, in August 2011, I'd won the Olympic test event in London and got everyone excited about my prospects in the actual Olympic road race a year later. The best thing to come out of that day, though, was a text sent to me by Brad that night. The gist, if not the verbatim message, was, 'Fuck all the grudges, fuck the issues with Dave, fuck everything. I want to be a part of you winning the rainbow jersey in Copenhagen.'

That had been another big moment.

Our next challenge with Brad before the race had been keeping him back until the last two or three laps, when he could act as our human Hoover – both pulling back breakaways and sucking the peloton along at such a rate that any fresh attacks or counter-attacks would be doomed. Brad had initially been reluctant, knowing that this was physically perhaps the hardest role in the team, and potentially the most pressurised; he wanted to get his job out of the way early in the race, but from our point of view that would have been like using a Formula One car for a milk-round. Brad eventually acknowledged that, too, and it was bad news for everyone riding against us.

This penultimate lap will be the only time in the race that I ride the finishing straight in the big ring. The circuit has been hard-wired into my memory for a year now: a right turn 300 metres after the line, past the Rudersdal town hall, down to the foot of the first, 300-metre hill, up and down again to the bottom of Søllerød Slotsvej, at 480 metres the longest and hardest climb on the course. Then it's a two-kilometre descent and another 650-metre drag before the relatively straightforward – and straight – second half of the course to the bottom of the 400-metre, steadily-rising home straight.

As we come towards the last ten kilometres, the last time up Søllerød Slotsvej, three guys are up the road but on borrowed time. That means the shit-fight for positions is about to begin; it'll no longer be single riders moving up on either side of the road but whole lines, whole teams, creating the conditions for a vortex or 'washing-machine effect' which could take me from fourth to fortieth wheel in a matter of seconds. It's paramount that this doesn't happen, and this is why and where we need Brad. I keep peering over Gee's shoulder, and Stannard's, wondering how the hell Brad's still there, but he keeps drilling – 55, 60 kilometres an hour, not only controlling our rivals but hurting them. When I watch the re-runs on TV later, the commentator will see Brad swaying left and right across the road, occasionally glancing sideways, and say that he's suffering and looking for a teammate to come through and take over. In fact what he's doing is using the whole width of the road to make it impossible for anyone to dive-bomb us, swooping down on the inside or over on the outside and setting off that vortex, that deadly spiral. Usually, in a long, hard race like the Worlds there are a certain number of riders, the thoroughbred *finisseurs* like Fabian Cancellara or Philippe Gilbert who could outride a group over the last five or ten kilometres. With Brad driving, they're seat-belted into the back seat of the bunch.

Ten to go. The Dutch rider Johnny Hoogerland gets a couple of hundred metres and joins the breakaway trio, but they're going nowhere. While it's fast, savagely fast, our secret all day has been the steadiness of our pace; it can be easier to go at a level 50–60 kilometres an hour than 52 then 54 and back again.

Nine kilometres to go and I'm already low on my bike, *in* my bike, as in with hands on the drops. Usually at this point I'd still be on the brake-hoods, head high, neck cocked and eyes peeled, but we're moving too fast to worry about who and what I can see. As we catch the breakaway, I'm certain it's the last we'll see of Brad on the front, but his legs are still pumping, two pistons stabbing the pedals. Six kilometres from home and he's still there. Five. Four and a half. Still Brad. Fucking incredible.

Finally, with four to go, Brad fades to the right and Ian Stannard is on the front and in the wind. Two seconds later it comes: a bolt of magnesium white, a flash in the far-right corner of my eye. The Aussie cavalry are galloping level and then past us on the right-hand side of the road. I don't panic. I never panic. This is one of the reasons – the main reason, I think – that I have a clear advantage over other sprinters, not just here in Copenhagen, but in every race. A sprint isn't a chaos bomb exploding in your sightline, it's not bedlam on fast-forward – it's a multiplication of problems to be solved quickly, usually instantaneously, but at the same time rationally. It's also a contest of freshness, not brute pace, and I generally have more energy and move faster than anyone else because I'm staying calm and clinical. I would even bet that my heart-rate is ten beats per minute slower than that of a lot of my rivals in the closing kilometres, not because I have a more efficient cardiovascular engine – I don't – but because I'm not getting flustered.

Part of staying cool is also, of course, staying focused on the process and not the outcome. When I know that I'm going to win, when that voice inside my head is telling me, 'Cav, you've got this,' it's also my subconscious warning to myself not to fuck up. That and a shot of confidence, not complacency – a last splash of the special tonic that quickens and gives HD definition and perspective to the film rolling in front of me.

Two kilometres out, though, it's a struggle to stay composed. On the far side of the road, in the shadows, riders of all different nationalities are pouring into the Aussie train's slipstream. Behind five Australian jerseys come Italians, Russians, Spaniards, Americans and French – the United Nations of fucking up my sprint train – and suddenly we're engulfed. I tell myself to be patient and have faith: faith in Stannard and Gee, the only teammates I now have left; and faith in how I can read the movements of a bunch, like a weatherman reads the path of a storm. Do only what I always do: stay not on the wheels but in them, not directly behind the rider in front, but almost between two guys riding parallel to each other ahead of me to give myself the room to move forward or back, left or right in a split second. I don't snap, although the urge is there, when riders and teams whom we haven't seen all day while we've controlled the race, guys like the Spaniard Carlos Barredo, start butting in, jostling and trying to barge us aside.

I'm lucid and alert, but inside the last two kilometres and 20 wheels back I know that I'm in a vulnerable position. If another train suddenly surges on the opposite side of the road I could instantly drop 20 wheels and out of contention. Luckily, in Gee and Stannard I've got two guys who are both exceptionally strong and immensely loyal. From where I am now, you'll get nowhere just following wheels – you have to go outside and into the wind, and to do that at 60 kph you need exceptional horsepower, which Gee and Stannard have. You – or I – also need that dedication, which I'd never question from this pair. The symbolism of me riding into the last two kilometres of a world championship road race behind two guys that I grew up with as a cyclist, with the British Federation and its Academy, will be something to reflect on and cherish later.

One-point-nine kilometres and we're still behind the Aussies, the Italians, Germans and Spaniards, tight to the barriers on the right-hand side. I can see Matt Goss five positions ahead of me, hunched over the bars, legs chopping. Muscles don't bulge from his calves like they do from Andre Greipel's, Marcel Kittel's or any other sprinter's – Gossy looks awkward, ungainly, but on an uphill finish like this one he could be the biggest threat.

One-point-eight and the arrowhead of the bunch sways towards the middle of the road. That movement opens a window of opportunity on the far right hand at one-point-seven: Stannard surges, makes it, Gee does the same, makes it, and suddenly they're snapping at the Aussie's heels, in second wheel and third. I also surge … but, maybe sensing I'm there, or guessing that I'll be following Gee, Gossy swings hard right and slams the window shut.

Fuck.

One-point-five and I've lost my lead-out man. One-point-four and I'm boxed. One-point-three and Stannard's on the front, Gee's looking around to see where I am but is dazzled and blinded by Italian blue, Australian and German white. Gossy lets me past but I'm not looking for Gee any more. I know that Gossy will come under me before the last corner, then I'll swing onto his wheel. It's risky but if I pull off. If I pull it off …

One-point-two. One-point-one. Then we're under the blue banner for the last kilometre. Nine hundred. The last, right-angle right-hander. Stannard slants his body and bike into the bend and is the first man to see the finish line; Gee, in second, tilts into the same arc. I'm ten positions back, Gossy's gone under me like I knew he would, and I'm fine here, I'm thinking now – I'm golden, this is good, real good. For days before the race we've debated whether to use the more aerodynamic, mid-section carbon wheels or the lower-section, lighter and zippier model, and finally I've gone for the latter because of the acceleration needed out of this last turn. As Gossy hugs the corner, an Italian rider tries to cut in. I kick, my bike fizzes in front of him and I know I've made the right choice.

Stannard's labouring now, about to pull off, and Gee's still turning to look for me. I shout: 'Gee, I'm OK!' Gee is the perfect spot to go for himself here, at 800 to go, and a lot of riders would, but not Gee. Gee would never do that. Loyal to a fault, Gee is. Would ride the cranks off his bike for you, Gee. Absolute legend.

Seven hundred and fifty. Three hundred more metres and then the road starts to ramp up. I stick to Gossy, like his shadow, or closer. I'm just waiting now.

Seven hundred. I see Gee drifting back on my right, level and then behind me.

Six-fifty. Now I'm just waiting. Waiting, waiting. Five-fifty.

Five hundred. The wind's coming from the right. I've felt it in training – laps and laps, practice sprints, testing gears, lines, lead-outs – and I've felt it on every circuit today. It'll blow and the group will drift, drift to the left, leaving clear air on the right-hand side of the road, where I am now.

Four-fifty. Four-thirty and the road starts rising.

Four hundred and they're drifting now. Just tiny amounts but they're moving. Heinrich Haussler's on the front, driving for Gossy, and he's veering, veering left and the whole group's swinging like a dragon's tail behind him.

Three-seven-five, three-fifty. It's going now. Haussler's dying and everyone's drifting, drifting left, and the window's creaking open. I've got an Italian, Daniele Bennati, on my right and a Dutchman, Lars Boom, on my left. I'm on Gossy, but here it fucking comes, earlier than I think. The gap's coming.

Three hundred and it's creaking ajar. Two-seven-five and it's halfway there. Two-fifty … come on. Two-twenty … a bit more. Two hundred and it's open, waiting, yawning – a gateway to paradise running up the barriers. I think I'll have a moment, a second in the eye of the hurricane, but no, I have to go: Fabian Cancellara, in red, sends a flare up the other side of the road and it's now or no chance.

Ten pedal revs and I'm past Gossy. Fourteen and I'm past Bennati. Fifteen and I'm past Cancellara and leading the Worlds. But there's still 100 metres to the finish and the lactic and the adrenaline are waging a chemical war in my thighs and calves and even my arms and this road's still going up at 75, 70, 60, 55 metres to go. At 50 it starts flattening but that breaks the rhythm and I've gone early and I've not got much left …

I look left, see Cancellara going backwards and no one else making ground. Forty-five to go and it's coming, it's coming, coming. *You're going to be world champion Cav, it's fucking coming.*

Thirty-five, thirty, twenty-five. Six-five more revs and it's over, Cav. Gossy's closing, I know he's closing but he's left it late and now I'm riding over the sponsors' logos and it's ten, it's nine, it's eight and it's five metres. I'm raising my fucking arms and the next thing on the road's the finish line and I'm the fucking world champion.

World champion. I'm the world champion.

chapter one

You think as a professional cyclist that you're used to pain. I've always said that it's a weird, twisted line of work that treats physical suffering as a part of the job description, like clocking on at an office. At least it comes with the benefit of desensitisation: a wasp-sting, a cramp, something that might have 'normal folk', non-cyclists, squealing in agony barely registers on our pain radar. We're harder, braver, more resilient than ordinary people.

At least that was what I thought until one night in a Majorca hotel room in January 2010, 18 months before my greatest day in Copenhagen.

I wasn't just squealing but crying and howling like a five-year-old girl. It was razor-blades, acid on an open wound, induced labour, five times up the most infamous of all major tour climbs, the Mortirolo in Italy, all of them at the same time.

I couldn't take it any more, and so I shuffled my body out of the bed sheets and alongside the wall. I cocked my head in the opposite direction then held it there as I paused to ask myself if this was really such a bright idea. Then I felt it again – a hot poker on my gums – and that made up my mind. Like a centre-forward leaping to meet the perfect cross, I lunged and flicked my head at the wall and waited for the thud.

Then it came. *Ahhhh, more pain. And relief.*

My logic, you'll have to admit, was pretty ingenuous: disperse or dilute the pain in my mouth by creating another one in my skull. It was the kind of thing that only I could have come up with. Had it worked? Depends what you meant by 'worked'; I was definitely in pain in two places. What I didn't realise at the time was that in those moments, on that bed in that hotel room in Majorca, the opening credits of a six-month waking nightmare were just beginning to roll.

It was my own fault, my own vanity that had done it. My bottom front teeth had always been crooked and over the previous few months I had finally decided to do something about it. Even now it strikes me as so superficial that I find myself wincing as I write, but it's one of those things that happen when you become more successful and, consequently, more intensely scrutinised. Ever since my debut pro season with T-Mobile, I'd been seeing photographs or videos of myself almost on a daily basis, in magazines and on TV, and over time it had made me more and more self-conscious about my looks. In those dark, thankfully long-gone days, whether in vanity or just insecurity, I would scour internet forums for comments about myself and come across the odd unflattering reference to my teeth. One of the worst was a suggestion for a 'look-alike' – a gorilla named Bingo from the old US kids TV series *The Banana Splits*, whose most distinctive trait was, you guessed it, his massive gnashers. There was no one remark or piss-take that did it, but over the last few months of 2009 I'd finally made up my mind: I'd get them straightened, or whatever it was that they needed, and be done with it.

And so I went to Paraguay. That's right, Paraguay. I was there for reasons other than my teeth – a holiday – but yes, that was also where I'd decided to have the operation. When I told people this over the months that followed, they reacted as though I'd gone and done it up a tree, hanging from a branch, or down some back alley. They clearly weren't aware that South America leads the world in cosmetic surgery. The clinic, which in fact was more like a hospital, was reputable and clean. Not cheap, either.

It wasn't there that the problems started, or even the next day when I went out training, but on the plane on the way to my HTC-Columbia team's second training camp of the winter in Majorca. I've had strict rules on aeroplane food ever since my time at British Cycling's Under 23 academy, before I turned pro. One of the Federation coaches, John Herety, who had trained at catering college in a former life, had some horror stories and two incontrovertible, inviolable rules: avoid seafood, and avoid ice cream that may have melted and been refrozen. Now, though, thanks to my new braces and a hole in my gums where a tooth had been extracted, ice cream was all that I could eat. It was a recipe for disaster: I spent almost the entire second half of the flight in the toilet cubicle, shall we say, switching ends. It was food poisoning, or a stomach bug, something totally unrelated to the surgery on my mouth. What didn't occur to me at the time was that I was vomiting over the open wound in my mouth. In doing so, I was setting in motion a sequence of events that, five months later, would take me to my lowest ebb, an emotional and professional macrocosm of the agony I experienced in Majorca.

The 2010 season was always going to be a vital one. They're all important – of course they are – but there were lots of reasons why in this one, in particular, I needed to hit the ground running: I'd be defending my Milan–San Remo title in March; I had a score to settle and a green jersey to win after missing out at the 2009 Tour de France; there was my first realistic crack at the world championship road race on a course that was potentially going to suit me in Australia; and finally there was the Commonwealth Games.

Off the bike, I'd had a difficult winter, with my mate Jonny Bellis nearly dying in a motorbike crash on his way home from a night out with me in Florence. My brother Andy, with whom I had a complicated and quite distant relationship, was going to prison for getting caught in possession of cannabis and cocaine. It had all been stressful and, with the season now about to start, cycling was going to be my sanctuary, my escape.

Another incentive to make it my best season yet – and a nagging worry – was that I still wasn't sure where I'd be riding in 2011. I had an 'option clause' in my contract, the ambiguity of which had already caused some tension. It could either mean that I would have to stay with HTC-Columbia on a wage that I'd already had offers to double elsewhere, or that I could leave, or renegotiate. The interpretation of the clause had already caused some disagreement between me and my team manager Bob Stapleton, as had what I suspected at the time to be Bob's tactics to make me stay: while complaining that he didn't have enough money to give me a better deal, Bob had been busy locking my best and most loyal *domestiques* into new contracts. His reasoning, as I saw it, was that if guys like Mark Renshaw and Bernie Eisel were sticking around, there was no way I'd leave, even if I stood to earn a lot more money elsewhere.

Making the issue even more fraught was what I saw as Bob's anxiety about the likelihood of me joining the newly formed Team Sky in 2011. Like a lot of people, Bob had added two and two together and made five: yes, Sky were British, yes, my coach Rod Ellingworth would be working as their 'race coach' in what would be their debut season, and yes, a lot of my mates were riding for them. But, I hadn't spoken to them about 2011, didn't have any immediate plans to, and I most certainly wasn't already trying to engineer a move.

I'd had a heated phone conversation with Bob over the winter and told him that he needed to chill out, stop issuing Sky with these 'hands-off' warnings in interviews and stop smothering me. I told him that it was like a relationship, and the more pressure he put on me to stay, the more likely it was to turn it into a self-fulfilling prophecy and I would leave. Even though we didn't broach the subject in Majorca, it was there, hovering in the back of my mind and Bob's every time we spoke, and every time we saw each other at races over the following weeks until it was resolved.

My back was also up about our co-sponsor, Columbia Sportswear, who was unhappy over promotional work that I'd been doing for my personal sponsor, Nike. I couldn't believe the gumption of Columbia, a company which had, relatively speaking, paid buttons to sponsor the team and been repaid in gold – hour upon hour of TV coverage, page upon page in newspapers and magazines, basking in the reflected glory of what was already being hailed as one of the most successful cycling teams in history. I partly blamed Bob here too: he had given Columbia exclusivity over the riders' clothing without consulting us, effectively overriding all of our individual deals. Nike, fortunately, had been good about it and said they would overlook, for example, me wearing Columbia clothing at press conferences and team presentations, just to placate Columbia. I, though, had started to resent every second, every occasion where I had to wear Columbia clothing, and would vent endlessly to our poor team press officer Kristy Scrymgeour. Besides anything else, I thought we looked like bloody idiots, standing there at team presentations at training camps or before races in full Lycra kit and ... Columbia hiking boots.

On top of these minor and major preoccupations, I now had my tooth. The vomiting and diarrhoea had soon eased after the flight, suggesting that it had been food poisoning, and I was able to go out for my first training ride the morning after arriving. My bottom jaw and my gums were aching slightly, but I assumed that was just the braces. Then I went to bed and it started: a pulse like piped electricity through my jaw that kept me up all night. The next morning I went straight to see one of the team doctors, Bohdan Wajs – or 'Doc Holiday' as I used to call him, since we didn't particularly get on, and I wasn't all that enamoured with his work ethic.

'Open wide,' he said.

I showed him.

'Ah, looks fine,' he said. 'You'll be OK.'

I trained again that day, with the pain still there, bad but bearable when I was on the bike, and then I went to bed again.

Three hours later I was head-butting a wall.

Harder, braver, more resilient than ordinary people? Hmmm, not sure. Maybe just more stupid.

It doesn't take long for your thoughts to start racing, extrapolating, retouching the vision of your future you'd painted in your imagination, when you're a professional bike rider and you have an illness or an injury. We may pride ourselves on our pain threshold but we learn early to be sensitive to our bodies, hypersensitive, and any niggle or ailment is invariably accompanied by an image of its consequences. The first sniffles or hint of a cold and we know instantly that's three, four days of training gone. Crash and break your collarbone and that's four, five, maybe six weeks out, and your entire season compromised

With the throbbing now spreading through my gums like fanned flames, I started wondering and worrying about the effect that all of this was going to have on my plans and goals for the next few weeks. For the second morning in a row, I went to find Doc Holiday.

'Look, Doc, something's badly wrong with this.'

He peered into my mouth again and reacted exactly as he had the previous day.

'Looks fine. Just take some Ibuprofen.'

I shook my head and, reluctantly, did what he said. Took Ibuprofen, way more than you ever should. It got me through until that night, when the now familiar ordeal started again: pain, tears, howls, shrieks, moans and not a wink of sleep.

This time I wasn't taking no for an answer.

'Doc, there's something not fucking right here …'

If he still wasn't convinced, he would be soon. I brought my thumb and forefinger to my mouth, clamped them around one of my bottom front teeth, and pushed. As the tooth moved, I felt the corners of my eyes fill with water again, and everything in my face tense into a rictus.

The doc's eyes widened, his expression turning from one of shock to horror. Our team chiropractor, who was also there, said he could see pus was oozing out. He said he'd hold me down, and I should keep pushing it. I tried, but I was almost passing out now. I barely managed to stagger to a team car, in which they immediately drove me to a dentist's. The dentist saw me straight away, and said it was the biggest abscess he'd ever seen in his life – or rather two abscesses, because there was one either side of the gum.

I've never been so glad to see a scalpel in all my life. Still crying, I felt the blade go in and, seconds later, a flood of relief.

It was over. Well, it would be after a course of the strongest antibiotics that the dentist said he was allowed to prescribe: antibiotics with their side-effect of more diarrhoea. I spent five days in that soulless hotel room while my teammates trained. By the end of the camp I was already 1,000, maybe 2,000 kilometres behind schedule, and had possibly already jeopardised both my Milan–San Remo defence and the first two or three months of the season. All because I didn't like the way my teeth looked in photos.

The training camp where I'd done next to no training ended in mid-January, about a week before what should have been my first race of the year: the Tour of Qatar. Instead my 2010 season was now going to start at the Ruta del Sol in Spain at the end of February, which gave me a month at my flat in Tuscany to get ready.

That month was miserable. Three things tend to affect a cyclist's motivation to train, and they're the weather, the company or lack of it, and your form. You'll find riders who don't mind the rain, or training on their own, but you won't find one who says that it's easy to get motivated when you're starting your training and going like a sack of cement. In that February I had the full house, the grand slam of motivation-killers: shit weather, no one to ride with and shit form. I did OK in the circumstances – 90,

100 dripping wet kilometres every day – but I was also cramming, panic training, still clinging to the hope that I might, just might, be ready for Milan–San Remo.

At the Ruta del Sol I managed to complete four out of the five stages, finishing only fourth in the lone sprint that I did, purely because I was lacking fitness. I then came second in the one-day race that comes immediately after the Ruta, the Clásica Almería, to the Dutchman Theo Bos. Bos had just switched to the road, having been one of the best sprinters in the world on the track, and predictably it was already being said in the press that Bos was the new sprint phenomenon, the young pretender who was going to take my throne.

I just laughed at stuff like that now. I'd lost the sprint at the Ruta del Sol because I was still out of shape, and the one against Bos because I'd ballsed up tactically. The day when I was fit, firing, in the right position and still got beaten, that would be the day when I'd start to worry. Whenever I read or heard anyone forecasting my decline, I didn't have to look very far into the past for reassurance: in 2009 I'd failed to win two of the sprints that I'd properly contested, and in only three of the ones that I'd won had I given it the full Monty (at Milan–San Remo, in the first sprint of the Tour de France, and in the last one on the Champs Elysées). When I pointed this out – and pointed out how much I'd won by on the Champs, approximately ten bike lengths – I was told that I was being arrogant. In fact, as usual, I was just stating the facts.

After Almeria came Tirreno–Adriatico, my last race before San Remo. Mark Renshaw and Bernie Eisel had come to stay with me for a couple of days before the race started, and we did some good training on the roads that were going to play host to the first couple of stages of Tirreno. Even so, I was under no illusions; I was going to get my head kicked in. In yet more shocking weather, that's exactly what happened for most of the week, until something started stirring in my legs on the last couple of days. I was hardly flying, but I was no longer creeping along either. Suddenly guys were riding alongside me in the peloton spotting the veins starting to protrude from my calf muscles, my legs starting to rotate not in a stiff, chopping motion but a fluid, rhythmic dance.

'Aie, aie,' they were saying to me. 'You're starting to go well, aren't you? Better watch out for you at San Remo ...'

And I would smile coyly, starting to believe a miracle might just happen.

But there would be no fairytale return. Part of the beauty of Milan–San Remo is that, of the 200 riders on the start-line, with the right weather or tactics, 100 of them can win the race. My team clung to that knowledge, mainly because we didn't have any better option. The previous year I'd sailed over the two crucial climbs of the Cipressa and the Poggio, and more or less won picking my nose; I could have ridden through the finish and done another 100 kilometres. This time round, my problems started with a broken wheel on the ascent of the first climb in the race, the

Passo del Turchino, and continued with a crash on the descent off the second one, Le Manie. On better form, I could have recovered from the chase back to the peloton after those two mishaps and still contended. But, for all that I'd packed in the kilometres over the previous month, I was trying to wing it. It didn't work and, sure enough, I was dropped on the Cipressa. Up the road, half an hour later, Oscar Freire was inheriting my title.

All things considered, though, mine had been a respectable performance. I was philosophical and proud of how I'd somehow contrived to get myself in reasonable shape after the winter that I'd had. Maybe things were looking up. Three days later I finally got my first win of the season at the Volta a Catalunya.

Three days after that, I had to leave Catalunya with the flu.

It was only March, but the press were already calling it an 'annus horribilis'.

Pretty soon, I'd stop being philosophical and start agreeing with them. It had been just over three years since my T-Mobile team's physiologist, Sebastian Weber, had looked at my fitness test results and haughtily informed me that my numbers weren't worthy of a professional cyclist. It had taken me a matter of weeks to prove him wrong, and since then the disappointments had been comprehensively outnumbered by the successes, the doubts by the certainties, the criticism by the praise. Having gorged on glory, I'd conditioned myself to expect nothing less.

Out of that mindset I'd created a winning recipe – but also the formula for a deep, insidious despair.

knew the feeling. It had happened once before in the winter of 2005 to 2006, not that I could really put a name to it at the time. Then, I was a 20-year-old world champion, having won the Madison that year with Rob Hayles in Los Angeles, but six months later I was in a dreadful state. My time at the British Cycling Academy was up, I still didn't know exactly when, where or even if I was going to turn pro, and all I had to keep me going through that winter were ritual batterings on the six-day circuit with Rob. I was living in Cheadle, near Manchester, with the track sprinter Craig MacLean, his girlfriend, and my old Academy mate Ed Clancy. Ed also had a girlfriend who, as the weeks went by, was becoming a permanent fixture at the flat, and who I couldn't stand. A pattern soon developed: she'd be in the kitchen, cooking for Ed, while I'd spend my days mainly trying to avoid her. My routine was to get up, train, then lie on the sofa, curtains drawn, with only a giant bag of Walkers Sensations for company. I'd finish the bag, go to the petrol station for another, and repeat. Needless to say, after a few weeks of this, not only was I fat, I was depressed, I think clinically.

This time, like then, the depression was going to creep up on me. After Catalunya, for the first time I'd ridden the Tour of Flanders, one of the races I'd dreamt of as a kid. I'd actually gone pretty well there – I finished almost half an hour down, but only after blowing completely near the second feed zone, where I'd been in the first group. We'd hit the Eikenberg, one of the narrow, gnarly cobbled climbs for which Flanders is infamous, and

I'd been passed by five groups in the space of a few kilometres. Boom, boom, boom, boom, boom – out of the arse, as we say. Nonetheless, I felt satisfied: my positioning had been good and I still believed that I could come back in the future and possibly win that race, given the right weather conditions. Unfortunately, the organisers would change the route in 2012, making it significantly harder, and now I suspect I might need more than just a sunny day and a headwind if I'm ever going to contend. A leg transplant might be more like it.

My spirits were OK when I left Flanders but over the next couple of months I started to get lonely and quite down. One incident stands out from the fortnight or so either side of Flanders. It was a minor irritation at the time, the kind of little drama that I can whip up like a chef does an omelette, but it was symptomatic of how rootless I'd started to feel. It was a midweek afternoon and my phone rang; the display showed an English number that I didn't recognise. I did something that I never did, except when I was as bored as I was that day: I answered. On the end of the line was Richard Moore, the journalist.

'Hi, Mark. Just wondering whether we could have a quick chat for a story I'm doing for the *Guardian* ...'

Because I had nothing better to do, I said OK. We chatted for ten minutes about my form, the Tour de France, and he asked for my reaction to some comments in the press a couple of days earlier from my teammate André Greipel, saying he should have been the leader at San Remo.

The next day, I can't remember whether someone told me to look at the *Guardian* website, or if I logged on myself. I can just remember reading the headline and thinking, 'Here we fucking go …'

'MARK CAVENDISH PUTS TEAM SKY ON ALERT AFTER CRITICISM OF ANDRÉ GREIPEL' read the headline. 'FUTURE WITH HTC-COLUMBIA IN DOUBT AFTER CRITICISING TEAMMATE …' To be fair, Richard hadn't written anything that I hadn't said. As often happens with these things, it was the way the story had been spun, the way he'd linked the quotes together, perhaps not maliciously, but still with a slant that was inviting trouble:

'[Riding in the same team as Greipel] is not a problem for me, because I'm a better rider.'

'Me on bad form is still better than him.'

'If Greipel thought he could win, he should have said it before the San Remo rather than when he's looking at the results sheet.'

'There's no chance whatsoever that he's coming to a bike race that I'm in.'

'There's no chance of Greipel winning a "monument".'

It certainly wasn't news at this stage that André and I had had our ups and downs. Having ridden on the same team for just over three years, there were two problems between us as far as I was concerned: one, André continued to make too many mistakes, lose wheels and thereby waste his teammates' hard work; two, he was basically a nice bloke and I wasn't. Not only could I be a dickhead, I could be very blunt (or, if you were being kind, honest). André and I had actually messaged each other a few times over the winter, spoken a bit at the team training camps in Lanzarote and Majorca, and both probably thought that we'd laid the old animosity to rest. What he'd said after San Remo, though, to my mind verged on delusional; I'd watched him at Paris–Nice while I was at Tirreno–Adriatico and I'd seen him making the same, familiar old mistakes. So I believed what I was telling Richard Moore; I just hadn't done it very tactfully.

With that one telephone call that I should never have taken, I'd pissed off Greipel, added to Bob's concern about me joining Sky, and served up yet more evidence for the already sizeable contingent of people who thought I was a mouthy, arrogant, disrespectful little upstart. The only small mercy was that the team seemed more angry with Greipel for what he'd said than my reaction to it.

There was always that unpleasant, sinking sensation when you dived into one of these controversies and this one simply raised a tide-line that had been inching higher since the start of the year. We were now getting towards late April and I'd won one race. Only I knew the pain that I'd felt in January, how many setbacks I'd had, how complex the overall picture was, but those intricate, textured portrayals never sell as well as the ones painted in broad brushstrokes, particularly in the mainstream press. 'Cavendish's nightmare year' was a titillating, convenient, catch-all hook.

All I could do to alter that view and stop the doom-mongering was to start winning. The Tour of Romandy looked like the perfect time and place: in spite of all the agitation, the sense of some invisible, dark force nagging and gnawing at me, my bike had been my refuge, and I'd trained well throughout April. Romandy is the French-speaking part of Switzerland, so you'd expect a bike-race there to be mountainous and hardly the ideal terrain for a rider like me. I knew, however, that at least one of the six stages could conceivably end in a sprint: that would be the day when I finally made my critics eat their words.

The race kicked off with a short prologue around Porrentruy. I've always liked and been good at short prologues, even won a few in my time, and rode well here to finish 17th. The next stage was a lumpy one through the Swiss Jura; although I could feel the form coming, slowly blooming through my legs, it was still slightly too tough for me, and I finished in a big second group.

Day three, then, was going to be the one. Had to be, because all that remained after that was a time trial and two final stages with profiles like an alligator's dental X-ray. I was familiar with the finishing circuit, because stages had finished in Fribourg with an almost identical loop when I'd ridden Romandy in 2008 and 2009. I also knew that it was going to be tough: on both of those occasions I'd been spat out the back on the final climb.

This time around, I floated over. The pedals were purring. I could almost have celebrated at the top of the climb, because by then I knew there was only going to be one winner. Instead I started thinking about what would be an appropriate way, besides the exhibition of sprinting I was going to give them, to respond to the journalists, the British in particular, who had been giving plenty of coverage to my lack of success so far in 2010.

The sprint itself proved trickier than I expected, if not for me then for my team. The wind was gusting into our faces and we'd committed early, which meant that everyone was doing mammoth turns on the front. I just had to sit tight, for Bernie to pull off, then Renshaw, and finally I went.

My kick was there, the spring, the zip, and I was never really in trouble. Fifty metres from the line I knew I was safe and that I was about to stick two fingers up at everyone who'd doubted me.

The problem was, I did it literally: clasping the inside of my right elbow with my left hand, I jerked my right arm upwards and raised my middle and index fingers in an emphatic V-sign. 'V' for victory. 'V' for, well … you know. In the moment or two after I crossed the line, it didn't really occur to me that I might have just ridden myself into yet more grief. Blood rushed to my cheeks, but in elation, not alarm or embarrassment.

'Better now?' Bernie asked through a huge grin as I turned around to thank him.

Of course I was. Winning was always the cure.

The first hint that I might be in trouble came in the press conference immediately after the stage. I didn't sugar-coat it: I said the gesture was intended 'to send a message to commentators and journalists who don't know jack shit about cycling'. Far from taking it personally, the journalists in the room chortled as they typed or scribbled.

That night, though, you could almost hear the storm rolling in, like thunder in the distance. It started with texts arriving on my phone, which were no doubt in response to stories appearing on the internet. The irony was that I'd provided all of those people who had been writing me off, the very commentators and journalists who were the targets of the gesture, with yet more ammunition for the storyline that they'd been peddling: Cavendish has lost the plot, it's all gone to his head, he's finished. Until this moment, I'd failed to realise two things: one, how people love seeing a meteoric rise but are even happier when it's followed by a precipitous fall, and, two, how cycling and I had outgrown the niche where the only attention we ever received in the UK was positive.

One journalist with whom I'd had a couple of run-ins in the past, Susan Westermeyer from the *Cyclingnews* website, had immediately called the International Cycling Union (UCI). What action did they intend to take? They said nothing publicly, but contacted Bob Stapleton, who then called me. One of the best things about Bob was that he never tried to curb my, shall we say, volatile tendencies. Perhaps he just knew that he'd be fighting a losing battle, but I think he also knew that I needed licence to express myself, within reason, on and off the bike. He also probably realised that my lack of filter made me highly marketable. Armstrong aside, Bob seemed to think I was the most charismatic and valuable name in the sport. It was just a shame that he tended not to bear that in mind when we were negotiating a new contract.

Bob said that the UCI were talking about banning me for the gesture. If they judged that I'd 'behaved in such a way as to blemish the image, the reputation or the interests of cycling or the UCI' I could potentially get a one- to six-month suspension and miss the Tour de France. Bob said they'd talk more some more to the UCI and see what happened, but one solution might be for me to issue a public apology and for the team to pull me from the race.

One of the texts I received that night was from a girl called Katy Nicholson-Lord, who at the time was working for my management company, Face Partnership. I'd explained to Katy why I'd chosen that particular victory celebration, the Churchillian salute, and she tried to be supportive while also, clearly, having some reservations about whether it had been wise. She did also say something else, though, that pricked my ears up: according to one version, the origins of the V-sign could be traced to the Battle of Agincourt in the 15th century, where British and Welsh bowmen took to holding up their arrow-shooting fingers – the same ones that the French would supposedly cut off if they took them captive – as a sign of defiance. Hmm, I thought, that's not bad, and asked Katy whether she'd mind me using that if the subject came up again. She didn't and so I tucked it away in my mental filing cabinet, ready to dust off when the need arose.

If I thought it might all have blown over by the morning, I was mistaken. The stage that day was a time-trial, and having finished early I was killing time in our team bus, waiting for the other guys to arrive, when Bob called again. Bob said that the UCI President Pat McQuaid had been hassling Brian Holm at the start that morning and that if we were going to avoid a ban the team needed to be seen to do something. He said that, as far as McQuaid and the UCI were concerned, if I was pulled from the race and issued an apology, they would only give us a fine of a few hundred Swiss Francs, which the team would pay. Bob was nice about it but I, naturally, was mortified. I was also adamant, in my 24-year-old mind, that it had been a riposte perfectly in proportion to criticism of what, essentially, had been just an unlucky start to the season. However, I was also sensible enough to realise that resistance was probably futile and that, for my own sake, and for my chances of riding the Tour de France, I should probably just take the punishment and be on my way.

A couple of hours later the team sent out a press release quoting my apology: 'I want to publicly apologise for the gesture I made on the finish line of the Tour de Romandy yesterday,' the statement read. 'I did want to make a statement to my critics but I realise that making rude gestures on the finish line is not the best way to do that. I apologise to everybody watching the race and especially the kids. I am not proud of releasing the feelings in that way. I hope I can redeem myself and show my feelings and passion for cycling with some exciting results in the next couple of months, rather than with a gesture such as the one [I made] yesterday.'

The following morning, in his weekly column in the *Guardian*, Richard Williams wrote the single most scathing piece about me that I'd had the misfortune to read since turning professional in 2007. Under a headline stating that my 'cavalier behaviour will sabotage a glittering career', he'd started with a reference to my ex-girlfriend. From there it got worse: my victory celebration had been 'puerile' and 'such behaviour should have been outgrown by a man of twenty-four'. He felt that Bob's decision to pull me from the race had been 'a judicious form of salutary humiliation'.

One thing that I wouldn't have disputed was what he'd written about how I usually acknowledged and was genuinely contrite about doing the wrong thing ... but not straight away. As Richard Williams put it, 'He acts first and says sorry – really, really sorry – later. And the funny thing is that you know he means it.' That was actually true. I lacked a form of self-awareness that would allow me to put my feelings and actions into perspective in real time. I was – am – good at being honest and self-critical after the event, but by then the damage has often been done.

This was also very relevant to Romandy, the consequences of what I'd done there, and my mood generally at that time, because here, too, I was blind to what was happening. Only months later, or perhaps now, could I or can I coldly analyse the build-up of pressure within me, the way that it was released, and judge whether it was acceptable or not. My objective last word on the matter now would be that I was entitled to vent my frustration, and did it in a manner that was consistent with my temperament, consistent with my level of maturity, and consistent with the state of my life at the time.

Would I do it again today? As a 24-year-old: yes. As a 28-year-old: no.

By way of a footnote, if you're wondering whether the 'Agincourt excuse' ever made it into the public domain, naturally I took the first good opportunity – at a press event in Soho the week before the Tour de France. Richard Williams was sitting in the front row. I made sure that I caught his eye.

Once the embarrassment and anger had passed, leaving Romandy early gave me yet another problem: I'd lost two more race days. Fortunately, the next week I was due to set off for the States, where I'd do a mini-training camp before competing in the Tour of California. Another issue that had set tongues wagging at the start of the year had been Bob 'insisting' that I raced in California rather than the parallel-running Giro d'Italia, which on numerous occasions I'd called my favourite race alongside the Tour de France. I was apparently 'furious' about this, so much so that it was another reason for me agitating to move to Team Sky. The reality was quite different: yes, I would have liked to do the Giro, but I could also see why the team, which had its headquarters in San Luis Obispo in California, wanted me in America. I'd enjoyed California when I'd ridden there in 2008, had a good relationship with the organisers, and was in fact quite happy with the decision.

In those few days before the race, though, as I trained and got ready, the loneliness really started to wear me down again.

Probably the single worst antidote I could have chosen was looking at the internet, but of course that was what I did. Having signed off from my last race with a V-sign, a lot of what was being written on cycling sites and forums didn't make for comfortable reading. Most nights I was so wound up that I couldn't sleep. I'd lie there, staring at the stars, waking for the world to wake up again and get back on my case. I kept thinking about something Rolf Aldag had said to me in Romandy: 'Mark, remember that the pen is mightier than the sword – you can't win.' That may have been, but I also just wished that they'd stop writing about me and leave me alone. It was a weird paradox: as my results and fortunes had dipped, some of the 'new friends' that had appeared from nowhere over the previous couple of years had started to drift away, all of which contributed to my sense of isolation, and yet here I was also yearning to be left in peace. At the same time, though, I'd never been so grateful for the support of the people who had stayed close to me throughout, especially Max Sciandri and the 'Italian family' that had formed around Max and me in Tuscany.

At least the race itself gave me some respite for a few days. On stage one to Sacramento I resumed normal service to win the sprint and take the race-leader's yellow jersey. My victory salute had been more, shall we say, 'traditional', and consequently my press conference was rather more light-hearted than had been the case in Romandy: as I walked into the room I was handed a first edition of the American version of my book, *Boy Racer*, which I proceeded to hold up to the journalists and cameramen, grinning cheesily for the entire duration of the conference.

Losing the jersey on a tougher stage was no real surprise or disappointment. Two days later, though, the curse was back. It was the 'queen stage', the one that the pundits had picked out as the hardest of the race, and, after battling in sweltering heat through the mountains of Southern California, I, Mark Renshaw and nine others chugged in 48 minutes behind the winner, Peter Sagan. We were out of the time limit and out of the tour. That was another two days of racing gone.

It was back to Italy and back to the drawing board. My next race was the Tour of Switzerland: this week-long tour might be the single least sprinter-friendly race on the calendar, yet in a certain sense it was also perfect preparation for the Tour de France and its mountains. There might be one, two opportunities at most for me to pick up a stage win in Switzerland, but there would be 2,000-metre peaks galore to crawl over, in readiness for the Alps and Pyrenees.

One time trial and two lumpy road stages in, we were still awaiting the first real bunch sprint. Stage three to Wettingen, though, looked destined to be my day, with only a couple of third category climbs in the final 50 kilometres potentially complicating matters – that and the fact that we had Tony Martin leading the race and needing protection. After a few skirmishes among the overall contenders on the last hill, it all came back together and I was safely sat on Mark Renshaw's wheel as we headed into the home straight.

With 200 metres to go, Mark was still thrashing down the middle of the road, but guys were now launching their sprints on either side of us. The first and fastest to go was my old teammate Gerald Ciolek. I jumped, took his wheel for no more than ten, twenty metres, then swung to the right to come around him on the outside. Another German sprinter, Heinrich Haussler, had gone around the left of Ciolek, who was fading in the middle of the road, leaving Haussler and I to contest a straight drag-race.

From 150 metres in, I didn't swerve, I didn't swing, I didn't veer – I simply maintained a trajectory slanting gently from the right to the middle of the road. I'll admit that on one of my best days I would have taken a straighter line and beaten Haussler comfortably. But relying solely on my speed, as I usually did, was a luxury; nowhere in the rules did it say that I wasn't also allowed to use tactics to close off lines. Other sprinters had turned this into an art form and been celebrated for it. Now I was just doing the same.

The line that I took was dangerous for one reason only: Haussler was sprinting up the middle of the road with his head down, not looking where he was going. As I moved across, ahead of Ciolek and towards Haussler, I expected him to see me coming and also start to edge towards the left-hand side of the road. Instead he went straight on, his eyes fixed not on the road ahead of him but on the tarmac under his wheels. With 100 metres to go, when I kicked down with my left leg and my front wheel jagged that way, Haussler seemed to sense that a collision was inevitable, imminent, and leaned as he braced himself. When it came, the smash was a spectacular one, with my front wheel snapping under Haussler's, my bike collapsing under me and me falling side-on onto the road surface like someone testing the springiness of a mattress. This bed, I'm afraid to say, was not very comfortable. The five riders who ploughed into me, including Ciolek, didn't work too well as pillows, either.

As is always the case after a crash, shock and total bewilderment set in before the pain. I sat surveying what was left of my bike, totally flummoxed for a second. I then took a quick look at the damage: road rash on my right shoulder, right hip and right knee. Nothing that seemed to be broken except my bike. Haussler was sat in the middle of another pile of rubble a few metres away. I honestly can't remember what he said, whether he even spoke, but it was pretty obvious at the time and from his comments later that he was furious and thought I was to blame. A story went around that I'd spat at him as I lifted myself up and wiped myself down; if I did do that – and, again, I swear that I don't remember – it certainly wasn't deliberate. I'm only mentioning it here to give the truest possible account of what actually happened. What I do definitely recall is Mark Renshaw having to ride me over the finish-line on the back of his bike, like a kid on his mate's BMX, because mine was a write-off. Maybe because that was an image that made a few people chuckle, maybe because I'd got up and on my way while Haussler was still down. I think that Haussler and others assumed that I didn't care whether anyone else was hurt.

It was weird with Heinrich: even before the crash and ever since I'd beaten him, by millimetres, to win Milan–San Remo in 2009, I'd had the feeling that he was harbouring some sort of grudge or resentment. Previously we'd been friends, but then it just flipped and I don't really know why. We'd never discussed it, and in 18 months we'd barely even spoken.

If Romandy had been a shit-storm, it didn't take me long to figure out that this was going to be a shit-cyclone. I had been given a 30-second penalty on general classification, a 25-point deduction in that competition, plus a token 200 Swiss Franc fine. The clear message was that I had been at fault; in the public relations stakes, the fact that Haussler and two other riders, Lloyd Mondory and Arnaud Coyot, had had to pull out with their injuries further cemented me in the role of villain. Haussler would end up missing the Tour de France with a knee injury that he'd aggravated in the crash.

Like at Romandy, I assumed that it would all have blown over by the next morning. I realised how wrong I was when we got to the start line, again in Wettingen. The flag went down, and nobody could move because there were riders blocking the road on the front row. I asked what was going on and was told that it was Haussler's team, Cervélo, and maybe one or two riders from Caisse d'Epargne and AG2R – Coyot's and Mondory's teams – who were staging some kind of protest. I asked what it was about. 'You,' I was told.

Some of the guys causing aggro were ones I'd have expected to be there. The riders who had been consistently the most hostile towards me ever since I'd started winning in 2007 were the grizzled, world-weary journeymen, often sprinters who I felt would always look for and find an excuse for their own lack of success. There were a few of them in there. Mainly, though, it was senior pros from Haussler's Cervélo team, including Thor Hushovd. Thor, of course, had complained about me before; at the Tour de France in 2009, the pressure that he put on the race *commissaires* to disqualify me on stage 14 effectively won him the green jersey.

Thor, Klier and the others were telling me that they weren't going to start the race unless I went home. I, in turn, was spelling out to them that I had no intention of pulling out and that their own sprinter, Heinrich, had been at least as culpable for what had happened the previous afternoon. This went on for no more than a minute or so, during which time other riders – Lance Armstrong among them – were getting impatient and wanting to start. Someone, I think Tom Boonen or Fabian Cancellara, finally forced themselves through the 'picket line' and that was that, the race was on, leaving the Cervélo riders standing on the line looking sheepish.

As it turned out, if Cervélo really did want me out of the race, they wouldn't have to wait very long; having finished that fifth stage 11 minutes off the pace, with my wounds still weeping into bandages and the fabric of my jersey all down my back and the left side of my body, I decided with the team doctor that I wouldn't start the next day. It was partly a physical thing, partly mental:

on the way to Switzerland I'd got the news that my gran, my dad's mum, had died, and that had been on my mind all week. Between that, the crash, and everything else dragging me down, I couldn't summon the motivation to suffer through the pain. And so continued an unblemished record of failing to finish races that now dated back to Milan–San Remo in March.

The following year, when we were riding for the same Great Britain team at the world championships in Copenhagen, I asked Jez Hunt, one of the Cervélo riders lobbying for me to be kicked out that day in Switzerland, why they'd done it.

Jez smiled coyly.

'Go on,' I said. 'Why did you do it?'

'It was to fuck with you before the Tour,' he said. 'Get in your head. We couldn't see any other way of beating you.'

Now, suddenly, it all made sense, but September 2011 was too late to find any comfort in Jez's explanation. This was June 2010. The Tour de France was three weeks away and I was a mess. Lonely, miserable, out of form, unpopular with journalists, fellow riders and even fans, after the highs of the previous two years, I'd somehow fallen into a pit of despair.

I had three weeks to crawl out. Three weeks to go from a version of hell to the Champs Elysées, the Elysian Fields, resting place of the virtuous.

chapter two

'Clunk, clunk, clunk.'

Although I had my head in my hands, I heard the noise just like the TV cameras saw the result. It was reported later that I'd thrown my helmet in a fit of fury, and that it had ricocheted around the inside of the bus, then down the stairs and onto the tarmac where journalists, TV crews and fans had gathered like wolves around a kill. Alessandro Petacchi had won stage four of the 2010 Tour de France to Reims, but as far as they were concerned I was the story. The truth was that I'd just placed my helmet on a chair, it had fallen off and toppled down the staircase. But the image, I'll admit, was a neat summation of my year and my Tour de France so far.

I sat with my head hidden under a towel, staring at the carpet through tears. Our team press officer, Kristy, put her arm around me.

'What's fucking happened? I don't know what's happened,' I blubbed.

The emptiness and silence of the bus were amplifying the tumult in my mind, creating a loud, almost visceral echo. Kristy had gone down to pick up my helmet, leaving just me and Bob Stapleton, who sat speechless at the other end of the bus. As the seconds passed, Bob's unwillingness or inability to say anything, offer any words of consolation, began to annoy me even more than what had just happened on the road. With 200 metres to go, when Renshaw had peeled off, I'd risen off my saddle and kicked – one, two, three, four, five revs – and then felt the muscles in my legs lock up. There was probably nothing that Bob could have said to make it better – and he certainly couldn't explain what I couldn't explain to myself – but his silence riled me.

Only now, three years later, can I hazard an educated guess at what was going though Bob's mind in that bus that day. I discovered recently that, for weeks before the Tour, one of my teammates, the Australian Michael Rogers, had been dropping none-too-subtle hints to the effect that he could possibly mount a strong challenge on general classification, if only the team would give him more support. Rogers had been enjoying his best season for years, having won the Ruta del Sol and the Tour of California, and the view that my recent antics made backing me a gamble and Mick the safe option had apparently gained traction with some members of the management. With hindsight, I should have put two and two together at the Tour of Switzerland in June: there, on the day of my crash, Mick had pulled out, purportedly to prepare for the Tour, when another of our teammates, Tony Martin, was leading the race. Tony went on to miss out on overall victory by 27 seconds. In Tony's shoes, I would have been more than a little miffed that Mick hadn't stayed in the race to help.

While Rolf Aldag and Brian Holm had dismissed the notion of Mick being our co-leader at the Tour without a moment's thought, sitting on that bus in Reims I can well imagine that Bob could see its merits, in retrospect, after five stages and not a sniff of winner's bouquet.

I had felt under pressure ever since arriving in Rotterdam on the Wednesday before the Grand Départ. The previous few weeks and months had forced me to think hard about how many of my problems had been self-inflicted, especially the ones created or exacerbated by stories in the media. Just the week before the Tour I'd done a press event in Bar Italia in Soho that reminded me, yet again, of the drawbacks of what I'd previously hoped and thought was just my 'refreshingly' blunt and spontaneous approach in interviews. There was no particular question or answer that set me off, no especially damning headlines the next day, but I had been my usual, spiky self. At HTC-Columbia I didn't feel that anyone was really giving me good advice on how to behave with the media, and most of the time I was going on instinct. I did, though, leave for Rotterdam that week having taken a vow with myself to steer clear of all controversy over the next three weeks. It was simply all costing me too much energy.

My performance in the pre-race press conference in Rotterdam, then, was uncharacteristically monosyllabic and, the journalists probably thought, disappointingly bland. Physically I was feeling pretty good: although the cuts from my crash in Switzerland hadn't fully healed and were still causing me some discomfort on the bike, I'd spent a few days on the track in Manchester and done some good sessions there with my coach, Rod Ellingworth. Since Sky had launched at the start of the year, with Rod as their 'race coach', he and I had had to change our arrangement slightly. I could no longer phone Rod and sound off about teammates or other riders, as I'd always done, given the obvious conflict of interests. He was, though, still the guy who could 'read' me best as a rider, and he was also in charge of the British national team for the Worlds in Melbourne later in the year. Before the National Road Race Championship the weekend before the Tour, we'd had a short get-together for the guys likely to make the team and discussed how we could accumulate more rankings points, thereby entitling us to a bigger quota of riders in the Worlds. The race itself was an absolute bloodbath, on a course like an Alpine Tour stage, with 4,500 metres of vertical climbing in Lancashire, and only 11 riders finishing on the same lap as the winner, Geraint Thomas. I didn't even finish.

With Geraint's team, Team Sky, making their Tour debut and aiming to win the race with Bradley Wiggins, all British eyes were on them on the day of the prologue. Meanwhile, I cruised to 126th place and was just glad to be up and running. If cycling was my comfort blanket when things were going wrong, my team was another insulating layer and the reason why being at races was a relief more than a hardship. Here, at the Tour the team line-up was pretty much the one I would have picked if I'd been selecting it myself. As one of the team leaders, I did have some input, and had fought hard for the Australian, Adam Hansen, to be on the team. Adam was a bit of a rare bird in professional cycling – a quiet yet also quietly eccentric Queenslander with a sideline in computer programming. He'd been fantastic for me on my first Tour but hadn't been picked in 2009, and Rolf and Brian were hesitating again. Adam was one of those riders who didn't particularly enjoy the rough and tumble of riding in a peloton, and his edginess made him susceptible to crashes.

'You watch, if we pick Adam he'll crash in the first week and we'll be doing the rest of the Tour with eight riders,' Rolf kept telling me.

I, though, kept insisting, saying that Adam would prove them wrong, that he'd be on the front for three weeks, that he'd be amazing. Eventually, they'd caved. Adam was in, with me, Bert Grabsch, Tony Martin, Bernie Eisel, Maxime Monfort, Kanstantsin Sivtsov, Michael Rogers and Mark Renshaw.

The first stage would be our first chance, my first chance. We'd been going about an hour when Rolf's voice crackled in my earpiece. 'Adam's down. Adam's crashed.' My heart sank: Adam had got up but we could tell from the snippets of information that were coming from the team car, and then when we saw Adam, that Rolf and Brian's fears had probably been realised. They were annoyed at him for crashing and didn't make too much effort to hide it. When Adam drew alongside the team car and asked what he should do, Brian looked back at him blankly.

'What do you mean?'

Adam was confused, too. 'Well, I can't ride,' he said. 'I think my hand's broken, my ribs, I can't brake ...'

Brian cut him dead: 'Brake? You don't need to brake. You're riding on the front of the bunch all day, anyway, so off you go ... '

Adam did his best for the rest of the day but was packing his suitcases the following morning. We were lucky that he was the only casualty; we'd never seen crowds like it, layered three and four deep along every metre of the route and spilling into the already narrow road. One crash was caused by a dog running into the middle of the peloton. It was mayhem. I've always said that most half-decent amateurs would be struggling or crashing even in the neutralised zone on first stages of Tours de France, such is the speed and tension, but this was something else.

One of my strengths, luckily, is my ability to focus on the task at hand, especially in the last 50 kilometres. In the winter we'd lost George Hincapie, probably the best 'pathfinder' in the pro peloton, but on Mark Renshaw's wheel I could still lock into autopilot. With eight kilometres to go, the obligatory first-day breakaway was caught, the lead-out trains were starting to rev, and I sat in Mark's slipstream like a stone in a catapult. In four years of riding the Tour de France, nothing much had changed in my routine: the half-hour, hour I spent doing my 'homework', memorising the next day's finish every night, visualising it, studying it in the road-book or sometimes on Google Earth was sacrosanct, as it was at every race. Today's map looked relatively straightforward but I'd made a couple of mental bullet points: a tight, right-angle right-hander with four kilometres to go; a wide but very acute right-hander at 2.1 kilometres, almost a U-turn, that looked nothing like the drawing in the road book.

The first one, we'd swooped and positively glided around. As we came out of the bend and onto a wide, straight road, though, the Lampre train surged and we were swamped. Garmin then went and I was ten, fifteen wheels back as we approached the second right-hander, until Mick Rogers surged and brought Tony Martin onto the front just as the road started to curve. I said that all I needed to do in the last 50 kilometres was stay on Renshaw's wheel; now, as we came into the corner, I took that a bit too literally and looked down to see his quick-release wheel skewer tangled in my spokes. It was only a second or two, but the timing and place couldn't have been worse; all I could do to stay upright was lean on the rider to the left of me, Mirco Lorenzetto of the Lampre team, while carrying straight on towards the barriers, where we both came down anyway. A handful of other riders taking a line between us and the apex of the bend, including the three-time world champion Oscar Freire, were collateral damage, also hitting the deck.

If nothing else, everything that had happened in the first six months of the year had taught me to roll with the punches. I don't know, maybe with my confidence as shaky as it was it was also somehow, perhaps subconsciously, a relief not to have to sprint. As the TV motorbike rode alongside me and the cameraman zoomed in to film my reaction, I lifted a hand off my bars, shrugged and smiled. It was harder to stay cool a few minutes later, when I rode over the finish line, around a corner and into the small crowd of fans and journalists gathered outside our team bus. Above the shouts of '*Allez Cavendishe*' and 'Hard luck, Mark', two or three English voices were louder and more noticeable than the rest.

'Cavendish, you suck! Go home!'

Standing either side of me, Kristy and our sprint coach, Erik Zabel, probably feared what was coming next. This, though, was the new, improved, ultra-phlegmatic, ultra-diplomatic Mark Cavendish. This Mark Cavendish turned, smiled at his new 'fans' and told them to have a nice day.

The next morning, my self-restraint would be tested again by *L'Équipe*'s coverage of the crash. The paper that two years earlier had anointed me 'The Mozart of the Eleven-Tooth Sprocket' (it sounds more poetic in French) had now decided that a more appropriate nickname would be 'Catastrophe Cavendish' or *'Le Pyromane'* – 'The Pyromaniac'. My performance in the first stage of the Tour, in their eyes, was worth exactly nought out of ten. The French Minister of Sports had even weighed in, calling me 'the bad boy of cycling'.

This all grated, just as it always bothered me to be portrayed as a 'dangerous' sprinter. Throughout my career, while always admitting that I was fearless, I'd also prided myself on never, ever being reckless. The risks I took were few and far between and were invariably calculated, endangering only myself. In that 2010 season I'd crashed three times, but because of who I was, the stage I was performing on, and the *schadenfreude* that was clearly such a popular disease, everything had been magnified and exaggerated. Again, for me, it was all part of the learning curve – finding out that the trappings of success included scrutiny and criticism and realising that I needed to adapt. Accepting that, though, and assimilating it, was going to be a long process, especially for someone as headstrong as me.

Only once previously, at the 2009 Tour, had I won the first bunch sprint of a major tour, so I knew how to bide my time. Here, though, I was going to have to be especially patient: stage two through the Belgian Ardennes was never likely to favour a sprint and turned out to be even more selective than we'd envisaged due to heavy rain. If that stage had been billed as a miniature Liège–Bastogne–Liège, on some of the same roads, the next one would be a passable imitation of Paris–Roubaix, the gruelling annual one-day Classic featuring long stretches on cobbled farm tracks in northern France. I'd always dreamt of racing Paris–Roubaix as a kid and now I fancied my chances of a good performance even if a win seemed unlikely. I was actually in a good position and starting to get quite excited until my handlebars and saddle came loose as we hit the cobbles; it was suddenly clear that my bike – Scott's new aerodynamic 'Foil' frame – was too stiff over the stones. The Foil was a fantastic bike but the less aerodynamic Addict, which

I'd used all year up to that point, would no doubt have suited the terrain better. I was not a happy boy.

With my wonky handlebars and sinking saddle, I was way out the exhaust. Renshaw performed absolute miracles to take me back into the bunch and through it like Lionel Messi on a mazy dribble, but then – BOOM – bodies and bikes clattered together again. Frank Schleck, one of the pre-race favourites, was down with a broken collarbone; I managed to stay upright and bunny-hop over another rider spread-eagled on the cobbles but by then everyone who had been in front of the crash was barrelling away into a cloud of dust. A few people said to me after the race that they thought 25th was a good result. I, though, was sure that I could and should have made the top ten and possibly won.

I took heart from the fact that the sprints were finally on their way – three nailed-on bunch gallops as the race wound its way down the east of France and towards the Alps. That night, after my roommate Mark Renshaw had dropped off, I lay with my eyes wide open for a few minutes, imagining those final 200 metres in Reims – like a bomb detonating down my thighs and through my calves, every cell ablaze with lactic and adrenalin, and then the explosion of joy on the line. I'd experienced it four times in the Tour in 2008 and six times in 2009. Nothing else in cycling quite compared.

I definitely woke the next morning, I definitely got on my bike and rode from Reims, and I definitely saw Alessandro Petacchi win the fourth stage of the Tour de France. The rest – the race itself, those final kilometres that I'd memorised, the lead-out and then those four, five pedal strokes before I sat up – are all still there but somehow the picture is foggy and drained of colour and noise. It was as though, when I'd finally nodded off the previous night, the lights had stayed off until the next afternoon.

It was as though the noise that had woken me wasn't my alarm but 'Clunk, clunk, clunk.'

There is one thing worse than losing a Tour de France sprint that you expected to win – and that's losing one and then having to spend the night in a Hotel Campanile. Over the course of a Tour, the races organisers, ASO, try to give each team an even spread of five-star luxury and two-star slumming, and Campaniles have become infamous among Tour riders for occupying a position very much at the more modest end of the scale. Right now, though, not even room service in the penthouse at the Mandarin Oriental could have raised my spirits. I was distraught and still at a loss as to how it had happened; never before had my legs abandoned me like they had on that finishing straight in Reims.

Luckily, I had Brian and Aldis.

I'd met Aldis years earlier, during a winter spent doing Six Days with Rob Hayles. Bald, Latvian and unfailingly good-humoured, over the previous couple of seasons he'd become *my* personal masseur, the guy the team sent to all of the big races where I was competing. Aldis could 'listen' to me and my muscles like no one else. Both he and Brian are also among the funniest people I've ever met. And what I needed that night, more than anything else, was a bit of light relief.

The one saving grace about that Campanile was its location – ironically, for us, in the heart of Champagne country. Sensing my anger and dismay, Brian, like pretty much all of the other staff and riders, had tried to keep well out of the way in the hour or two since the stage-finish, taking himself off for a jog in the vineyards. He had then showered and come to the masseur's room where I lay on the massage table, waiting for Aldis to get to work. When I turned to face Brian, my attention was immediately drawn back to Aldis and the clink of three glass tumblers.

'Here,' Aldis said. 'I'm going to give you something that'll make you feel better.'

Grinning, he took a bottle of vodka in one hand and one of the glasses in the other. As he poured, his smile widened. He then opened a can of Sprite and filled the glass almost to the top. He then did the same in the other glasses. It was barely a single shot of vodka – certainly not enough to get me drunk – but, in the circumstances, it was the perfect medicine.

Within a minute or two Brian was telling stories, Aldis and I were giggling away, and what had just happened on that finish line in Reims seemed to belong to a different age, a different world.

Then, when we'd stopped laughing, just as he was about to leave, Brian turned serious.

'Cav,' he said, 'is there anything we can do to help you? Would you rather we didn't go for it tomorrow, didn't go for a sprint? You know, because if …'

'Brian,' I said, interrupting him. 'Don't worry about anything. I'm going to win tomorrow.'

The fact was that suddenly, for some reason, I felt ready. The team's confidence in me had also not wavered; the previous day, Kanstantsin Sivtsov, a climber by trade, had spent the entire day tapping out a steady pace on the front of the bunch, just to keep the breakaway within a safe distance. Now he'd do the same on stage five. Again, it was hot, and getting hotter as we rode into *La France Profonde* – the dry, desolate breadbasket of central France. A three-man breakaway had gone away early in the stage but that wouldn't give us too many headaches providing that we got the timing right. With six kilometres to go, we duly reeled them in.

The sprints in the 2010 Tour were different from 2008 and 2009. We were getting next to no help on the front of the bunch, were consequently having to commit two or maybe three even before the lead-out really started to wind up, and therefore looked less dominant than we had been in 2009 in the final ten kilometres. This stage conformed to the new pattern; when we gobbled up the last survivor from the break, José Iván Gutiérrez, this was Lampre's and Garmin's cue to try to swamp us. Garmin, in particular, were exceptionally strong, so it was pointless us trying to wrestle back control. There was no real need, either, as I could trust Renshaw to pick a pocket somewhere in the first ten positions and all I had to do was follow him. It sounds easy and he made it look easy, but Renshaw was a magician: there were other lead-out men with his speed, his instinct, his anticipation, his aggression and his bike-handling, but no one else had assembled the full armoury. Along with George Hincapie, he was the only rider I'd ever ridden with whose judgement I would take over my own. With Mark, it was like riding a tandem.

Even with Renshaw at his best, I still needed a bit of luck. Or a favour. Geraint Thomas momentarily snuck in between Mark and me with 1,500 metres to go, boxing me in. 'Oh, Gee,' was all I needed to shout; Gee eased to the side and let me through.

At 1,000 metres to go, Mark was coming up on the outside of the Garmin train, shoulder to shoulder with Thor Hushovd. Oscar Freire was also fighting for the last Garmin wheel, while I stayed glued to Mark.

At 750 we swung right around a right-angle bend and then into the home straight …

Mark looks around, 600, another look, 550, he's still waiting, waiting, just holding me there. It's 450 and he doesn't move, then 400 and he's starting to slide out, alongside the Garmins, then past them. It's 350 now and I'm praying my legs don't fucking let me down, not again, not today, Cav. It's coming now, 300, and it's open, wide open, and if you can't win from here, Cav, it's fucking wide open. It's 250 and it's 240 …

Mark's fading to the left and I'm going to the right. I kick and know, I know straight away: one kick, one pedal stroke and I know. I've won. I know.

And I win. Finally I win and the nightmare's over, all six months of it.

I scream and I turn to see the guys and it's chaos, bedlam, people grabbing me, pushing me, hitting me with cameras but I don't care because I've won. And then the tears come. The tears come.

I don't know what it was that set me off. It may have been seeing Geraint as we got changed behind the podium, him going to collect his white jersey as the leader of the young riders classification, me as the stage winner. I'd like to say it was linked to the experiences I'd shared with Gee growing up together as cyclists, all those times we'd talked and fantasised about doing this, the poignancy of us standing there behind a Tour de France podium together. Really, though, I think I was just ready to let it all out.

When it was my turn to go up on the podium, I'd composed myself, but then I heard the Tour anthem, the few bars of classical music that they play just as you're about to walk up the steps to the stage, and I went again. This time the tears came in uncontrollable floods. As someone pointed out to me later, I'd cried at some point in every Tour de France I'd done. This time we were barely a week in and within the space of 24 hours there had been tears of sorrow and tears of joy.

The interviews I'd given until that point in the Tour had been almost comical – except for the journalists having to contrive stories out of my quotes. In my desperation not to court any kind of controversy, I'd turned myself into a parody of the PR-pandering monosyllabic sportsman. One day I'd been asked whether I was already too far behind in the green jersey competition to have any chance – the kind of question that infuriated me – but I'd responded with a forced smile and parroted, 'I'm looking forward to the rest of the Tour.' Now, when waterworks had stopped pumping, I could finally relax in the press conference and in front of the cameras. Standing and 'supervising' me, Kristy didn't know whether to feel relieved or petrified.

If my demeanour had changed overnight then so had the tone of the coverage in the press. Here's a little sample of the next day's cuttings:

Het Laatste Nieuws (Belgium):

CAVENDISH SENDS HIS TORMENTOR TO HELL IN MONTARGIS: Cavendish found a wonderful way to exact sporting revenge. He came off Renshaw's wheel like a man possessed, staring into infinity. Immediately after the finish, tears streamed from his bulging cheeks.

Gazet Van Antwerpen (Belgium):

CAVENDISH WINS AND BREAKS THE TOUR SPELL

Le Figaro (France):

THE 'CAV' BRIDLED: The 'bad boy' who burst into tears. The fifth stage of the Tour de France has marked the awakening of Mark Cavendish and unveiled his human face.

Guardian (UK):

MARK CAVENDISH'S PYROTECHNICS BLOW FIELD AWAY

I didn't mind the fickleness, because I was often guilty of the same thing myself. I certainly preferred that to Bob's reaction as we'd driven from the press conference to the hotel. 'Well, just make sure you keep that up now,' he said, or words to that effect.

The insinuation that only if I kept winning would he be satisfied, that no more mistakes were allowed, momentarily popped my balloon.

Bob should never have doubted me. My teammates, *most* of my teammates, at least, never had, and my faith in them was bullet-proof. The next day's stage, another flat one to Gueugnon on the edge of Burgundy, was going to reflect that and, I think now, encapsulated in a single sprint everything that was special about my understanding with Mark Renshaw.

The team had headhunted Mark at the end of 2008, after Gerald Ciolek had signed for Milram and left me without a lead-out man. When our *directeurs* first mentioned Renshaw as a potential replacement, I'll admit that I wasn't particularly enthused. My only real contact with him prior to that had been physical, literal – I'd shoved him out of the way in a sprint in the 2008 Tour. Beyond that I'd not really noticed him, which I didn't think was a particularly good sign. But I'd given it my blessing anyway, and he'd joined. We'd got on well enough at training camps that winter, though to say that we'd hit it off instantly wouldn't be strictly accurate. Mark is still fairly quiet, and you might think a bit standoffish at first. More to the point, our first race together had been the Tour of California in 2009, and our first sprint there had been a disaster. I'd lost Mark's wheel on the way in to the finish, he'd carried on and done his own sprint to come third, and I was livid. That night, after the stage, I went to see him in his room.

'Listen, mate, what you did today ... that's not on.' I didn't raise my voice, but he clearly got the message. From that evening on, our understanding was practically telepathic.

Before stage six to Gueugnon, the planning and homework was key. This was another area where Mark and I were perfectly in sync, and in which Mark was the model pro. The previous night, after my win in Montargis, we'd done our routine, painstaking virtual recce of the final kilometres on Google Street View. Whatever conclusions we drew from that, as usual, Erik Zabel would then go ahead of the race to test, and relay his observations back to Rolf in the team car. Rolf would then give us the vital information over race radio. Victory or defeat on this stage, we realised, was going to hinge on the final corner – a right-angle left-hander at 800 metres to go. The message from Erik was that it was blind but, if we took the right line, we didn't need to brake.

Intel like this took on even more significance now that we couldn't necessarily dictate terms in the final two kilometres. Mark's role also became more important for the same reason. It's a common misconception that a lead-out man is just a second-rate sprinter, someone who can sprint at 55 kph and whose finish line is the 250-to-go sign, but who can't sprint at 60 kph from there to the finish. In reality, the two jobs are totally different. When he's not part of a team riding like aerobatic display planes – with riders peeling off at predetermined points until only the sprinter is left – a lead-out man's work will often consist of multiple explosive efforts, or one long one very close to his maximum power. After that, the sprint, those last 250 or 200 metres, aren't about how many watts I can put out, they're about how many I can put out when I'm on the limit, because I should already be on the limit when I'm on my lead-out man's wheel.

Mark's other fantastic asset, in addition to the ones I mentioned earlier, was his ability to stay cool. This was another thing we shared. Both of us treated sprints like a maths exam: something you'd revised for, watching videos, studying maps, imagining what questions you'd be asked, visualising your answers, and then on the day thinking as quickly as possible, but never forgetting to do just that – think. In everything you ever read or see about sprinting, great emphasis is placed on the speed, the danger, the thrills and the adrenaline, and I think perhaps some sprinters get caught up with or perhaps fall in love with that tear-away image of themselves. Neither Mark nor I ever thought of ourselves or our jobs in those terms; our approach was calm, studious, clinical. What I've said before about staying physically fresher by saving emotional energy also applied to Mark.

This was a classic example: we were swamped by Garmin in the penultimate kilometre and their train rattled headlong towards that last left-hander with 800 to go, while Mark 'laid off' them – hung back ten or twenty metres. By doing that, we knew, thanks to our prep and Erik's, that we could freewheel around the corner while the Garmin riders, Julian Dean and Robbie Hunter, had to slow and then accelerate again into the finishing straight. We weren't trying to dive-bomb them out of the bend – just save a few pedal revs, a few watts, which would then make the difference for Mark when he started to wind it up, and for me when it was time to go at the 250-metre mark.

The previous day's sprint, like all of the others so far in this race, had been a 'power sprint'. They'd been an exercise in strength more than speed. I'd had to labour the gear, churn rather than spin it. This one was much more up my street. I kicked and knew instantly not only that I'd won but also that my jump was back to its springiest, fastest and most deadly. I won by two bike lengths from Tyler Farrar, easing up in the last 20 metres. While I hugged my teammates – and this time held back the tears – the Spaniard Carlos Barredo and the Portuguese rider Rui Costa were grappling with each other on the tarmac, this after Barredo had detached his front wheel from his bike and used it to wallop Costa over the head.

The Tour could get to you like that – I knew it better than anyone. It could be cruel but it could also be kind. Three days after wondering whether I would ever win again, I was suddenly two stages to the good.

As the years and Tours passed, my confidence and ability in the mountains had followed a steady upward curve. Even so, every now and again you'd still get a stage which, a bit like Carlos Barredo's carbon rim, hit you and left you dazed. Stage seven of the 2010 Tour was one such day: on paper it was only a *moyenne montagne* or 'medium mountain' stage through the gently sloped, wooded Jura range, with a crescendo of fairly minor climbs culminating in the second-category ascent to the Les Rousses ski resort; in reality it turned out to be a brute. It was the perfect example of how it wasn't the route that determined the difficulty of a race but the way that the riders chose to tackle it. Perhaps more than any other race, because every kilometre of the route carries value for some rider, some team, some sponsor, the Tour was permanently beholden to a butterfly effect which would jolt it out of a fragile equilibrium and into balls-to-the-walls chaos. On this stage, all it took was one of the French teams, Bbox Bouygues Telecom, to miss the key break of the day and the next three or four hours were turned into a groaning, aching procession of agony.

The heat was unbearable. On the penultimate climb, Bernie Eisel, Renshaw and I had slipped behind the *gruppetto*, the last group on the road. We chased and had regained contact at the foot of the final climb, but by then panic was starting to spread through the *gruppetto* about missing the time limit. The humidity that made a stifling sweatshop out of the peloton early in the day had now also built into a huge bank of storm clouds over our heads. It all contributed to the growing sense of urgency – and the quickening pace. Every 100 metres or so, someone, somewhere in the *gruppetto* would scream at the riders at the front to slow down. We finally crossed the line 59 seconds inside the time cut. When I was later asked to describe the suffering I'd endured that day,

I could only liken it to having your nails pulled off your fingers very slowly, one by one.

After a day like that, you wake the next morning wondering how you'll ever survive the same again – or harder. All that gets you through is knowing that there are other guys in the same boat, or even worse off due to crashes or illness. Over the course of a career as a cyclist, through experiences like mine at Les Rousses, you also become accustomed, almost brutalised, to making demands of your body that it simply wasn't designed to fulfil. You either let that reality overcome you, or you overcome it with pure bloody-mindedness.

In the Alps, just like every year, I did precisely that: I suffered but I survived. Up the road, in a parallel universe, there was apparently a bike-race happening, the Tour de France. We'd get back to the bus after mountain stages, hear maybe from the *directeurs* or on the TV that Andy Schleck had attacked Alberto Contador, that Armstrong was struggling, or that Cadel Evans had blown on the Col de la Madeleine, and we'd react as you do when your mum tells you that a second cousin has just graduated from university, or Maureen from down the road is moving house. It was news, but only of very vague interest to us.

Most of the time, your sphere of consciousness and concern narrowed as the race progressed and as your fatigue levels crept ever higher. Eventually, you'd get to the point where you only really cared about your teammates, but for them your empathy was intense. Perhaps that's what made stage 11 such a bitter blow, even though it was me who crossed the line first and took my third win of the Tour.

It had been another exemplary HTC-Columbia performance, on another hot day and another only gently undulating stage, until 500 metres from the finish line in Bourg-lès-Valence. Garmin had, as usual, left the work to other teams before a late surge, this time under the kilometre-to-go kite. Bernie Eisel pulled off, leaving Renshaw and the Garmin rider, Julian Dean, going shoulder-to-shoulder, toe-to-toe on the front, with me and Tyler Farrar respectively tucked in behind them, both ready to jump. It was a routine finale until Dean started inching left, brushing Mark with his elbow, and Renshaw responded by leaning across and nudging Dean three times with his head (others said it was more like the movement of a rutting stag). It was too early for me to go, 400 metres from the line, but too risky to stay, and so I steered wide of Renshaw on the left and flew up the inside of the barriers. I've always had the ability to 'go long' – hold my speed over 15, sometimes even 20 seconds – and it's also one of the few aspects of sprinting that I actually 'train', insomuch as I finish every training ride with one very long sprint. Here, I held off Farrar and Petacchi comfortably, but there was a sheepishness, a distant hint of doom in the faces that ought to have been elated when I crossed the line. Within minutes, the Tour's competitions director, Jean-François Pescheux, announced that Renshaw had been not just disqualified, *déclassé* in the stage, but '*exclu* du Tour de France': sent home in disgrace.

Pescheux and I have – and had – always got on OK. With his permanently furrowed brow, narrowed eyes and upside-down smile, he didn't always exude charm, but I generally felt that his own career as a rider in the 1960s and 70s had attuned him to the riders' needs and their difficulties. Now, though, in my opinion, he'd been swayed by a series of factors that ought to have had no bearing on his decision: my 'bad boy' reputation and the sheer volume of interest in me and my team; the fact that Renshaw and I were suddenly dominating the sprint finishes in this Tour; the exposure of the Tour and the pack mentality of the public; failing to realise that although the last of Renshaw's three 'head butts' was definitely intimidating, out of order and worthy of a disqualification from the stage, what Julian Dean had done was actually more dangerous. That was the bottom line, as I still see it: Renshaw was actually using the only available means to keep himself and Dean upright, given that the rules forbid you from taking your hands off the bars. Had he allowed Dean to keep veering across him, they could easily have locked bars and brought me, Renshaw and 20 guys around us down.

What really annoyed me was the lack of consistency. Barredo had got a slap on the wrist for throwing three punches at Rui Costa and clobbering him over the head with a wheel. There were shoves and scuffles in nearly every bunch sprint that were at least as likely to cause someone serious injury, only they went unpunished. It stuck in the throat to see Garmin's manager, Jonathan Vaughters, scuttling immediately off to lodge a complaint with Pescheux and the race jury. A year earlier, Garmin had been chasing down George Hincapie, our rider at the time, apparently because they couldn't bear the thought of an American rider not in their team taking the yellow jersey. To me, this was just the latest evidence that they spent far too much time and energy trying to stop us winning, and not enough on themselves.

We could complain all we liked, but it would change nothing. Mark was devastated as much by the fact that he was going home as the damage that had been done to his reputation. As a rider, you sometimes felt that you couldn't live with the Tour, yet you also couldn't live without it. While the riders in the race envied the guys with their feet up at home, the guys with their feet up at home would have given anything to be self-harming their way around the French countryside for 21 days.

There were certainly days in that Tour when my team and I both wondered whether I was going to miss Mark Renshaw at all – because it seemed quite likely that I'd also soon be on my way home. The problems began on stage 13 to Revel, which was sure to represent my last chance of a fourth win before the Pyrenees, and was an outside chance at that. In the morning I'd told my teammates that I was confident of surviving the third category Saint-Ferréol climb, which crested 7.5 km from the finish; I felt I could get over in the main peloton or within striking distance, and that if they worked I wouldn't let them down. As the Cervélo and Milram teams accelerated in an effort to drop me on the climb, I had duly buried myself, bent almost at right-angles over my bike, swaying wildly from left to right. Alexandre Vinokourov, who had attacked in the final kilometre of the climb, led by around 15 seconds as I reached the summit and began my descent. I could barely make out Michael Rogers's back wheel, the display on my SRM power meter showing 550 watts, or for that matter the zigzags of the steep, descending road; for a few seconds I was actually blacking out, fainting on the bike. I only knew that the gap was rising and that it would take the descent of my life to catch Vinokourov. The irate cries of 'Cavendish!' from other riders as I cut one bend after another shook me back to full consciousness, but it was all in vain. Vinokourov held on to take the stage by 13 seconds, and my 'winning' sprint was to be first of the losers.

The result, though, was less alarming than the goose bumps that ran all up my arms when I peeled off my jersey in the team bus. I didn't need to ask a doctor; I knew that I was getting ill. The next morning began with shivers, a splutter and, if you'll excuse the overly vivid description, a missile of greenish-brown phlegm into the toilet bowl. If I'd been apprehensive before about the three consecutive Pyrenean stages coming next, now I was consumed with dread. The first one to Ax 3 Domaines was an ordeal, but I scraped through in the *gruppetto*. That was also the day when Brad Wiggins told the press that he was 'fucked' and wasn't in good enough form to contend for the Tour. I'll make a confession: I thought Brad's fourth place in 2009 was as good as it would ever get for him.

The coughing was getting worse, the fever in me was rising, but, with the *gruppetto* as my life-raft, I somehow struggled ashore again the next day at Bagnères-de-Luchon. Now I only had to survive one more stage before the second rest-day. But what a stage. In the 1910 race, the first one ever to take on the Pyrenees, one of the Tour riders, Octave Lapize, had branded the organisers 'murderers' for inflicting the consecutive torture of the Peyresourde, Aspin, Tourmalet and Ausbisque passes upon the peloton. To celebrate the 100th anniversary of that first foray into the Pyrenees, we were facing the same quartet of climbs – the 'Circle of Death' as Lapize called it.

Alessandro Petacchi, the Lampre sprinter, had come to see me at the start that morning to discuss ways to make the day as painless as possible. From Bagnères-de-Luchon, the stage route reared straight up and over the Peyresourde, and Petacchi and I agreed that it would probably make sense to form a *gruppetto* almost immediately, on the lower slopes of the climb, and then settle in for a long day of nervously watching the clock and calibrating our effort to sneak inside the time cut.

The plan was quite sound but based on the assumption that I would be strong and healthy enough to follow the *gruppetto*. As it was, when the gun went that idea went up in smoke: dropped immediately on the Peyresourde and, with Bernie Eisel and Bert Grabsch at my side, I could only watch forlornly as the *gruppetto* disappeared over the summit. We then got news through our earpieces that Petacchi and Lampre were hammering down the descent in a bid to put me out of the time limit, out of the green jersey competition that Petacchi was leading, and out of the race.

One of the by-products of spending a lot of time trying to beat time cuts is that it forces you to become a fearless descender. Ask most cycling fans or commentators and they'll tell you that Vincenzo Nibali or Samuel Sanchez is the best descender in the world, but they'd soon change their mind if they saw the majority of guys who regularly ride in the *gruppetto*. Once, at one of my teams, I told the team manager that I couldn't ride on the tyres that we were being given by our sponsor because they simply wouldn't have withstood the rigours of *gruppetto* riding. I was told that the team's general classification leader used the tyres and got on just fine. That just underlined the widespread misconception: GC riders simply don't take the same risks as we do, simply don't have to.

Lampre certainly weren't going to gain any time on me on the way down, but the gap was still substantial as we started the next climb, the Col d'Aspin. Jens Voigt had crashed on the descent of the Peyresourde, and he now helped us to make good ground for the first half of the climb, before pounding up the mountain on his own. After another breakneck descent, we caught the *gruppetto* at the foot of the Col du Tourmalet – one of the highest passes in the Pyrenees and the climb that had prompted Lapize's 'Murderers!' diatribe in 1910.

I was now shivering with fever. To make matters worse, Ivan Basso, the reigning Giro d'Italia champion, was also ill and reduced to riding in the *gruppetto*, the etiquette and strategies of which were clearly all new to him. Basso had started to fret about the time-limit and ride full-gas, not realising that we would gain minutes on the front group over the last 60 kilometres from the summit of the final climb, the Col d'Aubisque, to the finish-line in Pau. Not only will a *gruppetto* by definition contain stronger riders on the flat, big *rouleurs*, than the front group of ace climbers, but everyone is expected to chip in with the pace-making. Admittedly, just because it's expected that doesn't mean that everyone does; every *gruppetto* has its share of passengers, usually Frenchmen who were attacking in the first five kilometres of the stage and later tell you that they're '*trop fatigué*' to do any work.

I was dropped again on the Tourmalet, with only Bernie now for company. At this point the calculators were out: how many seconds per kilometre could we lose on the Tourmalet and the Aubisque, how many minutes would we have to recoup on the flat, and was it all going to be in vain anyway, because I'd be too sick to carry on? The game of yo-yo continued on the Aubisque. Now I was on my knees, certain that even if we made it inside the time limit I'd be going home. As we lost sight of the *gruppetto* again, I started unloading all excess weight: my bottles, food, radio. Bernie, Grabschy and Tony Martin, who had now also waited with us, took all of them. Yet again, miraculously, we rejoined the *gruppetto* at the bottom of the descent of the Aubisque.

Then, with 20 kilometres to go, disaster. I punctured.

I reached down to squeeze the radio mouthpiece under my jersey.

'What the … Oh fuck!'

I'd forgotten that Tony Martin still had my radio. My team-mates were already pulling away and out of sight, so I had to go old-school – raise my arm and wait for the team car to arrive. Five, six, seven team cars passed me. Eight, nine, ten. Where was our second *directeur sportif*, Allan Peiper, in ours? I looked dolefully into the windows of the passing team cars, hoping that one would stop to give me a wheel, but they all swished past. I was still shivering, my punctured tyre was juddering, and there was still no sign of Allan. Finally I found a good Samaritan in the last car – from the Astana team which had no real interest in dumping me out of the time limit. The Astana car stopped, gave me a wheel, and paced me back up to the convoy. They had saved me.

Allan, I found out later, had stopped for a toilet break.

Half an hour later, I crossed the finish line in one of the biggest *gruppettos* I'd ever seen, almost 100 strong. If before that stage I'd thought I knew my limits, over the six hours that I'd spent on my bike that day I'd entered a new dimension of suffering; I'd crossed a Rubicon where it becomes more than bloody-minded, more than masochistic, both of which descriptions imply a certain degree of will and consciousness. This hadn't been that. This had been a boxer lifting himself off the canvas after a knockout and staggering around a ring, concussed, inviting yet more punishment only because that obligation is implicit in what he sees as his job

– a boxer will go on boxing, a Tour de France cyclist will go on cycling, come what may, until it becomes an impossibility.

When we arrived back at the hotel that night, my new roommate, Bernie Eisel, nearly had to haul me into the lift. I then got undressed and doddered off into the shower without closing the door. Ten minutes later Bernie wondered why he hadn't heard the water running. He promptly stuck his head around the door, exploded into laughter and reached for his phone to take a picture: I was sitting, cross-legged, fast asleep in the bottom of the shower.

The 'rest-day' is one of the great misnomers of professional cycling, given that it's standard practice for most guys to ride anywhere between 50 and 100 kilometres. For me, though, this one lived up to its name. I stayed in bed the whole day and had food and drink brought up to my room. It was hardly ideal preparation for the next day's final Pyrenean extravaganza finishing on top of the Tourmalet, but by now I was lurching mindlessly from one ritual pummelling to the next. As it happened, the configuration of this last mountain stage – with large portions of valley road between the three climbs on the route – was always going to make for a generous time limit, and I got through without too much difficulty. Whatever the bug or illness that I'd caught was, however, it appeared to be staying for the duration; I got into the bus parked a couple of kilometres the other side of the Tourmalet summit that day, pulled on a woolly hat, and found a corner to curl up in a ball.

That night, Aldis told me that I was too ill to even go to my massage, and the next morning Brian Holm said he was forbidding me from starting the stage. I argued for a while, Brian held firm, then I argued a bit more and he finally relented.

'Come on, Brian, it's a flat day,' I'd said. 'I'm not even thinking about sprinting, I just want to recover and make it to the Champs Elysées.'

My first memory of the stage, 198 kilometres from Salies-de-Béarn to Bordeaux, was of coughing and seeing a bullet of brown phlegm launch itself out of my mouth and onto a groove in my handlebar stem, where it stayed. That and a withering pace which, bizarrely, seemed to be blowing away cobwebs in my aching body. To my astonishment, my legs were starting to feel light, elastic, powerful, and so I went back to see Brian in the car.

'I actually feel OK, you know,' I said.

Brian nodded and reached for his intercom: 'Guys, Cav thinks he can do it, so we'll ride for the sprint.'

My team duly delivered another masterclass to get me into a good position with 1,500 metres to go and, from there, without Renshaw, I just 'surfed' the wheels. Having had a miserable first Tour, Sky were desperately trying to salvage something and they led into the final straight. This was interpreted by some as a sign that there was already a deal in place for me to join Sky the following season. In reality, I was just flitting between wheels like a bee buzzes between flowers, looking for the sweetest nectar, the best slipstream. From Bernie's wheel, I'd jumped behind Julian

Dean, then Thor Hushovd, before seeing Petacchi swing across the road as he wound it up, and then following him, passing him and winning by four bike lengths.

The podium presentation that day was one of the more memorable ones of my Tour de France career. Tom Cruise and Cameron Diaz were in town promoting their new film, *Knight and Day*, and were guests of the Tour de France organisers. Naturally, I gave Cameron Diaz my winner's bouquet.

There were now just two stages left. First there was a long time-trial that would act as the decider in what had been a close-fought battle for the yellow jersey between Alberto Contador and Andy Schleck. That was an irrelevance for me, unlike, of course, the grand finale on the Champs Elysées. Contador held off Schleck, as expected, in the time trial, and now it was left to me to fill in the other expected outcome on the Champs.

A lot of people will remember the side-on film of that sprint – of Thor Hushovd entering the frame, then Petacchi, and then me suddenly appearing like an Exocet on the other side of the road and tearing towards the Arc de Triomphe and my fifth win of the Tour. Three months later they would play the clip in a montage of the best moments of the 2010 Tour at the official presentation of the 2011 race. At the very instant when I roared into shot, the audience laughed as one. Sitting beside me, Thor Hushovd glanced in my direction and shook his head, smiling.

What people didn't necessarily see or hear at the time was me momentarily losing my position as we entered the last two kilometres, and a voice over my shoulder saying, 'Come on, Cav!' Only Tony Martin could have towed me back to fourth wheel, with the peloton already in one line, as we swung off the Rue de Rivoli, into the Place de la Concorde, and onto the Champs.

I'd ended the Tour with five stages: one fewer than in 2009, five more than I probably feared when I sat sobbing under that towel in Reims after the fourth stage. Having insinuated that I was finished, that the fame had gone to my head, that I was too preoccupied with girls and fast cars to train, the media were now drooling.

My own single regret was that, once again, I'd come up tantalisingly short in the green jersey competition – 232 points to the winner Alessandro Petacchi's 243. If I'd carried on sprinting that day in Reims, and not stopped pedalling the second I knew I couldn't win, eventually coming in 12th, that would have been enough. Hindsight, of course, could be a bastard.

After everything I'd been through over the previous seven months, I was certainly in no mood to complain that night in Paris, not about the race anyway. Our team's post-Tour party, however, I wasn't too enamoured with. As usual, it had all been arranged at the last minute, with our logistics manager being asked to find and reserve a venue with 48 hours' notice, on the night of the biggest event in the Parisian sporting calendar. She'd done the best she could, but we'd ended up in a pretty mediocre restaurant, and not even sitting around tables but all packed in around a buffet table. To me, at the time, this was yet more evidence that the way we were over-performing and over-delivering on a budget that shouldn't have entitled us to half of that success wasn't being appreciated, in both senses of the word. It also showed a lack of recognition for something else, something more fundamental: we'd just completed the Tour de France.

I went to bed early, just after midnight. The founder of the race, Henri Desgrange, once said the Tour was 'a crusade, a pilgrimage, a lesson and an example'. For me, this one had certainly been one hell of a journey.

chapter three

My last fight with Bernie Eisel had happened a month earlier, on the Col du Tourmalet during the Tour, and for us had been pretty standard stuff. As stragglers in the *gruppetto* flicked around a bend and out of sight, like a cat's tail through the crack of a pantry door, Bernie and I had known that it was time to start doing some sums.

'Cav, I know you're ill, mate, but we can't fuck around here. We have to go faster than this. Come on.'

Bernie's accent – like an Austrian loudly impersonating an Australian, which in some ways he was, or vice versa – could usually be guaranteed to make me smile, even if only internally. Hearing this, though, I had glared at him.

'Bernie, we can lose ten seconds a kilometre if we get two and a half minutes back on the descent, which we will. Don't nag. Just let me fucking ride ...'

'Cav, I'm telling you, mate ...'

'Bernie, no. It's under control. Ten seconds per kilometre ...'

And so it had gone, until I'd ended the argument by stroppily pedalling over to the other side of the road. The fans on the climb must have been scratching their heads: why were two teammates battling to beat the time cut riding up the mountain parallel to each other but three metres apart, both with faces like smacked backsides?

That had been the Tour. As usual, we'd soon put it behind us – before the summit, as I remember. Now at the Vuelta, Bernie and I were at it again. Toys were flying out of prams and the Seville roads were peppered with expletives. Our teammates could only look on, silently wincing behind their sunshades.

'Look,' I said one last time, 'if you listen and we get this right, we will definitely win this today. But if anyone doesn't want to listen, they can fuck off now.'

With a 'Fuck you, I'm off then,' Bernie swung his bike around and rode off.

This wasn't, I'll grant you, the most auspicious note on which to start my first Tour of Spain or Vuelta a España. After the Tour I'd skipped the beach, skipped the lucrative post-Tour criterium races, where I could now easily command five-figure appearance fees. I had raced just twice, at the Tre Valli Varesine and the Coppa Bernocchi in Italy, before arriving in Spain. My goal over the next two, maybe three weeks if I decided to do the whole Vuelta, wasn't stage wins or the points jersey but to fine-tune my form ahead of the World Championship road race in Australia. That would take place on 3 October, exactly a fortnight after the end of the Vuelta.

Here I was, though, on the morning of the team time trial that would open the final Grand Tour of the 2010 season, contemplating Bernie's one-man mutiny. As he clipped shoes into pedals, swung his front wheel around and set off in the direction of the team hotel, I turned to face my other seven teammates, still rooted to the spot and speechless.

'Right, anyone want to join him?'

On this occasion, at the Vuelta, as on others with me, Bernie thought that there was a point where helpful advice and encouragement ended and verbal bombardment began, and that I didn't know where to draw the line. He had done team time trials with me before, seen me perform the same General Eisenhower impersonation, but this time he reckoned that I was going too far. I disagreed. On the eve of the race we'd done a ragged first run-through, not on the race route but just to practise the rotation and cornering, after which I'd reminded everyone – admittedly in my usual, forthright manner – of the importance of holding a steady speed. We then repeated the effort, putting what I'd said into practice, and smashed it.

'Right, if we all do that tomorrow, we'll win the team time trial,' I'd announced as all grabbed drinks and cooled down.

The TTT itself had been scheduled for the evening, sensibly given that the temperature in the day was edging 40 degrees. This also gave us time for a proper practice run, this one on the route itself in the morning. And that was when Bernie started to lose patience. Now admittedly, I'd taken my I-dotting and T-crossing to a new level of fastidiousness by sketching the corners on pieces of paper before we set out, but as I kept telling my teammates: 'If we get 80 per cent of the technical aspects of this time trial right, we won't win. If we get 90 per cent right, we might win but we might not, and if we get 100 per cent right we'll definitely win,' Having laboured this point, it then annoyed me when we began our morning recce and I could hear Kanstantsin Siutsou and Lars Bak yammering at the back of the line as we approached one key bend.

'Right,' I said, slamming on my brakes. 'You're not paying attention, so we'll go back and do it again.'

This was when Bernie kicked off.

'No, I'm not doing it again. No way. You need to chill out.'

At this point, insults flew back and forth across the road, with neither of us going to give an inch. So Bernie went back to the hotel.

When I asked, no one else wanted – or dared – to join him, and we finished the practice lap with eight men.

An hour or so later, I got back to the hotel and the room that I was sharing with Bernie. I pushed the door, walked in and there he was.

'You're a dickhead,' were his first words.

'No, you're a dickhead,' was my reply.

And that was it over: within thirty seconds we were best mates again. Not only that, but when we got onto the course for one very

My infamous two-fingered salute after winning stage two of the Tour of Romandy in 2010. Not my smartest move, but I'd spent the start of the season ill in bed, the critics were all over me and it was an emotional response in the heat of the moment.

Blood, sweat and tears.
Above: Carrying the
scars of a particularly
tasty crash during the
final run-in on stage two
of the Tour Down Under
in 2011. **Left:** After a
pressured and difficult
start to the 2010 Tour
de France, returning
to winning ways with
the fifth stage was
undoubtedly one of my
most emotional victories.

It doesn't always go to plan. **Right:** A crash during a packed final sprint on stage three of the Tour of Switzerland saw me fined and docked points. **Below:** I lost out on stage two of the Giro in 2011 by the width of a wheel rim when I felt Petacchi rode across my line. The jury saw differently, but I had the consolation of wearing the maglia rosa the following day.

Left: It's all part of the circus – loading out the HTC-Highroad team in the Puy du Fou at the official team presentation of the 2011 Tour de France.

Below: Celebrating winning my fifth stage of the 2010 Tour. Despite this success I narrowly lost out to Petacchi for the green jersey.

Right: Everything's gone green – I got my first grand tour points jersey in Madrid in the Vuelta, 2010.

Below: Celebrating on the finish line on the Champs-Elysées to finally take the maillot vert in 2011. There's no more dramatic place on Earth to win.

The high point of my career as I emotionally receive my world champion medal and jersey after the Elite Men's Road Race in Copenhagen, 2011.

I look ecstatic and was … up to a point: the elation was also tinged with guilt, as I pulled on the rainbow jersey without the lads whose selfless performances had won me the World Road Race. **Below**, I hug Geraint Thomas moments after crossing the line.

The fame game. Once you reach a certain level it becomes as intense off the bike as on it. **Left:** Here I am promoting British technology with David Cameron in Woking in 2011. **Below:** Shaking hands with French President François Hollande after a stage win in Brive-la-Gaillarde in 2012.

last practice lap that night it was poetry in motion. We'd intended to take it easy – and it felt like a breeze because we were technically perfect – but our time on that practice lap would almost have put us on the podium in the race proper. When we finally did roll off the start ramp, only this time holding nothing back, we replicated the same fluid turns and clockwork rotation and went on to win by a relatively comfortable margin of ten seconds. The team had decided that I would cross the line first and so take the red leader's jersey in the event of victory. It was one of the best wins of my career to date: I was ecstatic, but I also felt slightly guilty that the rider in red at the end of it wasn't Matt Goss. Gossy was so strong that day that he could have ridden away from us.

The three weeks in Spain started as they were set to continue. I loved the Vuelta. The loneliness, the lack of any real anchor in my life, the restlessness that had gnawed at me all year, were still there under the surface, but racing a Grand Tour was the best way to keep my mind occupied, purely by virtue of the fact that I was on my bike and among friends. I was single at the time, but in Bernie I had a fairly convincing substitute spouse only minus the romance; we slept in the same room, spent more time with each other than with anyone else, bickered constantly, but, just like our row over the time trial, the arguments would be explosive and quickly resolved. When Bernie had to quit the race on the fourth day because of a virus, for a day or two I felt completely bereft.

Without Bernie, without Renshaw (who'd had a long season and been left out of the Aussie Worlds squad because they were worried that he'd be tempted to work for me!), without Tony Martin, I was working with a brand-new, you could say makeshift sprint train, but one that could still deliver me in style. Gossy was flying, and he was doing a fantastic job, but he was different from Mark; his style was jerkier, more erratic, and it took more balls to follow him. In the first week there were four bunch sprints, and I didn't win a single one, mainly because I'd got it into my head that it would take a long sprint to win on the Worlds course in Melbourne, and that I needed to simulate that here. I was kicking with 350 metres to go and dying before the line. Eventually, though, we were bound to win one, and in a technical finish on stage 12 into Lleida, Gossy dragged both of us so far clear going into the last corner that for a second I hesitated, hoping that Gossy would carry on to take the win himself, only for him to nod me through. The next day we dominated again, so much so that I didn't even have to sprint off Gossy's wheel – I merely carried on at the same speed as he peeled off. I even had time for a bit of showboating, bunny-hopping over the finish-line. With hindsight that wasn't particularly wise: going by the letter of the law, I really ought to have been disqualified, as lifting both wheels off the ground was considered 'dangerous riding'. The jury overlooked it, I think perhaps because they knew they should really have relegated Tyler Farrar for blocking me in a sprint earlier in the race, but had turned a blind eye there, too.

The two back-to-back wins had given me a solid lead in the points competition. Consequently I now felt duty-bound to push on through to Madrid, nurturing my form ahead of the Worlds as I went. We also had Peter Velits riding high in the general classification, and I was determined to help him wherever I could. Above all, I was enjoying it; if the Giro was three weeks of beautiful chaos, and the Tour just a huge, slick and scary machine, the Vuelta was the decaffeinated grand tour – with all of the flavour of the other two but minus some of the stress. There were hardly any journalists, late starts, and stages that generally settled quickly, with a break going down the road and the peloton slowly cranking up the pace to bring them back in the closing kilometres. The one element that wasn't to my liking was the climbs – the Lagos de Covadonga, the Bola del Mundo and other horrors that had more in common with rock climbing than professional cycling.

I managed to get myself one more win, in Salamanca on stage 18, again superbly set up by Gossy. It would have been two more, I'm quite certain, had I not pinged a spoke four kilometres from the finish in Madrid on the last day. With my brake pads rubbing on my rear rim and my power meter showing that I was putting out 800 watts instead of the usual 500 just to stay on Gossy's wheel as we entered the last kilometre, I was in knots by the time Tyler Farrar snuck past me to nick it on the line. I consoled myself with my first victory in the points competition of a major tour and only the second ever by a British rider, after Malcolm Elliot's in the 1989 Vuelta. I was delighted with my form and increasingly confident about my chances of pulling on another jersey: the rainbow jersey of the World Road Race Champion.

The following day I flew back to Tuscany, but it was only a short stop; I'd made plans, with the other two members of the British team for Melbourne, David Millar and Jeremy Hunt, to fly to Australia early and get acclimatised. The size of each nation's team at the Worlds is determined by the rankings points scored by riders from that country across that season, and it hadn't been a vintage year for British riders; I'd had my slow start from January until June, and Brad Wiggins had, by his own admission, flopped badly at the Tour after his fourth place the previous year. That had left us low on rankings points and with a team of only three riders, whereas other nations would have as many as nine. Luckily, among the stronger nations were those who had sent guys to recce the course or seen it on video and also decided that the best bet would be riding for a sprint finish; they would control the race.

One of only two Austrians to qualify for the race, Bernie had also gone out early and he, Jez, Dave and I trained together in the week before the race. In my desperation to hold the form I was taking out of the Vuelta, I was pushing harder than the other guys up the climbs, doing extra kilometres when they headed back to the hotel at the end of rides. All three of them and Rod Ellingworth, my coach and the GB team's that week, kept telling me that I needed to calm down. They told me that I was doing too much, but I was adamant that I was getting even stronger than I had been at the Vuelta. As the days passed, I convinced myself that I was going to be the world champion, even to the point where, in interviews, I was employing a tactic that had worked for me before Milan–San Remo in 2009: I started bluffing. I told the press that, having now seen and ridden on the course, I'd realised that it was much harder than it had looked on paper and on tape and, actually, I had no hope of winning.

'I'll have to revise my ambitions,' I lied, holding back a smirk.

Sadly it was the course and my rivals who had the last laugh, and Jez, Dave and Bernie who could say, 'I told you so.' The race started in Melbourne, and from there we would ride 83 kilometres to Geelong before completing 11 laps of a 15.9 km circuit. I, though, hadn't even got to Geelong – hadn't even made it out of Melbourne, in fact – when I already knew that my confidence had been badly misplaced. Within minutes of us rolling over the start-line, we'd come to the bridge curving gently over the Yarra river. I'd shifted my weight forward and into the slope, lifted myself up off the saddle … and felt my legs turn to timber. There was no spring, no zip, nothing. It dawned there and then that I would not be going home with the rainbow jersey. In fact, I wasn't even going to finish the race. I abandoned with three laps to go.

My turbulent 2010 season had almost drawn to a close, but before I could put my feet up I had one more long flight and one more important race. The Commonwealth Games wouldn't rank particularly highly on a lot of eligible riders' lists of priorities, but, for me, as a Manxman, they were a rare opportunity to compete in the island's colours. It was also a chance to give something back, and to ride with guys I'd been training with since I started cycling seriously in my early teens. The 2010 Commonwealth Games, held in Delhi, were being snubbed by a lot of top riders because of concerns over venue safety, terrorist threats and hygiene standards. I summed up my feelings on the matter, perhaps going into a bit too much detail, in the press at the time: 'The guys who stayed away made a mistake. If you look at the chance of catching disease in India; if you look after yourself you won't catch anything. As a single guy you run a risk if you sleep with a girl. Risks come with everything.'

These weren't the only comments I made that caused quite a stir in Delhi. For a few months now, my frustration with Bob Stapleton's seeming inability to offer me an improved deal, and also his failure so far to find a sponsor that would secure the team's future beyond 2012, had been slowly simmering to boiling point. As far as I could see, no progress was being made on either score. As I've already touched on, Bob had also started trying to tie my most trusted and valuable *domestiques* to long-term deals, I suspected in an effort to also somehow shackle me to the team. The latest contract renewal to be announced had been Renshaw's a few weeks after the Tour, and I'd made no secret of my disappointment to Mark. I'd told him to wait, promised that I'd get him the deal he wanted, but he'd gone ahead and committed to Bob for another two years before I'd been able to offer an alternative. He said that it was good money and at 27 he had to start thinking long term, about retirement and his family. I could understand that but still disapproved; it was in both of our interests, both sporting and financial, to stick together, and his new deal made it conceivable that we would be on different teams from the end of 2011, when Bob's contract with HTC ran out, if not earlier.

My status with HTC-Columbia had been uncertain for months. In the spring, before Tirreno–Adriatico, Bob and Rolf Aldag had arranged to meet me in Tuscany, supposedly to discuss my future and the team's. We'd booked a table at a restaurant near my house in Quarrata, sat down, made small talk almost for the entire meal, then finally got on to business over dessert.

'So,' Bob said. 'What do you want to stay with us?'

I'd answered bluntly, honestly and without any hesitation. 'More money, Bob,' I said. 'I want more money.'

Bob asked me how much.

'How much am I worth to you? That's how much I want,' I replied.

Bob said he'd have to go and see what he could come up with. The atmosphere when we left the restaurant, suffice it to say, hadn't been as jovial as when we'd arrived.

I should probably make it clear at this point that money both was and wasn't the real issue. I felt that Bob was reaping the benefit of the naivety that I'd shown in signing a contract that I'd negotiated myself in 2008 when I was 23, and which severely underestimated my future value. The bonus scheme was also almost non-existent. Accepting these terms had been my mistake, I would acknowledge, but at the same time I wanted

Bob to show some recognition of the fact that I was worth at least double the salary that I was earning, and verbal offers that had come from other teams were proof of it. I was desperate to stay with what I regarded as by far the best team in the world, HTC-Columbia, and I was willing to make a financial sacrifice to do so, but there was a point where loyalty ended and stupidity began. As the first flush of rookie exuberance and the novelty fade, the realisation sets in that, ultimately, it's your job, your livelihood, and you're a professional. You can't undersell yourself, which is effectively what I ran the risk of doing if I pledged my future to Bob for half of my real value, then went on winning and gaining tens of millions of pounds' worth of exposure for a corporate sponsor.

As things had stood in the spring, I was contracted to Bob and the team until the end of 2010, and there was an 'option' for me to stay on similar terms in 2011. This clause had been the source of intense speculation in the media, along with a lot of uncertainty. Initially it wasn't clear whether it was my option to stay another year or Bob's to keep me. Finally, though, I'd given the contract to my lawyers and, to my dismay, they'd confirmed that the option merely served as protection for Bob as the team owner, in the eventuality that we had no sponsor and the team had to fold. The fact was that in 2011 HTC would continue to fund us for at least one more year, the team would continue, and therefore I was obliged to stay. Which was fine – as long as Bob showed willing, and there was some more money in the new contract.

It hadn't taken long after our dinner in Italy for him to call another meeting. He was in the UK, he said, and could I meet him in his hotel at Heathrow airport, where he'd be waiting to get on a plane back to California. I did a quick bit of research and found out that I could get to Gatwick from where I was training in Italy but not Heathrow, not unless I took two trains and jumped through several logistical hoops. Bob couldn't change his arrangements, so we had a dilemma, which, as I tapped away on my laptop trying to solve, I explained to my Italian mate, mentor and confidant, the former rider Max Sciandri.

Max, who was born in Britain but couldn't be more Tuscan if you bottled him and called him Chianti, leaned forward in his chair, claiming to have a solution.

'Cav,' he said, in his languid Anglo-Italian drawl. 'You're probably going to sign the biggest contract of your career when you're there. Why not just take a private jet?'

Private jet? Fuck. Rod was always telling me to travel first class if it meant training or racing better when I arrived, but a private jet?

'Priva … I don't know about that, Max.'

'Look,' he said, 'you're going to sign a massive contract, plus it'll make a good story, won't it?'

Max had convinced me and, in any case, there were no other options: I forked out the two grand an hour that it would cost to hire plane and flew to Heathrow. It's just possible that I walked down the airstairs and towards the terminal building at Heathrow with a little more swagger in my step than would ordinarily be the case.

Bob was staying in one of the big, corporate hotels inside the airport complex, I think the Hilton or the Sofitel. I'd asked my manager, Chris Evans-Pollard, to come with me since I didn't want to be sweet-talked as I now felt that I had been at the 2008 Tour, when I'd negotiated a new three-year deal on my own. Chris and I found Bob waiting with Rolf Aldag in his suite. He seemed surprised that I'd brought Chris, and immediately asked whether he and Rolf could have a few minutes with me alone. I said no, that I wanted Chris there, to which he replied that we might as well all leave then. We finally agreed that Chris would wait downstairs.

Bob was a tough customer to deal with. In some ways he was your archetypal Silicon Valley millionaire, having made his fortune through the sale of his telecommunications company to T-Mobile in 2000 (the press commonly referred to him as a 'billionaire businessman', which he didn't like and said vastly overestimated his wealth). T-Mobile and the teams that they sponsored had been his pathway into professional cycling, and since taking over what was then the T-Mobile men's team in 2006, he had seen us become the most successful 'franchise', as he liked to call it, in the sport. About 5 ft 9 in tall, with a grey goatee beard that gave him an affable, avuncular air, he could be the 'Cuddly Bob' that the journalists loved or, when it came to business, a hard-bargaining American businessman. He never raised his voice but he had a slow, deliberate tone that could freeze over like a lake. He could be intensely demanding and sometimes ruthless; as riders, we were all slightly intimidated by him.

Here, now, with me sat opposite him in his five-star suite, he clearly had a strategy. He and Rolf had launched straight into their masterplan for the next two years: what riders we were going to sign, what races we were going to target. Money and contracts weren't mentioned. After five minutes of this, they could see me getting excited. I could feel myself edging forward in my seat and also, I suddenly sensed, getting lured in.

'Hang on,' I said, interrupting. 'I don't want to go any further without Chris being here.'

Reluctantly, they agreed and Chris was allowed into the room. Finally we got to the nitty-gritty. Bob handed me an envelope, which I opened to find a letter, a letter of intent, essentially a pre-contract agreement. I looked at the figure he was offering, then the duration of the contract.

'OK,' I said, 'but I only want one year.'

Bob was taken aback. So I explained: I wanted a new contract, overwriting the old one, for just the 2011 season, not because I had any intention of going somewhere else after that, but as a gesture of goodwill. I wanted Bob to show me what I was worth to him as a rider, not as a speculative punt that he might be able to lock in for less than my eventual market value.

This, Bob said, he couldn't and wouldn't do.

'In that case, I have no choice but to give you this,' he said, handing me a letter.

I quickly skim-read what was written on the piece of paper. It essentially spelled out that the option clause was valid and that I would have to stay with the team, on the same money, in 2011.

Not too much more was said. Like at our meeting in Italy a few weeks earlier, neither party left with what we'd come for.

After this in March, the weeks had passed. Bob was fully supportive after my injudicious celebration and 'diplomatic' early withdrawal at Romandy, and then at the Tour of California seemed ready to announce good news – possibly, at last, a new sponsorship deal that would guarantee the team's survival beyond 2011 and, just maybe, the brand-new contract that I was after. He called us all onto the bus after the last stage, in which Michael Rogers had wrapped up overall victory. We listened expectantly, only for Bob to feed us an even more oblique, non-committal version of the spiel I'd heard at home in Tuscany: 'We want the team to stay together, but you have to be fair. You have to do it for the right reasons ...' Meaning, as I understood it, that we should all ignore the far more lucrative offers raining down from other teams and stick with Bob, come what may. More than once that spring and over the summer we'd heard that a new sponsor was in the pipeline, that a deal was maybe just days or weeks away, but every time it came to nothing.

There had been no real progress over the summer, as far as I could discern, and I was now resigned to Bob holding me to my contract, with no pay rise, and the team continuing to operate on the same threadbare budget in 2011. I still had no burning desire to ride in another team's colours, and was immensely proud that, for the third year in succession, we had won nearly twice as many races as the next most prolific team in professional cycling's top tier. Our achievements were made doubly impressive by the exodus of high-class riders that took place at the end of every season. Our riders were not only successful but clean, thanks largely to the anti-doping ethos that Bob had implemented and quite aggressively publicised since taking over the team in 2006. That stance, combined with our victories, had become a double-edged sword in that our riders were heavily in demand and able to command salaries that Bob simply couldn't afford. The career of a professional cyclist is rarely much more than a decade long, and most will generally, understandably, follow the money. This was another thing, I thought, that Bob failed to appreciate: there were several guys on our team, not just me, who were willing to make financial sacrifices, within reason, that most in the sport wouldn't contemplate in order to stay.

In spite of everything, we still had the best staff, the best work ethic, the best camaraderie and the best equipment of any team. In my mind, this and Bob's expertise and connections in the business world made his failure to find a new sponsor all the more unfathomable. It upset me that Bob could have created something so special, so beautiful, so unique, and that he couldn't take the necessary steps to stop it from falling apart. That disappointment tinged with sadness had been building in me all season, and I'd decided to give it an outlet now at the Commonwealth Games.

In my pre-race press conference I was asked about the expectations that I now had to deal with at every race. This was a good enough opportunity ...

'I've got great family, great friends, great teammates,' I told the assembled media. 'It's nice. People around me appreciate when it's like that, but I'm not sure if my team does. Not my team as a whole, but the manager. I've not been offered a new contract yet I don't know why that is. I'm committed to a contract I signed a few years ago, [but] there's been no goodwill, no bonuses, nothing. I feel kind of abused for what I've achieved.'

The journalists in the room thought Christmas had come early. One now asked whether I was committed to HTC for 2011.

'I've been told I'm contracted to stay, so I have to do it,' I said. 'At the end of the day, I'm never going to stop racing because I love racing and I'm going to race with my teammates because they love to race as well. Fundamentally, I ride my bike because I love to ride my bike, but obviously [because of] the pressures, it's a normal person's life that I've lost. You should see the benefits coming with that, and I don't get them at the minute, and I'm a little bit disappointed at the minute with that ...'

'We're the most successful team on the planet and something is wrong when we don't have enough sponsors,' I went on. 'Ninety-nine per cent of people on the team, riders and staff, are not just performing, but over-performing. There are a couple of people whose job it is to get new sponsors and it's frustrating when they can't and we suffer for it. I'm just frustrated because I've been massively underpaid this year and next because for some reason we can't get more sponsors.'

As I put the microphone down, for once, I could foresee the repercussions with 20/20 clarity. My comments would be huge news in the cycling press and would infuriate Bob, not that he ever responded publicly. He was also too smart and too keenly aware of what was at stake to enter into an ugly, tit-for-tat argument; I remained the team's most valuable rider and his best bargaining tool in the hunt for new investment, particularly with cycling enjoying such a boom in the UK.

Bob also had me exactly where he wanted me: under contract for one more year.

It was ever so slightly ironic that I'd talked about being underpaid at the Commonwealth Games, because Delhi showed emphatically that money wasn't the primary motivation in my career. The Isle of Man's team in the road race would be six strong, and of those six I was the only elite professional. Among the other five were a pair of promising Under 23 riders in Tom Black and Mark Christian, plus three decent amateurs with fulltime jobs: Andrew Roche, Graeme Hatcher and Chris Whorrall. Andy was an electrician, Chris worked for the post office and Graeme for the water board. They were all talented riders but, by rights, really ought to have been out of their depth in a race where Australia, to cite just one example, were fielding a team consisting entirely of elite pros. I didn't care, and was also keenly aware that, for most of those six guys, riding the Commonwealth Games would be one of the most memorable experiences, if not the most memorable, of their sporting lives. While our team's inexperience put us at a major disadvantage, I could still realistically aspire to a podium finish, and I felt that I owed it to those five guys to at least give them something to ride for. Regardless of where I was going to finish, I also adored riding with the Manx lads; we'd raced together, trained together, gone out together and, above all, taken the piss out of each other and laughed together for over a decade.

The road race was 167 kilometres long on a pancake flat course theoretically suited to sprinters. The lads had all been given a job for the first 100 kilometres, after which I knew it would unrealistic to expect too much. They were all buzzing. As predicted, a break went up the road early, and at my instigation our yellow and red Isle of Man jerseys promptly poured to the front. The Australians, by far the strongest team in the race on paper, weren't represented in the break, and had a good sprinter in Allan Davis. I was confused as to why they weren't chasing, so I rode alongside Allan in the bunch and asked.

'It's too early for us to work,' I was told.

'Allan,' I replied, 'I've got a fucking electrician, a postman and a plumber up there. You really think it's too early for you, with your six full-time pros?'

It cut no ice. We carried on working without any help from the Aussies.

For all the guys' brilliant work in the first half of the race, I was always likely to be isolated, overpowered and outmanoeuvred in the finale, and so it proved. New Zealand still had three riders in contention with three laps to go, Canada two and Australia two, whereas David Millar for Scotland, Luke Rowe for Wales and I for the Isle of Man were the only men left for our respective teams in a small lead group. Ploughing our own lone furrow, none of us had any chance, so we chatted and decided that we'd work together to at least try to get a win for a British rider. The Aussies, Kiwis and Canadians were now hell-bent on dislodging me, and were attacking repeatedly to that end. A pattern developed: Dave Millar, mainly, would mark the moves, I would then bury myself to get across, whereupon another rider would ping off down the road. Eventually, the bombardment was always going to wear me down, and finally did as we began the last lap. Dave had latched onto the five-man group that rode into the finishing straight to contest the medal positions, but could only take bronze behind New Zealand's Hayden Rouslton in second and ... Allan Davis in first. I ended getting up seventh. I was disappointed not to have rewarded my teammates for their effort but had relished a rare chance to truly *race*, rather than just sitting in my teammates' wheels and wait for a sprint. That had become my day-job at HTC, but part of me missed the kind of racing that I'd been forced to do in Delhi – the chess on wheels, the thrust and counter-thrust. I ended the day feeling exhilarated.

I was due to fly home the next day, but partly because there was nothing or no one to go home to, and partly because I was loving Delhi, I decided to change my flight and stay until the end of the Games. If I was going to stay, I wasn't just going to spend the time swanning around the athletes' village trying to look cool in my sunglasses, or growing my sideburns; I was going to make myself useful to the Manx riders who were riding the time trial three days after the road race, Andrew Roche and Graeme Hatcher. It was their Tour de France – and I wanted them to get the same attention and support that I would expect at the Tour. People were surprised to see me pumping up Andrew's tyres, filling his drinks bottles, wiping him down after his warm-up and following him in the team car on his ride, but I had a fantastic time. Andrew ended up finishing 12th and Graeme 21st. Dave Millar, who had played wife, soulmate and partner-in-crime for the week in Bernie Eisel's absence, took the gold.

With the Commonwealth Games, the most eventful and testing season of my pro career to date had drawn to a close. The final balance sheet said that I'd picked up 11 race wins plus my points jersey in the Vuelta a España. My teammate, André Greipel, had won almost twice as many races, without ever truly challenging me for the role of HTC-Columbia's senior sprinter. Now 28, André had still never ridden a Tour de France, and had realised that he perhaps never would as long as we were both in the same team and I was fully fit. As a result, he had no choice but to leave at the end of 2010 and he duly signed with the Belgian Lotto team. André and I hadn't ridden a single race together for two and a half years, since the 2008 Giro d'Italia.

From my point of view, professionally, the first six months of 2010 had contrasted sharply with July, August and September. On a personal level it had been a strange, often unsettling year. In many respects I had felt unfortunate and sometimes a victim, whereas in others I was fully aware of the need to take responsibility for mistakes of my own making. The abscess in January had caused me a huge setback in my training but I shouldn't have ridden the day after the initial operation and I shouldn't have eaten that ice-cream on the plane. It was my brother Andy's fault that he'd ended up in prison, but I should also have worked harder on our relationship before that and perhaps shown him more sympathy and empathy. Though the press had occasionally twisted things that I'd said or rejoiced a little too much in my failures, coming across as moody, arrogant or impolite in interviews would only encourage them to do that in the future.

These were just a few examples of what boiled down to the same thing – the need to mature and make better decisions. I wasn't the only 25 year old with a few rough edges to smooth, but the past few months – far more than 2009 – had opened my eyes to the responsibilities that came with my growing profile. While rationally I could tell myself that pressures necessarily came with the privileges of being famous, wealthy, admired, it was still sometimes hard to compute and accept those stresses.

I returned home to England and a packed, three-week schedule of media and commercial commitments that acted as a reminder of exactly this Catch-22. My base was the swish Sanderson Hotel in central London, and every day brought a different party or product launch and a different crowd of people hanging on my every word. It wasn't their fault; I'd been, and still occasionally am, starstruck in the company of childhood heroes or stars that I'd meet at precisely this kind of event. At the same time, I'd started to see through it all, and I'd find myself having perfectly pleasant conversations with people while silently telling myself that they were interested only in *what* I was, what fame and success represented to them, and not *who* I was. After a few days and nights of this, I noticed that it was having a perverse effect on me: rather than alleviating my loneliness, it was actually exacerbating it. I'd go back to my sleek, modern, luxurious hotel room and notice not the flat-screen TV or the art on the wall or the designer furniture but how empty it felt, and how empty it all made *me* feel.

I was young, single, rich, famous and only truly happy when I was on my bike. Something, I knew, had to change.

chapter four

As couples do, Bernie and I had booked to go on our holidays together. For the 2011 season, the team's bike supplier was to change from Scott to Specialized, and to smooth that transition and get us all fitted up and familiarised with the new equipment Bob had arranged for our first training camp of the winter to take place in California, near the Specialized headquarters. Bernie and I decided to go out early and spend the whole of November 2010 having ourselves some fun, sunshine and training in Santa Monica. Our bachelor pad for the month overlooked the beach and the Pacific, with Bernie's grooming products taking up approximately half of the square footage.

The week before flying out, I'd attended one of what seemed like endless parties and product launches that month, this one for the gym equipment manufacturer Technogym. During a casual chat with one of their PR people, I'd mentioned the Santa Monica trip, and he'd said that was a coincidence, because they would also be there for the end of a Help for Heroes charity walk from

New York to LA. He explained what Help for Heroes did and that among the participants would be former soldiers with serious injuries, some of them amputees. I was impressed and said I'd definitely go along.

On our second day in Santa Monica, sure enough, I'd gone down to the pier, where the walkers were due to arrive that morning. There were a few people milling around, clearly waiting for someone or something, but my contact wasn't answering his phone and I was left standing on my own. After a few minutes there was a bit of commotion and more people started to arrive. I got chatting to the chef preparing food for the walkers, and as we talked a burst of bright red over his shoulder stole my attention; I turned, looked and saw a brown-haired girl in a scarlet T-shirt emblazoned with the logo of the *Sun* newspaper, denim shorts and Converse shoes. She was smiling, pouting at a photographer army-rolling along the floor as he took her picture.

'Who's that?' I asked the chef, my eyes having widened.

The chef shrugged and said he didn't know.

Even before his answer, I'd made up my mind that I was going to talk to her, or at least try. But I was also running out of time: the walkers had appeared on the horizon, jogging towards us, before slowing to a walk just as they reached the pier. I figured that gave me a couple of minutes, so I took my chance.

'Look, you can tell me to fuck off if you want,' I said, 'but I saw you were on your own and I wondered whether you wanted some company …'

At chat-up lines go, it was, well … I'd given her the option of telling me where to go, and she'd not taken it. We spoke for a few minutes – long enough for me to mention that I was a professional cyclist, and for her to make it clear she didn't have a clue what that entailed or who I was – before she was hauled away for some sort of presentation on the stage. As that got underway, I noticed her stealing occasional glances and smiling at me, and I naturally smiled back. Then, when it was all over and the crowd started dispersing, I turned to leave and saw that same red T-shirt flash in front of me.

'Hey!'

Initially, I think that my only audible reply may have been a gulp.

'I'm going now,' I said.

'Oh well, if you want to meet up later …' she replied.

My phone was out of my pocket and the number saved before you could say 'fastest man on two wheels'.

That afternoon dragged horribly. Bernie and I went out to buy some groceries, but all I could think about was why this girl – 'Petra' or 'Peta' she'd said her name was – was taking one, two, sometimes three hours to reply to the text messages that I'd been sending. I said to Bernie that she clearly wasn't interested, but that, just in case, I'd try an old tactic and add her as a friend on Facebook. I just had to get hold of her surname, so I opened up Google and typed in 'Peta' and 'the *Sun*'.

The search results flashed onto the screen, and my jaw dropped. She was a glamour model, a Page 3 girl.

'Bernie,' I said, 'Come and have a gander at this. Here's why she's not interested...'

After that initial shock, I told myself that I had nothing to lose and still headed out to the bar where she'd said she'd be. We stayed for a couple of hours, in a large group, then she asked whether I'd like to go on with them to another bar. I told her that I didn't drink, she said that was fine, so on we went. At two or maybe three in the morning the gathering spilled out onto the pavement, with me still completely sober but the others less so. Peta and I arranged to meet the next day for lunch, before she flew home. I ended up taking her to Ago in West Hollywood, which as well as being reputedly the best Italian restaurant in LA is owned by Max Sciandri's parents, Scarlett and Agostino (or 'Ago'). Scarlett and Ago ate with us and, when Peta had left, gave her an emphatic thumbs-up.

Rob Hayles, my old world championship madison-winning partner, was flying out to join us, and it was a good job, because Bernie had practically been dumped. Over the following few days and weeks I'd come back from training to spend two, three, four hours on Skype to Peta. The last thing I'd been looking for from our trip to LA had been a girlfriend, but I'd fallen quickly and hopelessly. She was intelligent, funny and beautiful. She had a four-year-old son, Finnbar, and even from the few hours we'd spent together and the conversations we'd had I could tell that she was a fantastic mother. As soon as I arrived at our training camp in December, I was telling my teammates and anyone else who would listen that I'd found the girl that I was going to marry.

Meeting Peta had transformed me and my mood within the space of a few weeks. That happiness in my private life had, in turn, spilled into my cycling; Bernie and I had trained well on our own and the other guys in the team could see it when we headed out for our first rides. Yet again, there had been an end-of-season exodus. Many had gone from the team for the key reason of our inability to match other teams' salary offers. André Greipel, Michael Rogers, Maxime Monfort, Adam Hansen, Vicente Reynes, Marcel Sieberg and Aleksejs Saramotins had all left, and were replaced by Matt Brammeier, Alex Rasmussen, Danny Pate, John Degenkolb, Gatis Smukulis and Caleb Fairly. Our *directeurs sportifs* had a deserved reputation as the best talent-spotters in the sport, but I still wasn't particularly enthused by some of our new signings. As it turned out, in most cases they would prove me wrong. It was certainly good to have Matt Brammeier, my old mate and fellow tearaway from the British Cycling Academy, on board. We'd both come a long way since our days of drawing giant equine reproductive organs on the window of our house in Fallowfield, Manchester. Brammy's journey had been a more meandering, stop-start one than my own, partly because of a horrific collision with a lorry on a training ride in 2007. He'd since spent four years regaining his fitness and grafting in small teams and finally, now, was getting his first opportunity at the top level.

The atmosphere at the camp, as usual, was excellent. We were spending the first week around the corner from Specialized's headquarters in Morgan Hill and the second further south in the Malibu Hills. The training was good, as was the weather, the roads and our new bikes ... the only thing that wasn't ideal was my relationship with Bob. In fact, there now was no relationship. The camp was symbolic in my mind as the start of the extra year, the 'option' year, when I'd be paid a similar salary as I had for the 2009 and 2010 seasons. I hadn't spoken to Bob since my outburst at the Commonwealth Games, and every moment was awkward in each other's company – or rather, in each other's presence, since I went out of my way to avoid eye contact and conversation. One day, after our official photo shoot, he stood in the doorway and put a hand on my shoulder as I left the set. I brushed it away and carried on walking. With a bit of hindsight, and perspective, I can see now that I was being petulant and that Bob didn't deserve that treatment. Months of frustration had festered inside me to produce that reaction. The fact that all communication between us had broken down put Bob in a difficult position when it came to courting prospective sponsors; if they were going to invest millions of dollars in the team, they would invariably want to knew whether they could count on the current team's most marketable rider, namely me, and that was a guarantee that Bob would have found hard to provide. This dilemma wasn't lost on a few of the more astute members of the team, and I know that, among themselves, they wondered and spoke about what could be done to somehow reconcile us.

Our *directeurs sportifs*, on the whole, didn't involve themselves in any of the politics. They, like us, appeared to be completely in the dark about the sponsorship negotiations and the probability of the team surviving into 2012. Nonetheless, along with the mechanics and masseurs, they too were starting to ask themselves where they'd be in a year's time.

If this was indeed going to be our last season, that threw up a frightening prospect: the camp in California would be the last time that we all got together, riders and staff, both the men's and our women's team. I was due to start my 2011 season at the Tour Down Under in January, so like a few others I wouldn't attend the second camp in the New Year. On our last evening in Morgan Hill, Specialized had laid on a party, after which the *directeurs* decided that we could all have a very rare night out. From the Specialized event in the hills overlooking the Pacific, someone had phoned around bars and restaurants in the area and finally persuaded one to stay open, or rather re-open for us. An hour or so later we had turned a quiet, suburban steakhouse a few miles away into a thumping school disco.

Later that night my smiling, semi-inebriated teammates were duly uncoordinatedly tail-spinning around the dance floor while, at the back of the room, the *directeurs* sat quietly sipping their drinks, half-amused, half-appalled by what they were watching. Brian, the deadpan, self-styled Danish style guru with a bizarre passion for all things English, from fried breakfasts with milky tea to the Sex Pistols – and Rolf, or rather 'Adolf' as Brian called him, the fastidious, affable German straight-man and serial butt of Brian's jokes. Next to them sat Allan Peiper and Valerio Piva. Allan had given me my first big break by allowing me to sprint for myself rather than lead out André Greipel in the 2007 Grote Scheldeprijs, where I'd gone on to take my first pro race win. Valerio had overseen my best performances in Italian races, but we'd clashed quite regularly, generally because he thought it was impossible to own a fast car and also be a fast bike rider, or eat lunch with your girlfriend in a Grand Tour and then go out that afternoon and do a respectable time trial. It boiled down to Valerio thinking that I was a 'Big Time Charlie', or least falling back on that clichéd image of me when things weren't going well.

I'd shared triumphs and disagreements not just with Valerio but all of the *directeurs*, and, in one way or another, those experiences had moulded me as a man and a rider. As I watched my team-mates shimmying and swaying unsteadily, drunkenly, to the music – or in a few cases quietly nursing soft drinks – I thought how strange we all looked and probably felt in this, a context that was completely banal to most people of our age.

It wasn't just tonight: we were forever in the same state of limbo, between what had been and still were our dreams and the real world which kept on turning while we turned our pedals. The night out was supposed to be an escape – but really it was the rest of our lives, the very existence of the professional cyclist, that was out of the ordinary. One day it would end and – depending on who we were, what we'd accomplished and what we'd learned – we would either parachute to a soft landing or drop down to earth with a thud. All along, though, our secret was the sheer joy that we took in riding our bikes together and winning. I think we were all still living half in hope, half in denial. In the event that Bob found the sponsor and the money, I knew it would be very hard to turn my back on everyone in our makeshift disco that night. But the future of the team was something that most of us chose not to contemplate. Better to live in the moment, dancing like we didn't care.

After California, I'd gone back to the UK for, among other things, the BBC Sports Personality of the Year awards. Not nominated in 2009, fourth in 2009, this time I finished seventh of the ten nominees. The winner, deserved in my opinion, was the jockey Tony McCoy.

I then flew to Tuscany, where I spent Christmas with Max Sciandri and his family. Although my training had gone smoothly in California and I'd rarely if ever been in better shape in December, one thing I'd learned in 2010 was just how much energy was required to sustain your motivation and form all the way through the year to the Worlds in late September. With the Worlds one of my goals for 2011, I had taken it easy either side of the New Year. A little too easily as it happened – by the time I left for Australia in the middle of January I was three kilos heavier than my usual weight at that time of the year.

Even when I was lean, I had never had the kind of muscles that would rise in impressive, contoured ridges just below the skin's surface. In races and on television, I always somehow managed to look fat. My weight was something that I worried about but also that I'd learned, with time, to control. Every year I'd take a month off at the end of the season and, having weighed 69 kilos at the Tour, I'd go up to 76 kilos by the time I started training again in November. It was the simple and predictable consequence of burning fewer calories than I consumed, and attending events and parties where I'd drink and eat things that during the season wouldn't pass my lips. It was also a question of structure; at that time I had none. I would be getting last-minute calls to attend such and such an event, in this or that location, and bought whatever food was available in airports or shops on my route. Other riders could perhaps do the same and put on no more than a couple of kilos. Unfortunately, however, my metabolism wasn't as fast as my sprinting or my backchat.

In spite of a few kilos of extra insulation, I wasn't worried when I arrived in Australia for the start of the Tour Down Under. It was enough just to be racing, bearing in mind that exactly a year earlier I'd been lying under a duvet, sick. I had none of the health issues that had beset me in the 2010 season, and I was much happier in my private life. In Australia, I felt strong … but fat, and any hopes I had of nicking a stage win or two ended with a bad crash four kilometres from the end of the second stage. If I finished battered and bloodied there, the next day insult was added to injury when I found myself in a group of stragglers on a hilly finishing circuit – and moments later we were slaloming in and out of traffic, the police and race marshals having prematurely reopened the road. Only thanks to some pretty nifty bike-handling did we make it to the finish unscathed.

After Australia, my next race was the Tour of Qatar in February. Completely flat, and essentially six different combinations of the same cobweb of roads crossing the Qatari desert, this race was notoriously fast, windy and good preparation for the spring season. For me, once again, it started terribly. At 2.5 kilometres long, the prologue was the kind of short, sharp effort in which I'd often excelled in the past, and, sure enough, at the first time-check I was still very much in the hunt for a win and the first leader's jersey of the race. The course was straightforward except for a couple of speed bumps. Supposing that the best way to hold my speed would be a low bunny hop, maybe just grazing or narrowly clearing the apex of the bump, I'd jarred my rear wheel on the first one but stayed in control. Approaching the second bump, I repeated the same steps; I jerked with my arms and felt the bike take off, but this time the impact was too heavy and catapulted me over my handlebars and onto the road. I'd hit my head in exactly the same place as in Australia and, though not as hard this time, it was enough to completely compromise my race. Because I was beaten up and not contesting any of the sprints, Mark Renshaw was able to ride for himself that week and also enjoyed the role reversal of having me as his *domestique*. He picked up one second place, one stage win and the general classification. Looking back, I think that Qatar was what convinced Mark that, if the team did fold, it was perhaps time for him to stop working for others and sprint for himself.

From Qatar, I hopped across the Persian Gulf, and finally took my first win of the season in the Tour of Oman. That week, Renshaw wasn't racing. In a certain sense, our paths were already beginning to diverge.

It was also in that period, as the spring Classics approached, that I made at least one firm decision about my future: I didn't want to carry on working with Bob, even in the increasingly remote eventuality of him finding a new sponsor. I'd assumed for a while now that HTC wouldn't renew their contract with the team, but they had shown an interest in working with me on an individual basis. The press had reported that there had also been conversations between Bob and the audiovisual retailer RadioShack, whose team needed to somehow reinvent itself after Lance Armstrong's second and definitive retirement, but those talks, too, would come to nothing. Bob was now so busy trying to win sponsorship that he was barely ever attending races, yet still implying in emails or via our *directeurs sportifs* that a deal of some sort was likely. I had lost all faith and patience with it; and couldn't now envisage a situation whereby we would continue to work together.

For a few weeks, at least, I think Bob had decided that whether I stayed or not wouldn't matter hugely. At Milan–San Remo I was put firmly in the shade by another HTC rider, Matt Goss. The pre-race plan had been for everyone to stick with me except

Peter Velits, who would work for Gossy. In the morning, perhaps because of nerves and not for the first time before an important race, I had felt suddenly nauseous and started vomiting. The symptoms continued once I had got on my bike, ultimately leading to my capitulation on the crucial climb of La Cipressa. I had been dropped earlier in the race, on Le Manie, and the entire team, even Velits, had stayed with me and exhausted themselves by towing me back to the peloton. This had left Gossy completely isolated in the front group, but he 'hid' brilliantly in the wheels and duly blitzed the sprint. To anyone who had known Gossy as an Under-23, it frankly wasn't much of a surprise. On turning pro, I think he had perhaps set himself back first by signing for Saxo Bank, who didn't support him as much they should have. In the last year and a bit, though, having switched to our team, Gossy's talent had finally bloomed.

I was thrilled for him. So, naturally, was Bob. With my victory tally for the year stuck on one, Bob may now have been less alarmed by the prospect of me leaving, since he had a ready-made replacement in Gossy. The reality was that we are completely different riders – Gossy is perhaps stronger and more versatile, though I am the faster sprinter. We are also very different people, for all that we had instantly clicked when he joined the team: Gossy is funny, outgoing but nothing like the same gift to headline writers (which is probably a good reflection on him!).

Despite feeling much fitter, the spring of 2011 was starting to bear a disturbing resemblance to the previous one. After San

Remo, my next big target was Gent–Wevelgem, the one Belgian Classic that has traditionally favoured sprinters, yet which had always eluded me. The most iconic feature of the race and the most important strategically was the double ascent of the cobbled Kemmelberg climb. On the first lap of the 2011 race I had punctured on the Kemmel and been forced to chase, but had caught and comfortably stuck with the main peloton when we tackled the Kemmel for a second time. The hard part was done, but then, as so often in the Classics, the race took an unexpected and, for me, irremediable turn. I was caught momentarily behind an innocuous-looking crash in the middle of the bunch, when I suddenly felt the back end of my bike jar and looked around to see the Movistar rider Ignatas Konovalovas with his front wheel jammed into my rear triangle. I stayed upright, but lost too many valuable seconds dodging the bodies that had also slowed or fallen around us and changing my wheel to have any chance of rejoining the main peloton. Gent-Wevelgem was turning into – and would continue to be – my bogey race: only once in three appearances to date in the 'sprinters' Classic' had I actually been able to *sprint* for the win (in 2008, when I'd finished 17th due to poor positioning).

My fascination with Gent-Wevelgem and the other 'cobbled' Classics ran as deep as the treacherous, jagged ruts between their infamous *pavé* stones. I'd realised very early that I'd never have the body shape to be a climber, and as a teenager learning about professional cycling I was drawn to the races which celebrated qualities that I did possess, like speed on the flat and tenacity. Since turning pro in 2007 I had also, very willingly, undergone Brian Holm's indoctrination in the 'cult of the cobbles': as far as Brian was concerned, the hard men of the north, the *Flandriens* such as 1970s Classics maestro Roger Vlaeminck, were gods. Other riders paled by comparison and were mere 'hairdressers' in Brian's eyes.

With Brian fuelling the passion that I already had, I had been pestering my team managers for years to let me take part in the most dangerous and punishing of the cobbled Classics: Paris–Roubaix. In 2008 Allan Peiper had made a bet with me: I could do Roubaix if I won two stages at the Three Days of De Panne and Gent-Wevelgem. I had kept the first part of the bargain but not the second, and Allan wouldn't cave. Now, though, partly because I'd shown some promise in the Tour de France stage that borrowed some of the Roubaix route in 2010, and partly because they couldn't take any more of my earache, he and the other *directeurs* finally relented. My best legs were also, finally, coming out of hibernation: after my second stab at the Tour of Flanders, where I had mainly worked for the team in the first half of the race, I had won the Grote Scheldeprijs for the third time the following Wednesday.

Paris–Roubaix itself was everything that I'd expected and harder. While the Tour de Flanders is also famous for its cobbles, the *pavé* in Paris–Roubaix are bigger and even rougher: imagine riding down a river bed in a shopping trolley, in places at over 50 kilometres per hour, and that will give you some idea of the sensation. For a day or two before the race, my excitement had been driving Bernie nuts, partly because he knew what was coming, and he couldn't comprehend how anyone would be relishing that amount of suffering. He had a point, although I would argue that my race might have been quite different had it not been for a mechanical problem and bike-change in the first hour. Complaining about punctures, however, or broken spokes or wheel changes at Paris–Roubaix, is a bit like booking a holiday in Manchester and complaining about the rain; it comes with the territory. I didn't make it to the finish in the legendary Roubaix Velodrome, but then neither did 86 of the other 194 starters.

April 2011 would also see me make another debut – on Twitter. My manager, Chris Evans-Pollard, had been extolling the micro-blogging site's virtues as a promotional tool for a while, but so far I'd resisted. Our team press officer, Kristy, certainly had nightmares about me opening an account. Finally, though, with Mark Renshaw also applying some pressure, I signed up at the end of April. Fortunately for all concerned, I did it at a time when I was content in my private life and didn't have too much free time on my hands. The days when I would spend whole afternoons reading the online cycling press and their message boards – and usually getting riled by something or someone – were now long gone.

One thing that I wasn't particularly satisfied about that spring was, funnily enough, the number of good commercial opportunities coming from Chris. In the five years since I turned pro, I had learned – slowly and often the hard way – that, while money would never be my primary motivation, ignoring the financial side of the job was irresponsible, and didn't do me any favours. Me being me, and being a perfectionist, I also notice and get annoyed when I can see someone in my team or entourage not achieving the standards that I expect of them, especially when that affects me. I had been with Chris for just over a year at this point, after my previous manager, Fran Millar, stepped away from athlete management and to take a job at Team Sky. I could theoretically have stayed with Fran's agency, Face Partnership, but she still owned some of the business and that clearly threw up a conflict of interests. Chris, who already managed Victoria Pendleton, seemed like a good alternative. He was in his mid-thirties, smart, personable and appeared to have significantly raised Vicki's profile. I had hoped that he would do the same for me.

I had been willing to indulge and give Chris the benefit of my considerable doubt until the Giro in May. The Giro, the race itself, was a good one for me, starting with another sensational win for us in the team time trial in Turin. Back in 2009 I had screamed at my Italian teammate, Marco Pinotti, when he lost my wheel on the final corner, fearing that it might cost us vital seconds and me the pink jersey. But Marco quickly corrected his mistake and all had ended well, with the team winning the stage and me in pink. It therefore seemed perfectly fair and natural for Marco to lead us over the line in the 2011 team time trial, particularly as he was wearing the Italian national time trial champion's green, white and red jersey, and the 2011 Giro was being billed as a celebration of the 150th anniversary of Italy's unification. He also deserved it, having ridden superbly. Marco and I could scarcely have been more different – he was studious, undemonstrative, totally disinterested in fast cars and designer clothes – but I had always respected him and even specifically asked to room with him once or twice at races.

I took the pink jersey off Marco in Parma the following day, for one day only ... but it was no cause for celebration. For the third time in succession I had failed to win the first sprint in a major tour Perfectly teed up by Renshaw, I had waited a split second too long. I had seen Alessandro Petacchi appear over my right shoulder and then deliberately swing left and right across the road to block my path to the line as I tried to get around him. My anger boiled over into furious arm-waving in Petacchi's direction as we came over the line, but ultimately what really got my goat was the inconsistency of the *commissaires*. I had lost points and, effectively, the green jersey at the 2009 Tour after a far less pronounced 'deviation' in Besançon. By the media's estimation, Petacchi's was a 'cunning old pro, showing *savoir faire*', whereas I was regularly portrayed as an 'outlaw' and a 'kamikaze'.

A week would pass before I had any chance to make amends, which I did emphatically with successive wins in Teramo and Ravenna. For a few weeks I had been troubled by a nerve problem in my back – a tiny twinge that caused a mental block more than a physical one, and which left me permanently bracing myself for those spasms when I kicked hard. Finally I was able to blank it out and let go, with the result being this pair of comfortable wins. After the second one, as the race prepared to enter the high mountains, I pulled out of the Giro, as agreed with the team before the race.

I knew Chris was coming to the Giro, but was surprised to spot him in the VIP enclosure after the team time trial in Turin. I asked him later how he'd acquired a guest pass. Oh, that was simple, he said, he'd just got in touch with the organisers and told them that he was Mark Cavendish's manager.

If I was already distinctly unimpressed then, I was furious when I discovered that Peta hadn't been allowed into the enclosure where Chris was enjoying Prosecco and canapés. That night I told Chris how much it had bothered me, while also bluntly informing him that I was far from happy with his work so far. I told him I would give him until December to smarten up his act, and that, if he didn't, I'd be looking for a new manager. To be perfectly frank, I didn't feel hopeful that much would change.

At the Giro itself, in truth, my frustration with Chris had very quickly been overtaken by much more serious and pressing concerns. I'd had the team time trial to worry about on the first day, the sprint in Parma on the second, and was wearing the pink jersey on stage three from Reggio nell'Emilia to Rapallo in Liguria. On that third day something else had occurred that had made not only the stage but also the entire Giro, and even our careers as professional cyclists, feel like an irrelevance: the Belgian rider, Wouter Weylandt, had turned to look behind him on the descent of the Passo del Bocco, stubbed his left foot against an iron rail running down one side of the road, spun out of control on impact and smashed into a wall on the opposite side. Around an hour later it was announced that he had died of his injuries.

Even before the descent and indeed before the stage, word had got around that the road down the Passo del Bocco was narrow, dangerous and tapered at the bottom, where the route hit the coast and a mad scramble for position would begin. With this in mind, having crested the summit adrift of the main peloton, Renshaw and I had embarked on one of our swooping skydives, catching and then passing more riders than we could count. One of these riders had been Wouter Weylandt. At the bottom of the descent, minutes later, we had slotted into a peloton where riders were already whispering in grave tones about a bad crash involving Weylandt. We heard nothing more until we arrived back at the team bus, the race having blown again on a climb before the finish to end my chances.

When confirmation arrived, silence descended upon the bus. I shivered. An hour or so earlier, he'd been riding at our side. They were his last moments of life.

We pulled up to our hotel and decanted out of the bus, heads bowed, speechless and numb. I found my room, got undressed and stepped into the shower. There, I burst into tears.

Weylandt wasn't a close friend but I'd always liked him. He had a big, bright eyes, a ready smile and a penchant for eccentric hairstyles, all of which were a reflection of his personality. We had crossed swords in the odd sprint, as I of course had with Wouter's best mate, Tyler Farrar. Tyler's team, Garmin, were staying in the same hotel as us that night, but Tyler didn't come down to dinner. What happened that day had put our petty squabbles into perspective; we were all part of the same family, all exposing ourselves to the same risks on a daily basis, and we'd lost one of our own.

The next day it was decided that we would pay tribute to Wouter by putting on a cortège, rather than a race. Each team rode for around 20 kilometres on the front, and scarcely a word was uttered all day. Fans lined the roadside with their applause and their banners commemorating Wouter and his race number at the Giro, 108.

It was both beautiful, moving and desperately sad. It also, inevitably, stirred up thoughts, images and memories that you usually went out of your way not to dwell on as a professional cyclist; the dangers the lurked on descents, in sprints, that I encountered and defied almost on a daily basis. On the evening of Weylandt's death and the next day as we rode together – each in a world of our own but probably all thinking the same things – I questioned my career, the way I rode, and whether I could carry on. This was the inner voice of sanity, reason, perspective – and yet this was the one that would soon be drowned out when our warped sense of normality returned in a few hours' time.

The only explanation was that love, our love for the sport, was deaf and blind.

chapter five

'It's not very logical,' admitted the Tour director, Christian Prudhomme.

It was October 2010, and in front of a crowd of cycling's glitterati at Paris' Palais Congrès – and one very happy Manx sprinter – Christian Prudhomme was revealing the route for the 2011 Tour de France. The lack of 'logic' that Prudhomme was referring to was the fact that, despite 15 Tour stage wins since 2008, I had yet to win the green jersey competition, nominally designed to reward the best sprinter in the race.

I'd come close in the previous couple of years. In 2009 Thor Hushovd and my contentious disqualification for dangerous sprinting on stage 14 to Besançon had cost me, then in 2010 I had been too unnerved by the sudden loss of power from my legs on stage four to mop up essential points. On both occasions I'd come within a whisker of winning the green jersey – but there was something fundamentally wrong with the structure of the jersey competition if I was dominating to the extent that I had, yet still losing out to riders stockpiling points in the two or three 'intermediate' sprints dotted along on the stage routes.

Prudhomme had agreed and decided that the rules needed to change. In 2011, he confirmed, there would be just one 'intermediate' sprint on every stage, not two or three, and these would be worth a whopping 20 points to the winner, with a sliding scale of points right down to 15th place. Under the old system only the first three riders at the intermediate sprints had scored, with six points for first, four for second and two for the third rider over the line. The revamp meant that opting out of the intermediate sprints, as I had usually done in 2009 and 2010, judging the risk of wasting energy too great and the reward too meagre, would no longer be an option.

Parallel to this, there was also now a bigger premium on winning stages than had previously been the case: every sprint would be worth 45 points, ten more than under the old rules. Even more crucially, there would now be a ten-point difference between first and second place in sprints at the end of stages, double what it had been in the past.

Based on Prudhomme's comments and these notable changes, it was widely assumed that I would be their main beneficiary. However, it was no foregone conclusion: a lot would depend on the placement of the intermediate sprints, which were only revealed a matter of weeks before the Grand Départ in the Vendée region; my task could theoretically been made even harder if, for instance, a large number of the intermediate sprints were placed soon after the major climbs.

One thing was beyond question, however: our commitment to banishing and avoiding the regrets of the previous two years. Mark Renshaw, more than anyone else, had been beating the same drum in the weeks and months leading up to the Tour: 'We're not coming home without that jersey.' Nothing was left to chance in our preparation: when the locations of the intermediate sprints had been released, we studied them, and formulated our strategy. At the end of May, we had even gathered at a training camp in north-west France to test-ride the first four stages, in the hope that local knowledge would help to give us a flying start.

My last major warm-up race, the Tour of Switzerland in June, didn't feature a single genuine sprint finish, as far as I could tell because the race organiser, a former pro by the name of Beat Zberg, thought that no one wanted to watch them. Nonetheless, surviving the glut of giant mountain passes that week had boosted my form and confidence. Further adding to my optimism, our Tour team had never been more singularly geared towards winning sprints. The eight express carriages on what I believed would be my fastest and best sprint train to date went by the names of Matt Goss, Bernie Eisel, Tony Martin, Danny Pate, Lars Bak, Mark Renshaw, Peter Velits and Tejay Van Garderen.

We were ready.

I wasn't the only one with high hopes for the 2011 Tour. British interest in the race had been steadily growing ever since the Grand Départ in London in 2007, and on Team Sky's second

Tour, Brad Wiggins had big ambitions in the general classification. A year earlier I would have endorsed Brad's own view that his fourth place in the 2009 Tour (later amended to third, after Lance Armstrong's disqualification) had been a one-off, the lucky coincidence of favourable circumstances. Over the first six months of 2011, however, I realised how wrong I had been. A cyclist can often gauge another rider's form at a single glance, based on things that he does at moments of a race that to the watching public pass completely unnoticed. The way he moves up the peloton after a toilet break, his positioning, how the muscles in his calves flex beneath the skin ... I had hardly seen Brad at a race all year but I studied him over the first week of the Tour and realised that he was a different animal from the one who had turned up 12 months earlier. Equally importantly, I'd heard the stories from guys who had been training with Brad at altitude, or others who had suffered on his wheel at the Nationals the week before the Tour, which Brad had won by 35 seconds from Pete Kennaugh and Geraint Thomas, and which I hadn't finished.

'Brad's flying. FLYING,' they all said.

'Never seen him this good ...'

'Could win the Tour going like that.'

All of which was making headlines back in the UK, which brought with it pros and cons, one being that my future was the subject of intense speculation when we arrived in France.

In June, various 'insiders' had told journalists that my move to Sky had already been agreed, which wasn't remotely accurate.

My fear when these rumours first started circulating had been that Bob might even use them as an excuse not to pick me for the Tour, or perhaps the Vuelta a España in September, which would be key to my preparations for the World Championships. Privately, I think it had crossed Bob's mind that Team Sky might be trying to hinder his search for a new sponsor. He had already seen five of our riders move to Sky at the end of 2009, with Michael Rogers joining them at the end of 2010. The demise of HTC would free up our riders for other teams. It wasn't just me in demand; the team was crammed with talent, between members of my lead-out train and winners in their own right. HTC folding would also clear Sky's path to something else: more race wins.

Bob wasn't in the Vendée for the Grand Départ, illness having kept him away. He therefore missed Philippe Gilbert winning the first stage finishing atop the Mont des Alouettes, a one-kilometre climb that most pundits had decided would be too tough for yours truly. In fact, it wasn't the climb that ruled me out but a puncture two kilometres from the line. Avoiding a crash in front of me, I had swerved and stabbed my front wheel on the crash barriers, punctured, and had to stop for a wheel change. There was then no way back into contention.

The next stage was one that we were all looking forward to and had prepared for on our spring recce: the team time trial. These were always the most stressful days for the *directeurs*, the mechanics and the riders, particularly with me around. In our press conference the previous week, I'd joked about how I went into

'*Full Metal Jacket* mode' before team time trials. Part of it was my desperation to do well and my perfectionism, but it was also sheer bafflement at the naivety of some professional bike riders about what this discipline required. While it mystified me, their failure to grasp even the fundamentals also made me realise what a fantastic education my coach, Rod Ellingworth, had given me and the other lads at the Academy when we were Under-23s. My pet hate was riders who would try to pull too hard or for too long on the front, just to comfort their ego; changes of pace, whether it was a guy slowing down because he'd been in the wind for too long, or suddenly accelerating, were poison for the team's momentum. I would never tire of emphasising it, even if my teammates were sick of hearing it: 'No fucking heroics!'

Two days before the Tour started, we had headed out, as a team, for a run-through on the race route. An Australian film crew had followed us, and, typically, I had kicked off about something or other, upon which Matt Goss had got the hump and told me to stop ranting, just like Bernie the previous year at the Vuelta. It had really been nothing but made a juicy little bit of footage for the Australian TV crew. When the clip was broadcast, for the rest of the media it was also an invitation to speculate about an internal rivalry between Gossy and me, fuelled by his win at Milan–San Remo.

In truth, all it had really been was me being myself in the build-up to the team time trial. It was the same on the bus within minutes of stage one ending, when I collared our sprint coach,

Erik Zabel, and began talking tactics and techniques for the following day.

'The first three men should be in their aero position,' I told him, 'the rest on the brake handles, so they can get as close as possible to the wheel in front and brake if they need to ...'

Erik had nodded wearily.

'Look, Erik, I know you fucking know, but we've got to make sure they know as well,' I'd said, jabbing a finger towards my teammates.

The next day we had barely turned a pedal before we'd had to rethink everything. Moments before riding together from the team bus to the start-ramp, our young American, Tejay Van Garderen, had muttered something about not having the right wheels for the windy conditions, and Bernie had got annoyed.

'You had half an hour to say something and you didn't say anything,' Bernie snapped.

Five hundred metres down the course, on the first left-hand bend, Bernie had clipped Tejay's rear wheel and gone down. Waiting for Bernie to get up and get back on simply wasn't viable: with Tony Martin, our strongest time triallist, drilling at the front as we exited the bend and hit a short rise, those who had been behind Bernie when he crashed now had to sprint to close the gap. It killed them, and the combination of this and our numerical disadvantage, with Bernie marooned back down the road, cost the team at least ten seconds – certainly more than the five that ended up separating us and the eventual stage winners, Garmin.

When we arrived back at the bus, Bernie, who is one of the most resolutely upbeat people I've ever met, looked suicidal.

There were no points awarded on the green jersey competition in team time trials, which left the standings unchanged after two stages: Philippe Gilbert, the stage winner on the first day, led on 45, while I languished in 24th place, having picked up five points in the intermediate sprint on day one.

The new rules took some getting used to. What was already clear, and had been since the announcement of the new points scale, was that while you didn't have to be winning intermediate sprints to challenge for the green jersey, neither could you ignore them. Tour stages tend to follow quite a stereotyped pattern, whereby at some point in the first two hours a breakaway group of four or five riders will shoot off down the road and consequently beat the main peloton to the intermediate sprint. In the old days this had often meant that the points on offer had already gone by the time we in the main bunch arrived, but now there were scoring opportunities for 15 riders, not three, and so unless there was a large breakaway, every intermediate sprint would somehow count.

It was interesting to see how my fellow sprinters had approached the intermediate sprint on the first day, and on stage three to Redon they were committing four or five men to the lead-out. A lot of it was down to ego, I'd decided, and the fact that sprinters are basically gladiators. For some, I sensed, it was about flexing their muscles more than picking up points. This was also something, I realised later, that the media would encourage by suggesting that the intermediate sprints were somehow indicative of what would happen two or three hours later on the finishing straight. That may have applied to other riders, but not to me; I knew what muscle damage was caused by even a seven- or eight-second effort, and how it could impact on your speed later when it really mattered. Despite that, here, on stage three, with five riders down the road, I had led the main bunch over the white line to take sixth place and ten points.

The good news as we headed into Redon, with the breakaway now caught, was that my legs were starting to sing. I clearly wasn't the only one in my team, but therein lay a danger to which we duly succumbed: in our over-eagerness to get to the first sprint, we'd gone too early. With four kilometres, Bernie had pulled off, leaving just Tony Martin, Gossy, Renshaw and then me, and even one of Tony's gargantuan efforts could only take us just inside the two-to-go barrier. At this rate, I'd be in the wind at 700 metres to go, not 200, so I decided to gamble: with 1,500 metres to go I let Renshaw's wheel go, allowing him and Gossy to pull clear. This would force the sprint trains behind me to surge, with the idea being that I would latch onto another team's train as they came past me.

I'd acted on instinct and the gamble didn't pay off. There were no gaps or good openings to slot into, no good wheels to follow. Riders had flooded past me on either side, leaving me submerged and too far back. I managed to get myself back into a reasonable position as we swung around the final bend – reasonable except for one thing: the rider on my inside was Romain 'The Menace' Feillu, who took us both wide and almost into the barriers. I unclipped my right foot from the pedal, ready to crash, but skidded like a speedway rider to stay upright. By then I was 50, maybe 60 metres behind Tyler Farrar and his lead-out man Julien Dean. In the last 500 metres I went like a cannonball but needed another 50 metres of road to catch them. Tyler Farrar held on to win, and I finished fifth.

If I'm honest, I can't say that I was thrilled for Tyler. There was something that never failed to wind me up about the way the media had built him up, the way he added to the hype by exaggerating the importance of my team in interviews, and not fully acknowledging that his was just as strong when it came to lead-outs. For all the talk, he'd only ever beaten me once in my career when I hadn't had mechanical problems or some other issue. I didn't rate him, and that day couldn't quite bring myself to congratulate him in my interviews after the stage. Instead, I made some typically forthright remarks about 'kamikaze Romain Feillu' and how he 'always causes havoc'.

What the journalists who had interviewed me on the steps of our bus didn't know was that when I'd gone back inside Mark Renshaw had given *me* a lecture. Apparently when I'd left the gap 1,500 metres out, he and Gossy had heard 'NO!', when in fact I'd shouted, 'GO!'. In any case, Renshaw said, it was a stupid move: 'the kind of thing might work at the Giro, but we're not at the Giro …'

My bad day at the office was not yet over. An hour after the finish, the *commissaires* announced that Thor Hushovd and I had been disqualified from the intermediate sprint and lost our points, supposedly because we had both deviated from our lanes as we fought to follow Philippe Gilbert's wheel. All that had really happened was that Thor had tried to jump in between Philippe and me, had leant on me slightly, and I'd leant back. The decision was farcical and everyone thought so. But then, equally, nothing really surprised me when it came from the *commissaires* any more ...

Once again, it was turning into a pretty miserable start to the Tour. There was no discernible improvement, either, after a hilly stage the next day through Brittany, won by Cadel Evans: I now trailed the new leader in the green jersey competition, the Spaniard José Joaquín Rojas Gil, by 48 points. He had 82, I was on 34.

The next day we stayed in Brittany, but I could have been back on the Isle of Man. It was green, it was gnarly and it was windy. The last 25 kilometres hugged the coast, and the last three had the feel of a roller-coaster ride, rippling up and over headlands. We had studied it on Google Street View and decided that a stage win was still well within my capabilities and had set off with that in mind ... until Erik Zabel radioed our *directeurs sportifs* halfway through the stage to suggest that it was harder than we'd imagined. Erik said that at three to go the road ramped up at 12 per cent and that I and the team would need to really dig in there to have any chance. That, when the road plateaued under the three kilometre banner, I decided, would be my finish line.

When it came, my chin was nearly on my top-tube, my vision began to fog – but I somehow made it over in fourth wheel.

A win from here was improbable at best, and would have rivalled the penultimate one of my six in 2009, at Aubenas, which I considered my best ever at the Tour. The task was made harder still when, with a kilometre to go, André Greipel barged me towards the barriers. The precedent had been set in the intermediate sprint two days earlier, with my disqualification for leaning on Hushovd: I couldn't retaliate, even if the impact had killed my momentum and left me 20 wheels back, surely out of it. Now I was sprinting for the minor positions, to pick up a few meagre points …

Or so I thought. With the road now rising towards the finish line from the 500-metres-to-go sign, I glimpsed a white jersey whose owner I mistook to be Brad Wiggins but was actually Geraint Thomas. I promptly jumped into Gee's slipstream, the lactic stinging my every sinew, and pushed and pushed until, 40 seconds later, I glimpsed the finish line through the spokes in my front wheel. Somehow, against all the odds, I'd won. Whether out of shock or exhaustion, I could barely even lift my hands off the bars to celebrate.

My press conference afterwards was the usual, sedate affair: I announced to the world's press that among them were 'ignoramuses' whom I'd been glad to shut up, threatened to sue a journalist who had misheard José Joaquín Rojas's account of a tangle with Alessandro Petacchi for suggesting that it had been with me, and finally semi-seriously admitted that we'd be there all night if I started talking about the 'problems in my head' to which I'd alluded in an interview the previous day. Poor Kristy, our press officer, stood to the side of the stage no doubt despairing.

After five stages, things were at least looking up for me and the team in the green jersey competition. Philippe Gilbert, who'd come second on the stage, was the new leader with 120 points, but after my victory I was within striking distance on 84. After stage six, another hilly one which lent yet more credence to my theory that the Tour organisers were on a crusade to eradicate bunch sprints, probably because they were fed up with our domination, the gap had widened to 144 points against 94.

A case, then, of one step forward, two steps back. But while stage six might not have suited me, stage seven seemed the perfect chance for me to close the gap again.

At the route presentation in October 2010 I had flipped open the information pack given to us by the race organisers, scrolled down the list of stages and felt my eyes immediately drawn to number seven. What grabbed my attention wasn't the fact that it looked to be only the second, nailed-on bunch sprint of the Tour, but rather where it was taking us.

I don't think Châteauroux's inhabitants will feel too aggrieved to hear me say that, by most measures, their town is not one of

France's most illustrious or memorable. It lies landlocked in the bullseye of France, surrounded on all sides by flat, featureless plains. Fifty thousand people live there, it has an impressive cathedral, some museums and a pretty old town, but even judging by the paragraph of tourist blurb in the Tour route book there aren't too many reasons to plan a trip.

Despite this hardly glowing reference, Châteauroux happens to be my favourite place in France. Why? Because it was there that I won my first ever Tour de France stage, in 2008, and there that my HTC teammates now offered a masterclass in 2011. This time around, the Tour's route planners had thrown a spanner in the works by positioning the intermediate sprint just 25 kilometres from the finish line, as the road doglegged from its southward course to the east. The danger was that, with the change of direction and the wind suddenly gusting across the road at a different angle, a team or teams would try to split the bunch as soon as we turned after the sprint. The way to make sure that we were all on the right side if the elastic did snap was for the whole team to swarm to the front the second I crossed that intermediate sprint line. Sure enough, within seconds of me edging out Rojas for the 11 leftover points, they were wrapped around me in a protective cocoon. It was just as well as Fabian Cancellara's Leopard Trek was soon applying exactly the kind of pressure we'd successfully pre-empted at the front.

Our last ten kilometres that day would have had connoisseurs swooning. It's often said that a sprinter's train sets a fast tempo to deter and soak up attacks, but really that's only its most rudimentary, in some way least important, function. The success of a sprint train is gauged by the amount of space that it creates and not its speed, although the two are intimately linked: the faster the train, generally speaking, the harder it is for other teams and riders to crowd around and cramp its last wagon, in our case me. Here, we flirted with perfection, our line extending out of the peloton like the barrel from a gun. Everyone went beyond the call of duty, Peter Velits even finishing his work with three kilometres to go, slotting back into the train, then returning for a second shift between the two and 1.7 to go mark. The sprint itself was a simple drag race, Greipel having kicked from a deep position then gone wide to the right as he appeared in my sightline, while I hugged the barriers on the left. There was no doubt that André had responded to having a team built around him this season, was making fewer mistakes, and had got quicker. While I still had the edge – quite accurately quantified by the one bike-length that was my winning margin here – André had emerged as my most competitive rival.

My victory celebration was premeditated, but nothing to trouble the censors, nothing like at Romandy the year before: I had simply tried to re-enact exactly what I'd done on the same finish-line three years earlier, lifting my arms above my head and gripping my helmet with both hands, this time in only mock disbelief.

Three years. It was hard to believe it wasn't more. The last time I'd won here, it had felt like I flicked a switch as I crossed the finish line, and with that my life changed. The disbelief had been real. Before Châteauoux I had won stages at the 2008 Giro d'Italia, my first in a major tour, but the Tour was and still is the only bike race where a stage-win could have that sudden, transformative effect.

Even at the time I'd been adamant that riches and fame wouldn't change me, and in a certain sense I'd been right, but on other levels I could see that, three years later, so much was different now. While I still adored my job, it had become that – a job – with high stakes and daunting responsibilities towards teammates, sponsors, the public and myself. For the most part I relished the pressure, and yet there were times when so many people's state of mind seemed to depend on what I did aboard my bike. That was what had got to me so much in 2010: while I was devoting all of my energy to putting myself back on track, the media in particular seemed aggrieved that I wasn't working to their timetable. For all that I was intelligent and experienced enough by then to have worked out the rules of the game, it still wasn't easy to learn, mature and grow at my own pace whilst constantly in the spotlight. This was especially true given my habit of reacting instinctively, heart throbbing from my sleeve. That same qualities that were 'raw', 'refreshing', 'endearing' when I was winning were flipped to become 'rash', 'tiresome' and 'obnoxious'; when I wasn't; depending on the day, I either reaped the benefits or paid the cost.

Ours was a fickle existence, and I was reminded of that moments after stepping off the podium in Châteauroux. In an interview with ITV's Ned Boulting, I discovered that Brad had crashed around 40 kilometres from the finish and was out of the race with a broken collarbone. The joy drained from me. I was crushed for him. Before the Tour, the excitement and curiosity among all of the British riders had been palpable. Now he was out of the race, a deep respect for the hard work that he'd done and the sacrifices that he'd made accentuated our sympathy.

If a British rider wasn't going to be wearing yellow in Paris, I could at least now make sure that one was wearing green. My second win in Châteauroux perhaps hadn't changed my life, but it had caused a major shift in momentum in the points competition. Rojas still led on 167, but I now trailed by only 17.

chapter six

The next two days after my Châteauroux victory would bring back more memories of my 2008 Tour, but this time ones that were not especially welcome. Familiar roads stirred up familiar thoughts and sensations, but this time they were not about victory but tiredness, pain and – when it was over in the evening – relief. In 2008 we'd also finished the first mountain stage of the race at Super Besse in the Massif Central and I was the point in the race when pain had taken up permanent residence in my legs. The 2008 stage that followed the one to Super Besse ranked among the most traumatic days I've ever spent on a bike, but with age I'd grown stronger and now it was a faint, dull discomfort rather than the chorus of aches that I remembered from 2008.

The second stage in the Massif Central in 2011 had a lot in common with that one in 2008, including the winner, Luis León Sánchez. At the back, Bernie, Mark Renshaw, Lars Bak and I toiled all day just to keep pace with the last group on the road, the *gruppetto*. This was a stage that didn't even register with most pundits as difficult or mountainous, and it was taken for granted that we would finish without too many problems. Little would the fan who looked at the results that night know that the whole day had been a battle with the terrain and with the voice in my head that told me this was ridiculous, inhumane, and that the Tour de France was barbaric.

The day featured seven classified climbs including the highest pass in the Massif Central, the Col de Pas de Peyrol and descents like sky-dives. That was challenge enough, and not helped by the knowledge that Bernie's descending tactics were weirdly incompatible with my own. Bernie takes strange, shallow lines, killing his speed on the way into corners and then bursting out of them, whereas I use my low centre of gravity to go in low and tight, feathering the brakes and then flicking my back wheel around at the last moment. If we ignore each other and do our own thing, we both go down equally fast, just in very different ways.

Now, as so many times before, Bernie and I rode the line between what was safe and what was possible just to stay close to the *gruppetto* and in the race. Others weren't so lucky: rain early in the stage had made the corners treacherous, causing crashes that put both Dave Zabriskie of Garmin and Alexandre Vinokourov out of the Tour. Later on, two of the five riders clear of the peloton, Juan Antonio Flecha and Johnny Hoogerland, demonstrated that bad weather was just one of the endless hazards at the Tour. Both had been riding towards a shot at one of those life-changing stage wins when a VIP car belonging to the French state broadcaster went to overtake them, swung into the middle of the road to avoid a tree and knocked Flecha to the tarmac and Hoogerland into a barbed-wire fence off the opposite side of the road. Hoogerland's shredded bib shorts, the 33 stitches in his left leg and his tears that night were among the lasting images of the Tour.

I felt desperately sorry for them. Neither Johnny nor Juan Antonio was the most popular guy in the peloton but I liked and admired them both. It was often the same: guys who never gave an inch, who would see a gap and go for it before anyone else got there first, who rode with the commitment that Juan Antonio in particular showed every day, were considered by other riders to be nuisances or often much worse. At the Tour, especially, the combination of everyone's frayed nerves and the way that a pack mentality could develop in the peloton over the three weeks could make a villain out of a guy like Flecha. I'd been misjudged in the same way, partly because of things I'd said in the press, partly for the way that my team and I moved around the peloton.

As feared and predicted, with the stages in the Massif Central, my green jersey challenge had somewhat stalled while Philippe Gilbert, a superior climber, forged ahead. Gilbert had reclaimed the lead in the competition with 217 point to Rojas' 172 and my 153. The next two stages, though, would see a return to less rugged terrain and another shift back in my favour. I was disappointed to lose to André Greipel in Carmaux on stage ten, particularly with a noisy contingent of Manx fans waiting to celebrate my victory alongside the finish line, but at least my second place cut into Gilbert's green jersey lead.

Even when I say that now – that I was 'disappointed' to lose to Greipel – it somehow jars. Not because it was André and because of our history together, but because early in my career there had always been a perverse sort of comfort in the agony of losing. If I didn't win back then, it could only ever be because I'd fucked up, and the self-flagellation that came next was my corrective device, the inner censor that demanded the same thing would never happen twice. The mechanism still functioned, as anyone unfortunate enough to be on the team bus with me after the majority of my defeats could have attested, but there had also been times when it was hard to be angry with myself because I'd been beaten by something special. In Carmaux on stage ten Greipel had executed a perfect sprint, whereas I had also been handicapped slightly by Renshaw's absence from my lead-out train. We'd had precious little help from other teams since leaving the Vendée, the fatigue was starting to bite, plus Mark had been on a bad day. Consequently I had to improvise on a technical, twisting finish, slotting in between Greipel and his lead-out man, Marcel Sieberg. I had also made a tiny mistake, but one that I could almost forgive myself for: finishes where you couldn't see the line at the moment when you launched your sprint had always caused me a few problems, adding fractions of a second of hesitation, shaving a handful of watts off my kick.

That night, Renshaw gave it to me straight: 'Tomorrow, when it's time to kick, you go. OK? No fucking around.' While I balked at the notion that I couldn't win without him – and the 2010 Vuelta had quashed that idea anyway – the next day's stage to Lavaur emphasised Renshaw's importance. The last hour of the race had been ridden in a deluge and the plane trees lining the road blocked what little light was coming from overhead. I tried taking off my glasses, but the spray from the road only made it harder to see. I decided then that I would wear my glasses and make this sprint the ultimate, literal testament to the 'blind faith' in Renshaw that I'd talked about in interviews: I'd simply lock my eyes onto his back wheel and kick, this time holding nothing back, as soon as he started to slow or pulled off. The outcome this time was a win by bike lengths.

If it felt good to reacquaint myself with that winning feeling, there was better news to come. My victory in the rematch with Greipel ended with me collecting two prizes on the podium: the stage winner's bouquet and the green jersey itself. With 11 stages gone the order from two days earlier had been reversed: Gilbert was now third with 231, Rojas second with 235, and I had 251. It was the first time I'd had the green jersey on my shoulders since stage 13 of the 2009 Tour.

As far as I could make out, there were now only three things that could stop me winning green: Gilbert, Rojas and the time limits in the Alps and Pyrenees. Gilbert and Rojas, I knew, would climb better than me and pick up points in the medium or *moyenne* mountain stages, but would almost certainly lose ground to me on the two remaining stages that were expected to finish in bunch sprints, in Montpellier and in Paris on the Champs Elysées.

The time limit was a more predictable enemy and one that had come close but so far never beaten me in the Tour. Critics thought they knew why: it was, could only be because I hung on to cars or relied on pushes from spectators in the mountains. These were accusations that had followed me throughout my pro career and become more and more insistent as I became more successful. There had been whispers from other riders, one or two more or less veiled allegations that made it into the press, and these had then been seized upon by the public.

I knew exactly where the accusations had started – at the Giro in 2008. That year one form of cheating led to another, with a few rogue desperados at the front – most notably Emanuele Sella – making a farce out of the stages in the Alps and Dolomites. That Sella was doped to the gills was obvious at the time but, without any proof, all we could do was try to hold on – quite literally in dozens of riders' cases. I would admit to you that I did it, and so would many, many other riders in that race. My crime was merely made worse, the riders who had survived the drug-fuelled rampage legitimately argued, because I went home from that Giro with two stage wins.

At the 2011 Tour I knew that another incident at this year's Giro would bring these accusations back to the fore again. On the first mountain stage of the Giro finishing on Mount Etna I'd come in just 25 seconds inside the time-cut. Such a narrow escape was in itself suspicious, the pundits had said, and even riders who had been minutes up the mountain agreed. The Movistar rider Fran Ventoso was particularly scathing and said that I should have been thrown out, with the Italian sprinter, Manuel Belletti, making a similar comment. Rod Ellingworth wasn't at the race, but he'd called me that night and put me on the spot.

'Did you do it, honestly?'

I told him the truth: we'd ridden like our lives depended on it, but we hadn't hung on to the car. The next day I said more or less the same thing to journalists, albeit in more colourful terms: 'If I piss, if I stop, if I crash, if I get a wheel change … I have the TV camera with me, I have motorbikes, I have helicopters, I have the ice-cream truck with me. If it's possible for me to cheat then I am doing a David Copperfield.'

As the Tour entered the Pyrenees, these sorts of accusations were bound to resurface. On stage 12 to Luz Ardiden I finished safely tucked into the *gruppetto*, with Rojas wrongly claiming that I'd been pushed by spectators on the final climb. The 13th stage to Lourdes was a slightly easier one and there had been no complaints. On the third and toughest day in the Pyrenees to Plateau de Beille, however, the familiar sniping started again. Tyler Farrar typified it, remarking in an innuendo-laden interview on American TV that I'd made a 'remarkable comeback' to rejoin the *gruppetto* late in the stage.

My comeback was remarkable, just not in the way that Tyler was implying. I'd been dropped on the third of six major climbs on the route, recovered thanks to Bernie and some more breakneck descending, but then had crashed as we started the plunge off the Port de Lers towards the foot of Plateau de Beille. The fall had cost us a minute, and with the *gruppetto* now bombing towards a valley where it would be impossible for the two of us to claw back any time, we radioed ahead to Lars Bak and Danny Pate to say that we needed them to drop back. They followed the instruction and were soon joining Bernie in a three-man time trial, while I hung at the back saving energy for the last climb. We'd seen our Emerald City – the silhouette of the *gruppetto* – halfway up Plateau de Beille, the day's final climb.

Tyler thinking that legs and willpower alone couldn't have saved me was understandable in one sense. I'd jumped to the same conclusions in the past: when you've only scraped through and done it on fumes, and a guy who's a worse climber or in worse condition than you also somehow makes it, you can't help but wonder.

Anyone accusing me, though, hadn't seen or had to put up with the 'special treatment' that the *commissaires* had reserved for me on this Tour. Partly because of the controversy at the Giro, partly because the TV cameras always zoomed in on me when there were 30 riders dropped on any given climb, so giving the impression that I was the only one, and partly because Rojas and his Movistar team had been in their ear, the race jury had seemingly deployed one *commissaire* solely to watch me.

That would have been OK if the gentleman in question had applied the same rules to me as to everyone else, but in the

Pyrenees there had already been inexplicable discrepancies: there were 'Barrages' whenever I stopped for toilet breaks – the cycling equivalent of Formula One's safety car, meaning that no car in the convoy behind was allowed to overtake and help draft you back to the bunch; I was told that I couldn't take bottles in the last 20 kilometres of mountain stages while other riders were merrily going back to their car for gels, bars and drinks. It made me paranoid to the extent that I wouldn't even go back to the car for my drinks at all, in case the *commissaire* accused me of taking 'sticky bottles' – holding onto the bidons as the *directeur sportif* handed them to me out of the car window and allowing myself to be dragged along.

The team spoke to the chief *commissaire*, Philippe Mariën – who is one of the fairest around – and explained that, in our opinion, certain rules weren't being applied evenly. He ultimately agreed and spoke to the *commissaire* who had been on my case since we left the Vendée. This guy had been a constant, irritating presence at my side, but at least his being there was good in one respect: it made a mockery of insinuations like Tyler's.

My only real objective in the Pyrenees had been survival. I'd not only accomplished that but was heading north and east towards the Alps with an unexpected souvenir: the green jersey that I'd managed to defend from Rojas and Gilbert thanks to some canny and productive riding at the intermediate sprints. The scoreboard now read Cavendish 264, Rojas 251 and Gilbert 240.

Despite the bigger gap back to Gilbert, I was now possibly more concerned about him than Rojas, and stage 15 to Montpellier showed why. In 2011 Gilbert had been without too much doubt the best all-round rider in the world, potentially deadly on almost any kind of terrain and at any moment of a race. On the road in to Montpellier, all it had taken was a few hundred metres of gently rising road to lure him onto the attack three kilometres from the line. The secret to reeling in this kind of attack was resisting the temptation to panic and maintaining a high but steady speed. Gilbert may have been the best all-round rider, but Tony Martin was peerless in this particular exercise. Gilbert was swept up two kilometres from the line and Peter Velits, Gossy, Renshaw and then me did the rest. It was my fourth stage win of the tour and extended my green jersey lead: I was now on 319 points, Rojas on 282 and Gilbert 248. Now we were talking …

With one week to go, albeit one predominantly spent in the Alps, I was confident but wary. Peta had come out for the second rest-day after my Montpellier win, for which our team had been billeted in a large, bland three-star hotel just outside a town called Loriol-sur-Drôme in the Rhone Valley. The scene in the hotel garden that afternoon showed two worlds momentarily overlapping – the bubble that we inhabited for the duration of the Tour and the normality that we'd left behind two weeks before: ordinary folk on their holidays discussing current affairs or the minutiae of everyday life; people who couldn't care less about the Tour. Then there were our partners and families with a foot in both realities, unsure of how to bridge the divide. We were protagonists in maybe the greatest show in sport and yet for many of us it was the last thing that we wanted to discuss. This, admittedly, was the paradox that those closest to us had to reconcile on a daily basis, and not only at the Tour.

For me, it was especially hard to completely switch off on rest days, even with Peta around. There were press conferences, interviews and team meetings. On this particular rest day, Bob, who had arrived at the Tour a few days earlier, and Rolf had asked me whether we could have 'a chat' in the afternoon. There was no need for them to tell me what it was going to be about.

I wanted Peta with me – as per my new policy with Bob and Rolf. They had no problem with that and the four of us sat down in a quiet, secluded corner of the hotel garden, well out of the earshot of the agents, journalists and fans who always found their way into the team hotels on rest days. Bob and I had barely spoken since I'd given him the cold shoulder at our training camp in California in January, but we'd at least been civil to each other in the limited and brief conversations that we'd had over the previous week in France. If he had a new sponsor, if the CEO or sponsorship director of whoever that company was had come to France and was going to talk to us, and if my teammates were keen, I knew that it would hard for me to walk away …

'Now,' Bob said, 'you'll have guessed why we've asked to talk to you. It's about your future and the team's …'

What followed wasn't a short discussion, but it can be quickly summarised: Bob said they had found a new, long-term partner but that the investment hinged on me committing to the project. As far as I could tell, it was exactly what we had been hearing for the previous two years. Too vague, too familiar. Perhaps it really was all different this time, perhaps it all could and would have worked out, but by now I'd lost patience. I wanted certainties, a concrete proposal, not another version of the promise that had been playing on repeat since the end of 2009. Having made my decision, I had now set aside the frustration with Bob and could answer him politely, even graciously, but also emphatically.

'Look, Bob, I'm really sorry,' I said, 'but it's a no.'

With that and a few more failed attempts to talk me around, we shook hands, got up and went our separate ways. With no hard feelings.

One by one, Bob and Rolf had spoken to everyone else on the team that afternoon. The impression that I got, though, was that nearly everyone, like me, had given up hope without yet making arrangements for 2012.

Our disappointment and sadness at the realisation that this was our last Tour together could have overwhelmed us in that last week, but my green jersey quest gave us the perfect distraction. It was the way that we had always dealt with the same uncertainties: by immersing ourselves in the job. The first stage after the rest-day had taken us to Gap in the foothills of the Alps and been one of the most dangerous from my perspective. With the second category

Col de Manse 11 kilometres from the finish, the likelihood was that Gilbert would finish inside the top 15 on the stage and therefore collect at least some points, as could Rojas. The nightmare scenario was a Gilbert win, but it didn't materialise thanks, ironically, to the man who had pipped me to the green jersey in 2009: Thor Hushovd. While Thor romped away to the stage and Rojas and Gilbert could only pick up a measly three and two points respectively, I had surprised myself on the last climb and for a moment even thought that I could sneak inside that top 15 and add to my tally. Unfortunately, as we'd neared the summit of the Col de Manse, a rider in front of me – a climber, in fact – let a wheel go in front of him, creating a gap that I wasn't able to bridge. Whereas usually in these circumstances I might have lost my rag, I was under strict instructions from Rod not to waste any energy in the last week, whether physical or emotional. I ended up finishing almost 30 places and two minutes outside the scoring positions, but still relieved that both Gilbert and Rojas had missed a major opportunity to eat into my lead. As soon as they were available, I loaded the latest standings onto my phone and sat in the bus studying the numbers:

Cavendish 319 points
Rojas 285 points
Gilbert 250 points

After another *moyenne montagne* stage in which I was the only one of the three of us to score – a single point at the intermediate sprint – the Alps and the final hurdles in the race for green loomed. For the next 48 hours that third opponent – not Gilbert, not Rojas but the time limit – would present the biggest danger. It was the guillotine poised above all of our heads, but especially mine as the weakest climber of the trio, with the potential to end not only my green jersey bid but also my race. Riders finishing outside the time limit might conceivably stay in the race, at the *commissaires'* discretion, but lose 20 points. You only had to open the road book, cast your eyes over the route profiles, consider the names of the climbs and what they represented in Tour folklore to realise that points might be easier to lose than to gain between here and Paris.

Just as the 2010 Tour had celebrated the 100th anniversary of the race's first foray into the Pyrenees, so this year the organisers had decided to pay a special homage to the Alps and their most emblematic climb, the 2,645-metre Col du Galibier. We would be going up the Galibier twice, first from the south and finishing at the summit on stage 18, and then from the north en route to Alpe d'Huez on stage 19.

The night before the mountain stages I did my usual homework, studying maps, videos and paying particular attention to the last two kilometres. It was fair to assume that a stage finishing at the top of the highest mountain in the Tour wasn't going to be decided in a bunch sprint, but many times in the past I had been racing the clock in the last two or three kilometres and found it useful, if not essential, to know the lie of the land. In readiness for those squeaky-bum scenarios, it is also vital to know the formula for calculating time cuts. This is too complicated to detail in full here, but in basic terms amounts to the winner's time plus anywhere between 9 and 20 per cent on top of that, depending on the winner's average speed, the type of terrain and length of the stage. Crudely put, the percentages and time cuts are more generous in the mountains and increase in step with average speeds. Paradoxically, then, fast stages often suited us.

In my early years at the Tour, Bernie had always taken on the role of timekeeper, not only on my behalf but the whole *gruppetto*. His would be that voice that you'd hear, an unmistakable, booming, Austro-Australian foghorn filling the valleys as you climbed: 'Guys, 32 minutes with 20 to go. Got to move now. *Allez*!' There was a science, a special intuition to *gruppetto* riding, and with time I had become almost as adept as Bernie at both the calculations themselves and judging the efforts required to squeeze in. And with the *directeurs* in the team car also keeping track and relaying time gaps, we had at least three different brains on the job.

Nothing could ever go wrong. Or could it?

'Fucking hell guys, you've fucked us over here.'

These were my bitter first words, hissed into the mouthpiece of my intercom radio, as I collapsed over my handlebars. They were directed at Allan Peiper and Valerio Piva in our second team car. All the way up the Galibier, Allan and Valerio had assured us that they had done their sums and that we and the rest of the *gruppetto* were easily going to make the time limit. We could coast in with no fear of missing the cut and thereby incurring a 20-point penalty. Hearing this news and the confidence with which it was delivered, we had relaxed and given up the mental arithmetic.

A panicked message arrived in our ears around a kilometre from the summit of the Galibier.

'Guys, we've made a mistake! You're in trouble here. You're going to be outside …'

To everyone else in the group except Gilbert, of course, this made no odds: they didn't care about losing points, and there was no chance that an entire *gruppetto* would be dumped out of the race for finishing *hors délais*. This was also why no one on other teams had thought to warn us that we were in danger. Why bother, when they were perfectly content with the present, leisurely pace, except perhaps Gilbert, who languished with us? This was also typical of the unwritten code governing the *gruppetto*: while it was mutually understood that *all* of the riders would share the workload (and hence keep the pace higher on the flat than it would be in an average peloton being driven by a limited number of riders and teams), they would only do so in the pursuit of a common interest; as soon as singular agendas encroached, in this instance our need to get me to the finish inside the time limit, it was no good looking to others for assistance. Ninety-nine per cent of the time – in other words when he doesn't happen to be in contention to win a points jersey – the *gruppetto* rider has only two, overlapping aims: avoid elimination by finishing in a group too large for the organiser to want to cull, for fear of 'decapitating' the race, and do it while riding as slowly and economically as possible, to conserve energy for the challenges ahead.

Needless to say, then, the atmosphere in the team hotel after my 20-point penalty on the Galibier had been confirmed, like my prospects of keeping the jersey, had noticeably deteriorated. Usually our two most meticulous *directeurs*, Allan and Valerio were no doubt mortified, but they also made the point that it was stressful for them, directing the team from the car. Whoever was in the wrong or right, one certain outcome of the whole fiasco was that, in future, I'd do my own maths.

There was now a real danger that I would lose the green jersey at Alpe d'Huez. The stage was unusually short at 109 km and designed for maximum thrills, with the ascent of the Col du Télégraphe beginning after just 14 kilometres, to be followed by the Galibier and then Alpe d'Huez. With the day consisting entirely of climbs and descents, it was going to be a back-breaking limbo dance to make it under the limit and avoid another 20-point penalty.

As soon as we hit the foot of the Télégraphe that day, I at least already knew that my doomsday scenario, elimination, wouldn't come to pass: I was going like a rocket. Bernie wished he could say the same. He, like Dave Millar, was having a shocker, a textbook *jour sans* or 'day without' as the French call it, so much so that both had fallen out of the back of the *gruppetto* and were already in a fight for survival on the lower slopes of the Galibier. With every update from the team car, my guilt at having left Bernie behind tugged a little harder on my jersey, until I finally turned to Tejay Van Garderen, my chaperone for the day in the *gruppetto*, and announced that I was going back for Bernie.

'I'm not going to Paris and winning the green jersey without him,' I said. 'If he gets eliminated, I go too ...'

Fortunately for all concerned, Bernie needed not martyrs but just a long, not particularly technical descent like the one of the Galibier to rejoin me in the *gruppetto*. Now the message from the *directeurs*, this time verified by us, was that we were heading towards another 20-point deduction. This time, though, it caused me no great alarm, since Rojas was paying for his efforts on the Galibier the previous day and also labouring in the *gruppetto*.

We would therefore remain as we were – unless I did something totally unexpected and attacked on Alpe d'Huez to distance Rojas, beat the time cut and save my 20 points. The idea was good and so were my legs, but I couldn't quite pull it off. Having picked my spot to accelerate, where the gradient eased two kilometres from the line, it took a kilometre to move through the *gruppetto* and off the front. That effort had cost me too much and Rojas was alive to the danger. We crossed the line together, and together with 82 other riders, 25 minutes and 27 seconds behind the stage winner Pierre Rolland ... and 18 seconds outside the time limit.

There was confusion about that limit and whether Rolland's time should have been rounded up to the nearest minute, as the rulebook seemed to state, but really it made no difference to what was now the key equation: Gilbert had made the time cut and avoided a points deduction at Alpe d'Huez, but he was now 50 points adrift and out of the hunt. It would be between me and Rojas, who remained 15 points behind. We had two stages left to ride, but one was a time trial in which neither of us was likely to gain or lose points. It would all therefore be decided in one final sprint showdown on the Champs Elysées.

While I respected Rojas and was in some ways surprised that he had never challenged for the green jersey before as he seemed to have all of the prerequisites, I didn't particularly like him. The controversy over the 'assistance' from fans and my team car that I had allegedly received in the Pyrenees had rumbled on throughout the race, and the press were suggesting that Rojas and his team were perpetuating it. The best way to silence them, of course, was by winning on the Champs.

As it transpired, I wouldn't have needed to: with a break down the road, I took seventh place and nine points at the intermediate sprint, two more than Rojas. My lead was now 17. Avoid catastrophe – a puncture or a crash – and I'd be unassailable. As we hurtled through the Place de la Concorde, around the right-hander which brought us onto the Champs, Gossy led Renshaw who led me, and Rojas and everyone watching knew the script from there.

At the exact moment when my 2011 Tour de France ended, hundredths of a second before anyone else's, I brought my hands to my chest and rubbed the fabric between thumbs and forefingers. The Tour was Cadel Evans's but the green jersey was mine. Just like Mark Renshaw had said, we weren't going home without it.

A few minutes later, as the team gathered for our ritual lap of honour around the Champs – the last one that we would ever do together – one of Movistar's *directeurs* strolled towards Brian in the area behind the finish line.

'Hey, *hombre*,' he said, 'I'm sorry about the business in the Pyrenees, with Cavendish. You know, saying he'd been pushed ...'

Brian looked up, quizzically.

'Yeah,' the gentleman said. 'No hard feelings. We were just trying to mess with Cavendish's mind.'

chapter seven

Abit like my green one before it, the 2011 world champion's rainbow jersey would be won months, no years, before I pinned on my race number.

One school of thought is that 'Project Rainbow Jersey', as it came to be known, dated back to a weekend in Manchester in 2003, when I'd bounded across the velodrome car park after my first meeting and training sessions with Rod Ellingworth and thanked him for 'the best two days I've ever spent on my bike'. Another is that it originated a few months after that, when Rod presented his idea for an Under-23 British Cycling Academy to Dave Brailsford and other federation top brass in one of the meeting rooms in the same velodrome. Rod had asked for around £100,000 to get the scheme up and running, and after some hesitation he finally got the green light to start interviewing riders later that year.

I had been in that first intake of six likely lads. In my interview, Rod asked what I hoped to achieve in professional cycling. I'd said honestly that I dreamt of winning stages in the Tour de France, then told a strategic white lie about also wanting to win Olympic medals on the track. Although I didn't realise it at the time, both Rod and I regarded the track as a rite of passage on the way to where we really wanted to be: making waves on the elite road scene. Lottery funding was allocated in reward for Olympic and World Championship medals, and it was much easier to obtain them (and consequently more funding to feed more success) in the velodrome.

Despite the initial track focus, Rod always had the same aim for me as I had for myself. I would turn pro in a major professional road team and one day compete in an attempt to win famous races: the Classics, stages and jerseys in major tours and the World Championships. In my first year as a professional I won 11 races. In my second I followed two stage wins at the Giro with four at the Tour, and in my third I put my name to my first 'Monument': Milan–San Remo. A world championship was the next milestone, and, together with the green jersey, was the most prestigious accolade that a rider with my physical characteristics could win. Rod knew this too, and since the middle of 2008 had been putting together an audacious plan to give Great Britain its first male world road race champion since Tom Simpson in 1965. He'd called that plan – you guessed it – Project Rainbow Jersey.

By this time we knew the venues for the next three world championships and a bit about the courses. Mendrisio in Switzerland would host the 2009 race and looked too hilly for me to harbour any realistic hope, but after that were two world championships with somewhat less undulating terrain: Melbourne in Australia and Copenhagen in Denmark. By 2010 I'd be 25 and about to enter what should be the most fertile years of my career. On top of this, the overspill from Great Britain's glories on the track were crystallising into a British professional road team, for which Dave Brailsford was already trying to secure sponsorship back in 2008. As far as Rod was concerned the coincidence of these factors represented a perfect storm … and one at the end of which we'd hopefully find a rainbow.

Even the first time Rod and I spoke about his idea, which at the time really was rather vague and fanciful-sounding, I already knew that there was no one better or more passionate, more thorough, more driven than Rod to take on the challenge. Whenever anyone talks to Brian Holm about the contribution that he had made to my development as a cyclist, Brian always smiles and thanks them for the compliment, but reminds them that it was Rod who had spotted my potential. It was Rod who had nurtured and moulded it, at a time when other coaches even at British Cycling had dismissed me as a physiological mongrel who 'didn't hit the numbers' they wanted to see in fitness tests.

'Doctor Frankenstein' Brian called Rod. Obviously, because he was the one who had created the monster.

Rod had ridden competitively in his youth but never at the very top level. Consequently, current or former professionals sometimes viewed him with a scepticism that, I can see now, was grounded in small-mindedness or insecurity. In the five years since I signed my first professional contract with T-Mobile, barely a week has passed without me putting into practice something that I'd learned with Rod, a basic skill or principle to which other riders were completely oblivious, or had once learned and had now forgotten or neglected. In two years at the Academy Rod had ingrained in us a kind of awareness – or mindfulness – that even a lot of top riders don't possess.

As I've already said, bike riders devote a lot of time to training their legs but not a lot to an equally important muscle: the brain. From the day I'd first screeched into the velodrome car park in my gold Vauxhall Corsa, with its 007 number-plate and *Goldfinger* windscreen sticker, Rod had stressed the importance of *thinking* about everything that we did, from using the £3,000 annual allowance that we received from the Federation to analysing strategies and tactics before and after every race.

Project Rainbow Jersey was the fruit of this approach. Instead of just rocking up at a World Championship with a ragtag bunch from assorted trade teams and trying to improvise, or starting to plan only once the team had been selected as most nations did, under Rod we expected to spend months, if not years, obsessing over the Worlds and working out which variables we could control in order to improve our chances. The very act of identifying it as an objective and giving the project a name focused everyone's minds. It instilled the kind of motivation that you could never take for granted in the Worlds, the one race a year when riders were asked to compete *against* the guys who for the rest of the year were their teammates.

Fostering that sense of a common goal, then, was going to be crucial. Rod had been given his mandate in 2008 and by the end of that year was already running structured, off-season training sessions in Manchester for the Academy lads and any British road pro who wanted to attend. In January 2009, I was one of 13 British riders in elite pro teams at the time to receive a group e-mail, with the subject line 'Pro Worlds Project' and a Word document attached. I opened the file and carefully read the three-page, bullet-pointed letter.

The key line, the one that made the hairs on my arms stand to attention, was at the top of the second page:

'Basic outline performance targets for the road race will be, 2009 Mendrisio top 20, 2010 Melbourne top 10, 2011 Copenhagen first, London Olympic Games first.'

The rest of the document was typical Rod: a pomposity-, mumbo-jumbo- and bullshit-free outline of the idea and the practicalities of what was going to happen next. Short training camps that trebled as team-building exercises, brainstorming sessions and opportunities to practise specific skills, such as lead-outs, would be one central component of the process. Rod wanted the first one to take place the week before the National Road Race Championship in Abergavenny at the end of June, a rare occasion in the season when the majority of us would be competing in the same place. A couple of months later he gave us a date and a time to report to a Best Western hotel in Newport for the start of our first mini-camp and meeting.

That evening in Newport, when we all shuffled off into a meeting room after dinner, I think we probably all expected a brief speech from Rod about the selection process, a quick discussion about the training we were going to do the next day, followed by an early night. But for all that he's a straight-talking, no-frills Northerner, Rod also knows how to inspire people – and that was clearly his intention here. When everyone was quiet, Rod formally welcomed us and then walked over to a chair in the middle of the room, draped with some kind of shawl or blanket. After a pause for maximum dramatic effect, like a cheesy magician, he lifted the material to reveal a white, silk cycling jersey. All eyes were immediately drawn to the horizontal rainbow stripes across the middle and around the sleeves. For those who hadn't already guessed, the garment's former owner was the late Tom Simpson, the only British rider ever to win the World Championship road race. Rod then pressed play on a DVD machine and gestured towards the grainy film footage now rolling on a projector screen of Simpson's winning ride in the 1965 Worlds. Rod later told me that he had borrowed both the jersey and the video from a British journalist who also happened to be Simpson's nephew, Chris Sidwells. Rod knew that Chris had a DVD and the jersey, had contacted him and arranged to meet him at a junction off the M6 near Manchester on his way to Wales. This kind of attention to detail was typical of Rod.

Rod had also prepared a montage of clips showing all of us in action, after which he'd turned to us and put a hand back on Simpson's jersey.

'So,' he said, 'how do fancy bringing one of these back here?'

'Fuck, yeah,' I think was my reply. Others might have put it more eloquently, but the sentiments were the same.

Rod reiterated what he'd said in his first group e-mail in January: Melbourne and Copenhagen could both end in bunch sprints, which would logically place me among the favourites. Having established and agreed on that, he then wanted us to split up into groups of three or four and talk about what kind of team we'd need to ensure a bunch sprint, and what kind of riders and roles would be involved.

After a few minutes we had all come to the same conclusion – it would take strength in numbers, which would mean scoring enough ranking points between us to put Great Britain in the top ten on the International Cycling Union (UCI) nations' rankings. By doing this, we could enter up to nine men – or as many as had scored at least one ranking point in the qualification period. Of the possible nine, come race day, two might do the hard yards at the start or in the middle, three might be there to wind it up in the last 20 kilometres, then a minimum of two or, preferably three, would be needed to shepherd and lead me out in the last couple of kilometres.

How we secured that many starting berths was another equally important conversation that we would have both that night and regularly over subsequent months. On paper it seemed straightforward – we all needed to collect as many rankings points as possible with good results in the counting events. The reality, though, was that a lot of the guys weren't paid by their teams to finish at the sharp end of races and to do so would mean abandoning their duties to their trade team leader. They would therefore have to be, if not sneaky, then at least a little bit smart. As Rod said, 'If you're at the end of a race and you can't win it, remember that fifth place is still a ranking point and could be useful for us ...'

Wherever possible, we needed to marry our goals and our teams' with what we were trying to achieve together. Another subject broached was how best to get ready for the Worlds: whether the Vuelta, which usually ended a fortnight before, was the ideal place to get into top shape or, to use Dave Millar's elegant expression, was a 'form-fucker'.

'It depends how you ride a Grand Tour,' Dave said. 'It is possible to just cruise around ...'

Hearing this, I glared at Dave, and a few of the other guys were shaking their heads.

'Cruise around?! Fucking hell, Dave, you might be able to do that, but we haven't all got your talent ...'

On issues like this, our individual preferences or opinions didn't necessarily matter. Once again, the important thing was that we were *thinking* about every ingredient, looking at the problem from all angles. Dave Brailsford had famously coined the phrase 'aggregation of marginal gains', and there was some of that in here, but really all we were doing was aggregating a lot of common sense and mixing in some passion, determination and a bit of camaraderie.

Every month, Rod continued to send his e-mails, with updates on our position in the nations' ranking, news on good recent results by our riders and titbits about the Worlds courses. Over a year before the actual race would take place, he'd been to recce and film the 2010 course in Melbourne. Anything that Rod thought could give us a competitive advantage, he would note, brief us about and ask us not to mention in conversations with riders of other nationalities or in interviews. On his Australian trip, Rod hadn't just gone to look over the Melbourne course but scouted out hotels and tested on himself the impact that different flight options had on jetlag. He had made the Melbourne trip almost exactly a year from the date of the Worlds, which in itself had been insightful.

'It was bloody freezing, six to ten degrees with a lot of rain,' he wrote in one mail. 'I really feel that most nations think it is going to be a hot Worlds and they will not be prepared for the shit weather. This is one area that we must not talk about. Let the others find out when they get there and it will be all too late.'

Not everything would give us an edge, but the only way to ensure that we weren't caught out was by covering every base, trying to pre-empt every permutation. The World Championship, like any other race, could hinge on the timing of a feed, a decent night's sleep on the eve of the race, or the comfort of your team kit – which is why, incidentally, Rod would send us some GB team kit to train in and get used to weeks before the Worlds.

For all the planning, certain lessons and knowledge could only be picked up in an environment like the one we'd find in Melbourne and Copenhagen – a World Championship race. Therefore, although we didn't think that we could win in Mendrisio, and although I wasn't riding, Rod still viewed the 2009 Worlds as essential testing ground. After years of going to World Championships and riding around almost aimlessly – so much so that in 2005 two British riders, Tom Southam and Charly Wegelius, had infamously accepted money to ride in support of the Italian team – Rod wanted everyone in a GB jersey at Mendrisio to at least execute a pre-agreed task.

With certain riders Rod had noticed something that I saw continually in my trade team: because they perhaps lacked one single outstanding ability – they weren't incredible sprinters, time-triallists or climbers – these riders could occasionally look a bit lost and directionless in races. If, however, you gave such riders a role or a function, they'd be transformed.

A great example of this was Danny Pate and Lars Bak at the 2011 Tour de France. Both were the kind of rider who, left to their own devices in a team with no stand-out leader, might have slipped into one or two breakaways over the course of the three weeks, but otherwise been fairly anonymous. But in my team their job was vital every day. With this new responsibility their motivation suddenly soared, and by the second week of the Tour Lars and Danny were toying with the peloton – accelerating into corners to stretch it, then slowing down to squeeze it, playing it like a concertina.

Similarly, even though we had never been likely to contend for the medal positions in Mendrisio in 2009 – and indeed our best-placed rider, Steve Cummings, finished in 52nd place, five minutes behind the winner, Cadel Evans – the guys who represented us had at least all ridden with some sense of purpose.

Over the winter of 2009–10 and the following spring and summer, we continued to get a monthly e-mail from Rod updating us on plans for Melbourne. Team Sky had launched in January 2010 with Rod employed as their 'race coach', which had forced us to change our working relationship slightly. Bob Stapleton and all of the other staff at HTC-Highroad rated Rod, so much so that it looked at one point in 2008 or 2009 as though he might join the team. When Rod went to Sky, Bob was too sensible to veto him remaining my coach, but the strength of our bond still put him on edge. As a concession to both Bob and Sky, Rod and I agreed to impose boundaries on what we discussed and keep it strictly related to my coaching. If I ever wanted to call and vent to someone about other riders, staff members or teams, now I either had to bite my tongue or save the bombardment for different ears.

When we did speak in 2010, as well as everything that I did on the bike, in racing and training, there was one stand-out recurring theme: how much – or rather how little – I rested. Simply put, my hyperactivity drove Rod to distraction. Any time that he called and I wasn't on my bike, I'd be with friends, out shopping, at a meeting – never *only* recovering. He had a point, and I did try, but he was fighting a losing battle. Occupying my mind with other things *was* how I rested and regenerated. Admittedly, in the first half of that 2010 season a lot of things competing for my attention were also causing me a fair bit of stress. Moreover, at that time I lacked the shield of strong management to give me the peace and headspace that I probably would still have filled, but perhaps would have done so more constructively and restfully.

As it turned out, my chances in Melbourne had been compromised even before we arrived. A combination of my poor start to the year, Brad's disappointing Tour de France and a slow first few months for Sky and their British riders left us badly short of points. We were in 15th place in the nations rankings, which would give us only three riders in Australia. As we'd discussed in that first meeting in Newport in June 2009, that was very unlikely to be enough.

Nonetheless, Melbourne would be a valuable and instructive experience. Rod arranged another camp prior to the UK Championships that June – this time in Burnley in Lancashire – which had helped to foster more of that team spirit and sense of a common goal that had taken root the previous year. And of course the race itself taught me that I needed to manage my form and handle it with care in the fortnight before the Worlds, not bleed

bleed it dry until there was nothing left. Essentially, in Melbourne I'd had to learn to lose the Worlds in order to understand how I was going to win it.

By the start of 2011 Rod and I had formed a clear picture of what it would take to execute Project Rainbow Jersey. In our favour, as well as the know-how we'd accumulated over the previous 18 months, we had a course that was far more conducive to the kind of race we wanted than Melbourne and certainly Mendrisio. While I'd had my problems with my weight and crashes early in 2011, it had also been a vast improvement on the previous year's spring and early summer. I had finished every stage race that I'd started before the Tour, having completed just one, Tirreno–Adriatico, in 2010. At the same time, I had consciously avoided packing too many aims and too much pressure into the first six months of 2011, having seen in the past how that could leave you drained of physical and mental energy by the end of the Tour de France.

The 2011 camp before the UK Championships was held at Foxhills in Surrey, which was also going to be our base before the 2012 Olympic road race. Jeremy Hunt, Russell Downing, Pete Kennaugh, Ben Swift, Ian Stannard, Alex Dowsett, Chris Froome, Roger Hammond, Adam Blythe, Daniel Lloyd and I were there for all three days; Dave Millar was skipping the Nationals to be with his heavily pregnant wife. Brad and Geraint Thomas were training with Sky and could only make it for a few hours. Whether Dave and Brad could work together continued to be a concern, and wasn't helped by our inability to get them together in the same room and talking. Brad's recent victory in the Critérium du Dauphiné and his impending one in the National Championships brought the dilemma even more sharply into focus, having put us comfortably inside the top ten in the UCI rankings. It was looking increasingly likely that we would have between five and nine riders in Copenhagen – five being the number that had already scored rankings points – and, on merit, Dave and Brad would be two of the first names on the team sheet.

A fortnight after the Nationals, Brad was crashing out of the 2011 Tour in Châteauroux. A fortnight after that I was leaving Paris with a green jersey and five stage wins to my name. The cloud, then, had a silver lining, although going into August we still didn't know a) how many riders we would be taking to the Worlds, or b) whether Brad was on board. As weekends went, the second one that month took a bit of beating: after Adam Blythe's fifth place finish on the third stage of the Tour of Poland (earning a single, but crucial, ranking point) and brilliant performances by Pete Kennaugh and Steve Cummings to finish in the top ten overall in the same race, we were suddenly certain to qualify eight riders as of the cut-off date of 15 August. Our prospects in Copenhagen were now looking very good indeed, a fact underlined by my win in the Olympic test event over the Box Hill course the day before.

The best news that day, though, wasn't that I had held my form from the Tour de France but the text message I received in the evening from Brad. He wanted to forget and move past the tension between him and Dave Millar, he said. He wanted me to win the Worlds, and he wanted to be part of the team, with Dave, that was going to do it. Everything, it seemed, was starting to fall into place. Well, as far as the Worlds were concerned, anyway.

For me personally the period immediately after the Tour had been tinged with frustration. But I had to accept that there were certain things that I just couldn't control – as much as that aggrieved me sometimes. I'd expected my manager, Chris Evans-Pollard, to fully publicise and capitalise on my green jersey success, particularly after my ultimatum following the incident with the press pass and the VIP enclosure at the Giro. But a fortnight or so after stepping off the podium in Paris, I'd still not had a single new endorsement and hardly any high-profile media appearances. I was clued up enough to know that opportunities were being missed.

By this point another incident had opened my eyes. After the Giro I'd received an invitation to the Champions League Final at Wembley from my sponsors Nike, and had a chance meeting there with Simon Bayliff, the agent for the England and Arsenal footballer Jack Wilshere. Simon had introduced himself and talked to me about his and his dad's love of cycling, and how they used to spend summers following the Tour de France in a camper van when he was a kid. I'd listened, intrigued, and then, when it was time to leave, Simon had handed me his business card.

I hadn't done anything with it until one day at Peta's house when my phone bleeped, and I looked down to see a text message from Lance Armstrong: 'Have you called Simon Bayliff yet?' It threw me slightly because Lance and I had barely spoken to each other since his second, definitive retirement at the end of 2010. I certainly hadn't talked to him about Simon, and didn't know at the time that Simon's agency and its founder, Casey Wasserman, had brokered the sponsorship deal between Lance's final team and the electrical goods retailer RadioShack in 2010. As I stood, puzzled, rereading the message, Peta urged me to dial Simon's number. When I finally called and Simon answered, he sounded pleasantly surprised, then asked whether I could come to his office in central London for a meeting in a few days' time.

A week or so later, and Simon was giving me a half-hour presentation detailing exactly what he could do for me, from the kind of endorsement deals that he could bring in to the way that he and the agency would help me to manage my time. I was blown away and immediately agreed to sign. When my joining Wasserman was later reported in the media, I think most people assumed that the agency had made a timely move to get a slice of the contract that I was about to sign with Sky. In fact I had kept them out of that deal. Which, with hindsight, was possibly a mistake.

In the short term, before I could put Simon to work, I had to let Chris Evans-Pollard know that he had run out of time. I'd said December, but if the green jersey hadn't spurred him into action I couldn't see what a few more months were going to change. I called him to say, as politely as possible, that my warning after the Giro hadn't had the desired effect and that I wanted to call off the collaboration. To Chris's credit, he magnanimously said that he understood and that we could stop there.

Despite this distraction, when I arrived at the Vuelta a España the week after the Olympic test event I was growing more and more confident about the Worlds. The Vuelta would start in Benidorm, as it had the previous year in Seville, with a team time trial.

Also as it had been in 2010, the heat was absolutely blistering.

We set off from a start-ramp positioned *on the beach*, surrounded by frazzled and bemused British pensioners on their sun loungers. From there, the course pointed inland and straight up a hill; Matt Goss and I were immediately gasping for air so hot and uncomfortable that it exacerbated rather than alleviated the suffocation. Without us, our seven teammates pressed on to finish third, while we puffed and wheezed like a pair of geriatric chain-smokers to eventually cross the line nearly three minutes behind.

Gossy said that his stomach had been troubling him for a few days. He thought it might have been light food poisoning compounded by the heat, in which case I, as his roommate, shouldn't have had any bother. I had felt nothing amiss in my stomach but also nothing at all – no strength whatsoever – in my legs. We crossed our fingers that it would pass, especially with stage two looking likely to yield the first bunch sprint of the race. The next day the team controlled the race for most of the first three hours, again in savage temperatures, but there had been no miracle recovery: Gossy had nearly fainted as he stepped off the team bus in the morning, and didn't make it to the finish in Petrer. I completed the stage, but didn't have the punch or power or legs to stay with the peloton in the closing kilometres, let alone sprint for the win. Stage three, taking us even further south to Totana in Murcia, was even hotter, hillier and more disconcerting. Again, I pretty much crawled over the line, this time 13 minutes behind the stage winner.

Even in milder conditions and good health, stage four in the Sierra Neveda mountain range in Spain's deep south would have been a terrifying proposition. With my legs mysteriously empty, it was pure hell: a breathless, sweat-drenched inferno for the 120 kilometres that I lasted before pulling over at the side of the road, gingerly putting one foot onto the tarmac, then two, and climbing into our team car. No sooner had I closed the door than a small swarm of photographers was buzzing around the car. I ducked and turned away to hide my face, then, realising that wasn't working, hid under a rain cape. The pictures of me trying in vain to shield my face were all over the internet within hours.

As we drove off down the route in the team car, whatever poison had flushed the feeling from my legs now started to seep into my thoughts. The Worlds might now be in jeopardy. There was, though, an even more immediate, practical issue to resolve: Peta and her son, Finn, had flown out from London that morning and were due to see me at the end of the stage. Not only would they not see me racing, but they would now be hoping I would go back to the UK with them, which would mean disaster for my Worlds preparation.

Even as I tried to recover from whatever it was that had made me ill, I didn't want any home comforts. It was a question of focus and concentration, as much as it was the lack of suitable training in the UK, the weather or the risk of putting on weight. Not that this was easy to explain to Peta. As most riders will tell you, we make a lot of sacrifices in a career as professional cyclists, but our partners make even more. The faint look of disappointment in their eyes as we break the news that the team has planned *another* training camp, or that *another* one of our teammates is injured and needs to be replaced in a stage race, is one that might become all too familiar, yet can still cut like a dagger.

The question that Peta, the team and also Rod were now asking was *where* I could go to train, if not at home in the UK or my place in Italy. Luckily Dave Millar, who wasn't riding the Vuelta, had already come up with the perfect solution: his friend and neighbour, the Garmin rider Christian Vande Velde, was away and I could stay in his place in Girona, Spain, and train with Dave. Another one of the guys who would be riding for me and Great Britain at the Worlds, Jez Hunt, was also going to be there, and Rob Hayles would also fly out. We could therefore make it our own mini-, pre-Worlds training camp. It sounded perfect – and the even better news was that Peta and Finn could come with me.

That was one problem at least half resolved. But there were others. I could train as much as I wanted, but since 2001 every single Worlds winner had also competed in the Vuelta – and without exception got a lot further than stage four. That was one worry. Another, which essentially stemmed from the same issue of my premature withdrawal, was that UCI rules forbade a rider to pull out of one sanctioned race and, before that event had finished, enter another one. This meant that I would not have raced for a whole month when I took my place on the start-line in Copenhagen and would near enough have ruined my chances of winning the Worlds.

In the heat and panic of the moment, Rod and my team had at first just wanted to know what was going on, why I'd pulled out. From the moment that I'd started losing teammates' wheels in the two or three kilometres of the team time trial in Benidorm, the media had launched into their usual game of Cavendish controversy bingo. What was it to be this time? The girlfriend? His weight? The money? Or that he couldn't be arsed? Rolf, Brian and the others knew better than anyone that it was all pretty much always total nonsense, but might still have wondered for a second whether there wasn't an ulterior motive, perhaps linked to this being HTC-Highroad's last ever major tour. Some of the phone calls exchanged between the *directeurs* that night, and between them and Rod, were by all accounts pretty fraught.

They, too, though, soon had to focus on practical matters. Providing that I could recover and get back on my bike again within a few days, Rod would come down to Girona and oversee my training with Dave and Jez, but that still didn't address our fears about my lack of racing. The Tour of Britain, eight days long and finishing the weekend before the Worlds, would be ideal, but of course the rules wouldn't allow me to take part. Or would they? Rod and Brian knew that there were precedents where riders had pulled out of one race and obtained permission from the UCI and the organiser of the abandoned race to start another. They came to an agreement: Brian said that he would try to find a place for me on HTC's Tour of Britain team, which already had been selected and was full of riders also desperate for competitive action before the Worlds, while Rod dealt with the race organiser and the UCI.

In the space of three or four days in Girona, the toxins in my muscles started to gradually drain away, and I discovered on my first two or three trainings rides that the fitness built up before the Vuelta was still largely intact. Rob Hayles had arrived with his family and joined Dave, Jez and me on the rides. Rob was training for what would be his last ever road race, the British Hill-Climb championships, and we butchered him. Christian's house is perched at the top of a tough, one-kilometre climb, and every day I'd whizz up and wait to take the piss out of Rob as he zigzagged, barely still moving, over the brow.

I was flying, not that I realised it at the time. On every ride or after it, I'd be pestering the guys to reassure me about my form: 'I'm going OK, aren't I? You think I'm pretty strong on the climbs ...?' Rob said later that the only thing more stressful than having to constantly put my mind at ease was maintaining my standards of cleanliness in Christian's house. Rob thought that I might suffer from OCD. To be fair, he wasn't the first to say it.

While we rode in the mornings and rested in the afternoons, Brian and Rod set about their respective tasks. Brian needed to persuade one of my teammates to vacate his place in the Tour of Britain, just in case I got the green light to start the race. The first person he tried was my old chum from the Academy, Matt Brammeier – good old, amiable, unselfish Brammy. There was just one problem: Brammy, who wasn't exactly earning a king's ransom with HTC, not only needed the racing before the Tour, but could also earn some cash in bonuses from the Irish Cycling Federation if he rode well at the Tour of Britain. From Brammy, then, it was a 'sorry' but a 'no'.

Brian looked down the list for another name to try. Peter Velits. Peter is a nice guy, and was riding in the Worlds but not expecting or expected to be in the shake-up on such a flat course. Brian punched in his number, and this time tried a different tactic.

'So, Peter,' he said after the initial niceties, 'you're doing the Tour of Britain, are you? Ach, that bloody race. The transfers in that race are a nightmare, aren't they? And the hotels?'

By this point Peter may just have sensed that there was a hidden agenda. But Brian went on to explain our dilemma, and because he understood and was a nice guy, Peter said that it was OK. He would just train at home in Slovakia instead. I later called Peter to check that he was sure, and even said that I'd give him some money as compensation. He told me not to be silly, that it was fine.

I now only needed permission from the UCI and the Vuelta organisers. Which Rod duly secured.

All that was left for me to do was concentrate on riding my bike. In Spain, the combination of Dave and Jez, fantastic roads and great weather meant that motivation was never going to be a problem. We had smashed ourselves, possibly clocking up more high-quality kilometres than I would have at the Vuelta. I then returned to the UK, to Peta's house in Essex, slate skies and torrential rain. But it didn't faze me; Rod stayed with me and I got myself back up to race speed on mammoth rides behind his moped, with another British pro, Alex Dowsett, keeping me company. We'd do 260 kilometres, the exact length of the race in the Copenhagen, the last 100 of which would be following Rod at 50, 60 kilometres an hour. I had rarely, if ever, trained so hard. And I was not about to start the Tour of Britain in supreme, crank-wrenching, chain-buckling form.

The race rolled out from Peebles in Scotland, and right from the off I could sense that friends, teammates and rivals could see that I was flying. I won that first stage to Dumfries, with Renshaw in second place. The stages ended early in the Tour of Britain and weren't particularly long, unlike the distances between one day's finish and the next day's start. For most of the riders this meant tiresome transfers in team buses ... but Rod and I were using alternative means of transport for at least part of the journeys. I'd wipe myself down, attend to my media duties, then get back on my bike and prepare to follow Rod for 50 or 60 kilometres on his moped. Stage two, incredibly, was cancelled due to hurricane-force winds, which meant that I still led the race. Twenty-four hours later I'd relinquished the race leader's yellow jersey but impressed everyone on a difficult, uphill finale in Stoke-on-Trent. At the hotel that night, Bernie Eisel added his voice to the growing chorus tipping me for the rainbow jersey in Denmark. In fact, he did more than just tip me – he said that it was in the bag.

If there really could be no such certainty, I did strengthen my claims and shorten my odds by easing to my second stage win of the race on the last day in London, a week almost to the hour before I'd hopefully be doing the same in Copenhagen.

The secret in that week, Rod and I knew, would be avoiding the mistakes of the previous year in Melbourne. Project Rainbow Jersey had been over two years in the making – nearly ten years if you traced it back to the birth of the Academy – yet its success would now depend on tiny details. There was the choice of kit – in my case a British cycling track skin suit, cut off three quarters of the way down the sleeves not for aerodynamic reasons but to keep my wrists cool, which in turn helped to keep my core body temperature down. This was something that I had first learned when I was a junior, bombing around sweaty indoor velodromes.

Then there was my bike – the Specialized Venge designed in conjunction with the McLaren Formula One team, with a custom paint-job and specially stiffened at the bottom bracket for extra zip in a sprint. The wheels we would agonise over for days – hesitating between a deep section carbon wheel, more aerodynamic but not as reactive, and a narrow section, which gave me more jump out of the corners but had a higher drag factor and therefore wasn't as effective at high speeds. Having trained on the circuit throughout the week and paid particular attention to that crucial, right-angle right-hander with 900 to go, I eventually opted for the latter. My positioning from that bend to the finish line – and the scope for correcting mistakes – would be more decisive, I thought, than my straight-line speed.

My tyres were also the source of some concern and a lot of discussion right up to the eve of the race. I adored the Continentals that we used at HTC, especially in the rain; Mark Renshaw and I still talked fondly about a descent we'd done in damp conditions at the 2009 Giro, on a day when the Spanish rider Pedro Horrillo had suffered a career-ending crash into a ravine, and we reckoned that we'd caught and overtaken five groups. They were the only tyres that I wanted on my wheels in Copenhagen, especially if there was any chance of wet weather, but Rod insisted the forecast was set fair and that the Continentals were the wrong option. He pointed out that, at the Tour of Denmark that year, on Danish roads surfaced with the same kind of tarmac we'd see at the Worlds, HTC riders had suffered numerous punctures. Still sceptical, I agreed to train on the Veloflex tyres that Rod was recommending ... and punctured on that very first ride. That settled it: I was going with my trusty Continentals.

Another of my equipment choices in Copenhagen would be the subject of scrutiny and debate – but not until weeks and months after the race. My helmet was a regulation road one that Rob Hayles had helped the manufacturer, Specialized, to adapt and make more aerodynamic. In the effort to save every watt of power, the helmet had been encased in a transparent carbon bubble covering the air vents. No one said anything at the time, and questions were only raised when the Lotto team's riders were prevented from wearing a similar helmet, this one with a removable cover, at the Tour Down Under the following January. The discrepancy stemmed from a rule-change that the UCI hadn't publicised, and from the fact that their equipment regulations in general tended to be a movable feast. They could have spared themselves and me some embarrassment, it has to be said, by not using a photo of me crossing the line in the now-offending helmet quite so prominently in the documentation that they finally released explaining the rule in March 2012.

These, then, had been the finishing touches to Project Rainbow, the last effort to second-guess the explosion of variables that would occur on the sound of that gun on the Sunday morning. It would be easy and perhaps tempting amid this eruption of imponderables to cling to faith, to trust in luck and natural talent, but Rod had begun this quest precisely because he knew that wasn't the way to win any bike race, least of all the World Championship. The advantages procured by what the press now delightedly bracketed among my 'marginal gains' might have amounted to tens, hundreds of metres over a 266-kilometre race. I ended up beating Matt Goss by less than one metre: he was also riding a Specialized bike, but a less aerodynamic model, and was also wearing a vented helmet and a normal jersey and shorts.

Those crucial, life-altering last 50 metres bearing down on the line that represented so much to so many of us – none of that was anything but the culmination of years and years of hard work. I had no more won the Worlds than Rod had won it, than Chris, Jez, Ian, Gee, Brad, Dave and Steve had won it. Than Adam Blythe, who had scored that vital single point that had given us an eighth rider. Than Dan Lloyd, who hadn't made the team, but had attended every training camp and whose congratulatory text message was the first on my phone. Than every one of the other hundreds of people who had in some way contributed to Project Rainbow Jersey.

That realisation would trouble me throughout what should have been the happiest evening of my professional career. At first I couldn't process anything: neither Brammy, who had ridden for Ireland, being the first person to embrace me in my first few seconds as the world champion, nor the Prince of Denmark, a huge cycling fan and another mate of Brian's whom we'd once met for a cup of tea, presenting me with my medal on the podium. My head was still spinning at a dizzying, disorientating cadence throughout the national anthem during which I surprised myself by not crying, or at the press conference or dope control.

By the time I'd dealt with the formalities, arrived back at the bus and clambered up the steps, my teammates were midway through their second, maybe their third happy hour. Everyone was drunk and raucously elated. Even Rod, who is the least proud and self-regarding person you could ever meet, took a photograph – just about the only one in his possession with any 'commemorative' value – and later made it the screensaver on his computer.

We drove back to the hotel, the bus throbbing with cheers, music and jubilation. The party then spilled into the bar, and grew in size and inebriation throughout the night. Peta and Finn were there, as was Simon Bayliff. The guys all had their own stories, different things that they remembered, different vantage points from which they'd seen me win. Dave and Jez had pulled over next to the big screen on the last lap, watched the sprint and almost forgotten to finish the race!

Everyone tried to savour the moment and the achievement – but I was struggling slightly. I'm loath to use the word 'anticlimax' but there was a certain hollowness to the joy at having realised an ambition that I'd held for so long. Perhaps I hadn't drunk enough, or, more likely, I felt uncomfortable that so much of the attention was being focused on me. As if *I* was the world champion and they weren't. Of course that was the reality – I would now wear the rainbow jersey for a year, the rainbow jersey that I had lusted after, dreamt of, grafted towards – but it somehow didn't seem right that there was so little recognition for *them*. I had executed my job perfectly, but so had they. I'm not just talking about money, bearing in mind that our federation didn't offer any bonus to divide up, unlike other nations, and I don't mean other kinds of material rewards. They would all get a nice watch – an IWC Yacht Club – specially commissioned and customised, with rainbow stripe detailing across the black face and each rider's name engraved on the bezel. There, too, I was indebted, to Steve Cumming's wife Nicky, who worked for the jeweller David M Robinson and had arranged to have the watches made in secret.

When I talked about recognition, I meant something that money couldn't buy – a unanimous, even if silent, acknowledgement that I was just one part, and not even necessarily the most important, of an extraordinary, unstoppable machine. They all looked happy enough, beer bottles in hand, staggering around the bar, hugging each other and singing. But, as the clock ticked towards one, I was tired and realised that ecstatic-yet-guilty feeling was one that I wasn't going to shake.

I thanked them all, said goodnight, and took myself and my rainbow jersey off to bed.

A few days later, incidentally, Rob Hayles went to collect the bike that I'd ridden in Copenhagen from the Manchester velodrome. When he located it in the British Cycling coach Shane Sutton's office, Rob looked down at the front wheel, did a double take, then squeezed the rubber with his thumb. Like the Spaniard Abraham Olano in 1995, I had won the World Championships on a punctured tyre.

chapter eight

This is not necessarily a detail that I'd like recorded in the annals of professional bike racing, as a footnote to the first British victory in the World Road Race Championship for 48 years, but soon after thinking 'I'm the world champion', another realisation flashed across my thoughts: 'Fuck ... Head and Shoulders.'

Head and Shoulders was the brand of shampoo that I had recently agreed to endorse, and for which I was due to do a major photo shoot two days after the Worlds. It wasn't dandruff that I was worried about, but – like in January 2010 – a damaged tooth. After the 2002 Giro d'Italia, the American Tyler Hamilton had famously needed 11 of his capped, having fractured his shoulder early in the race and using teeth-grinding as a way of displacing the pain. I'd done something similar over the previous six hours (admittedly without the broken bone, but also without the drugs that Hamilton has now admitted were fuelling him), and it had left me with a smile more suited to Halloween than a major advertising campaign. I had no choice but to clear the diary over the next two days, call off interviews, fly to Manchester and go straight to my dentist. If you look at the adverts we shot later that week, I think you'll agree that he did a pretty good job.

In my first fortnight as the world champion, I'll admit that not too much of my time was spent on a bike. There were public appearances, meetings with Simon Bayliff, and, finally, days and evenings to be spent with Peta and Finn without fretting about what I was eating, how long I was staying up and what impact it would have on the next day's training.

As well as my new manager, I was going to have someone new helping me to stay on top of things – a role that roughly matched the traditional job description of personal assistant but was in actual fact more like a human Swiss Army Knife.

In 2010, partly promoted by Rod Ellingworth's constant insistence that I got more rest, I'd realised that my afternoons and evenings were filled with tedious admin and practical chores, and that it would be beneficial if someone could lighten that load. One of my mates from the Isle of Man, a guy called Rob Dooley, worked in a bike shop and was looking for a change of direction and scenery. I asked him whether he'd consider being paid to act as my odd-job man and Dools had leapt at the chance.

Dools was a lovely guy but, bless him, a bit chaotic. It didn't matter for the most part because he generally did what I asked, plus I trusted him and liked having him around. There were, though, times when the disorderliness not only annoyed but also alarmed me. One day in the spring of 2011 particularly stands out: I'd got a call one afternoon – it was from either the BBC or the Giro d'Italia organisers, I can't remember which – to ask whether I was free to go to Sicily and ride up Mount Etna for a preview of the forthcoming race. It was short notice but I had no prior engagements and so I said, yes, why not. The next day I duly did the ride, the BBC filmed it, and then we all went back to the airport to catch our flights home.

I thought no more of it until, around two weeks later, a letter from the UCI dropped onto my doormat. I opened the envelope, looked down the page, and gulped. The only three words that I remember were 'missed test notification'.

I should confess straight away that it was naïve and irresponsible to trust another person, whether it was Dools or anyone else, to fill out my anti-doping whereabouts form. These log-sheets had to be continually, accurately updated to allow dope-testing bodies to locate riders for out-of-competition controls. If they were unable to find you and take samples, you got one 'strike'. Three strikes or 'missed test notifications' within the space of 18 months added up to a full-scale anti-doping violation, a ban, and an irredeemably damaged reputation. I was now on one strike.

Dools's excuse was that, although he'd known about my change of plans and change of location for the day, he hadn't been able to access the internet and log the new details. I thought it sounded a bit the-dog-ate-my-homework, but I gave him the benefit of the doubt and we moved on.

There were further issues over the summer before it all finally came to a head. The catalyst was an unfortunate mistake by my HTC teammate Alex Rasmussen, or rather three pretty half-witted ones, because that was how many 'missed test notifications' he had chalked up. The team had no other option but to terminate his contract and immediately send him home from the Tour of Britain.

When I heard the news I suddenly felt an odd, ominous chill. I picked up my phone and immediately scrolled through my contacts to the number of my UK Sport anti-doping liaison officer. When he answered, I asked whether he could look at my whereabouts information and tell me what it said for today's date.

'Sure,' he said. 'Here it is. You're in Italy.'

I kept my composure long and well enough for the correction to be made, thanked him, then ended the call and straight away phoned Dools.

There was no 'Hey, Dools, how are you?', no platitudes, just a very abrupt one-line question: 'Where am I right now?'

'The Tour of Britain,' said the sheepish voice at the end of the line.

'Oh, OK,' I replied. 'So how come on my whereabouts form it says that I'm in Italy?'

This was the final straw. As I put it to Dools, 'If I get three missed tests, you're going to lose your job but I'm going to lose my career. My career. Do you realise what that means?'

There was nothing that he could really say.

I adjusted my tone, ended my rant, and got to the crux.

'Look, Dools, thanks for all you've done, but I can't take these risks. You can't work with me any more. I'll pay you for the next month, even if you're not working, but I can't keep you on.'

Dools didn't take my decision particularly well and this was the end, sadly, not only of a working relationship but also a friendship. I now needed someone to replace him, but fortunately didn't have to look too far or hard. Since the start of the year, Rob Hayles and I had been vaguely discussing some arrangement whereby he could help me when he stopped racing at the end of the year: losing Dools had now put me in a position to offer Rob something akin to a full-time position. The fact that Rob had been a top rider, the man who had partnered and mentored me to a first world title on the track in Los Angeles in 2005, not to mention that he was one of my best mates, clearly made him the ideal man for what he would tell you can be quite an onerous role. Although I have a lot of friends and there are a lot of people who want and try to get close to me, Rob was and still is one of a tiny handful who, I know, accept and love me for the person underneath the personality. He can be hilariously funny, sick with it, and he can be infuriatingly laid back for someone as highly strung as me. Even so, it would be very difficult to find someone with a bad word to say about him.

As my 'Mr Fix It', Rob was superb from day one, pretty much ensuring that all I needed to do was get up, get dressed and get myself on my bike. He frequently stayed at our house and became part of our family; I was part of his, with his wife, Vicky, a more than capable and very straight-talking second mother.

On 4 August Bob officially ended his efforts to keep HTC-Highroad alive beyond the end of 2011, having been unable to secure replacement for HTC as the main sponsor. After informing Bob and Rolf during the Tour that I wouldn't remain patient any longer, wouldn't entertain any more promises or even statements of intent from them, I had thought that would at least bring some clarity to my ideas about 2012.

With my new status as World Champion and all of this upheaval in the period either side of the race, it was no real surprise that my training suffered and I had raced only once more, in the French end-of-season Classic Paris–Tours. When I woke on the morning of the race, I was so terrified of getting humiliated in my first outing in the rainbow jersey that it took a stern talking-to from Rod to make me go ahead and race. I managed not to disgrace myself but was never really in with a shout, either, ending up finishing 42nd.

With that fairly anonymous performance and a round of handshakes and goodbyes, my time with the team known in its final incarnation as HTC-Highroad came to an end. Perhaps neither I nor my teammates appreciated the poignancy of the moment at the time, but we all began to realise later what a remarkable, unique team it had been and what a tragedy its demise was. Over four seasons the men's and women's teams had amassed a staggering 509 wins, 50 of which had come in stages of major tours. This made us not only by far the most prolific team of our era but one of the greatest of all time.

What made it even more remarkable was that when Bob Stapleton took over what was then the T-Mobile team from the previous free-spending (and, as has subsequently been proven, ethically dubious) regime, he was suddenly working with a heavily reduced budget. This resulted in across-the-board pay cuts and some controversial redundancies among the riders. Despite operating on limited means, he, as Brian Holm put it, 'whipped our arses' and instilled a winning mentality and team spirit that became infectious. At the start of every season Brian told himself there was simply no way we could sustain the same level of success, the same fairytale, and yet every year we somehow managed to punch way, way above our weight.

I wondered, though, whether this same pattern of over-achievement wasn't eventually our undoing: Bob seemed to assume that we would maintain the same standards on our frugal salaries, and that sponsors would come running to buy into such an uncommon, inspirational underdog story. As I told a journalist in an interview in 2010, 'Bob thinks it's Hollywood and he's Steven Spielberg.'

What I saw as his misjudgement and ingratitude – or certainly his failure to understand how uniquely efficient the team had been – had of course soured our relationship in 2010 and 2011. The lack of a satisfactory pay rise or new contract for me were symptomatic of the same thing: him thinking that we'd happily all carry on getting our arses whipped, with no credible promise of a change or reward at the end of it all.

I realise now that I was unfair in my assessment of Bob. He wasn't intentionally depriving me or anyone else of the money we deserved: he simply didn't have it. The signs of our poverty were everywhere you looked, from the fact that our bus was just about the only one without a shower to the team failing to pick up the Swiss franc fine that I had incurred for my V-sign at the 2010 Tour of Romandy, as they had promised.

Scandalised by the doping controversies that had rocked the team in 2006 and 2007, T-Mobile had effectively paid to have their contract with the team rescinded and their name disassociated from us: that money ended up accounting for a large wedge of our budget for the next four seasons. Columbia and then HTC had both chipped in, but they had paid a little for a lot of exposure and success and therefore been spoiled. When Bob later went to them to talk about a contract renewal and upping their investment, I can imagine that they balked: why would they pay full price for what we'd previously given them at a huge discount?

The other recurring problem with cycling sponsorship was that it was *too* effective for brand awareness. The exposure was so fantastic that companies often felt that they had already derived more-than-adequate benefits after only one or two seasons, and therefore didn't need to stick around for the long haul. For this reason and others, the business of cycling sponsorship didn't follow the same basic logic or patterns as most others, and I wondered if that was something Bob may not have fully grasped. It occurred to me that with the HTC deal running down and their interest in renewing dead, Bob was perhaps approaching big corporations without considering the single most important factor that seemed to predispose companies to sponsor cycling teams: a love of the sport, usually the CEO's or a marketing director's, which meant that sponsorship wasn't only a strategic initiative but something that they also did for fun, a flight of fancy that they could also justify on business grounds. Perhaps I'm presuming too much when I say that maybe Bob wanted to sign the deal, take their money and go off and run a brilliant team, when a lot of sponsors wanted more engagement and influence than that. Or maybe Bob was just unlucky.

In my final analysis, I'd stand by what I thought at the time: everyone at HTC was over-delivering in their jobs, except the people or person whose responsibility it was to find backing for the most successful, cosmopolitan and attractive team in the sport. That person – although it pains me to admit it – was Bob. On the other hand, I would also admit that I regret the lack of empathy I showed for Bob and my lack of appreciation. What Bob accomplished by taking an under-performing team riddled with systematic cheating and turning it into the best organisation in the sport – and also one of the first to truly combat doping from the inside – makes him worthy of a place among the best managers that professional cycling can ever have seen.

On 11 October, two days after Paris–Tours, the worst-kept secret in professional cycling ceased to be: after months of speculation and weeks of serious negotiations, it was announced that I had signed a three-year deal with Team Sky.

The deal might have seemed inevitable, but what I hadn't been prepared for, as the lawyers on both sides hammered out the small print, was the collateral effect on friends and current teammates. I had told Mark Renshaw to wait for me to sign for Team Sky before considering any of the other lucrative offers that he'd had, and even said that I would cover lost earnings out of my own pocket if the Team Sky deal didn't come off. As the days had passed, though, Mark had started to get edgy and couldn't perceive any real desire on Team Sky's part to sign him. Meanwhile, on the back of the success that he'd tasted at the Tour of Qatar in February, the Dutch Rabobank team were trying to tempt him with a big salary and the chance to try his hand at being their front-line sprinter rather than a lead-out man. Mark had finally called me to say that he was going with Rabobank, and I'd said that I understood why he made that choice, while deep down thinking that he could have been more loyal and held off for a bit longer.

Brian Holm had been in a similar position – with my solemn word that I'd find a way in for him at Team Sky, but, like Renshaw, not detecting any real will to take him on from Team Sky. Brian also had other options, the best of which seemed to be the Belgian team Omega Pharma–Quick-Step. They were a notoriously old-school outfit, unglamorous and proud, which appealed to the wannabe old rocker in Brian, a man who held Thin Lizzy and Roger De Vlaeminck in equally high esteem. I still didn't think he'd accept their offer – and was shocked to receive a text from Brian one day in early August announcing that he'd said yes. I text back: 'You're fucking kidding me.' But, alas, he wasn't.

There was more to my decision to join Team Sky than just the fact that they were a British team which met my asking price and employed riders and staff whom I had known for years: in signing for Team Sky I was also buying into a vision for cycling in the UK that I shared. BSkyB wanted to grow the sport on all levels and their investment reflected that, spanning the track, the road and recreational riding. While money does matter, it has also always been imperative to me to believe in and like any company with which I associate myself. That's been the case with Nike, who have sponsored me since the start of my career, and with Oakley; it also applied to Team Sky, now that I was aligning myself with their brand. When I turned pro I made a vow to myself never to bow to PR bullshit, never to be untrue to myself, and I'm proud to say that I've never really deviated from that principle – often with some fairly incendiary results.

Having essentially spent my entire career in the same team up to that point, I couldn't have been more excited about the change of scenery. Team Sky represented the best of both worlds – the familiarity of many of the riders and the staff and the novelty of a new environment. After the austerity of HTC, I was looking forward to new and well-funded ways of working. Our first get-together was a two-day meeting in Milan at the end of October to discuss the season just passed and plan for the next one. My expectations were high, but this surpassed them. Dave Brailsford made a speech that captivated everyone, about what the team had already achieved and what our targets for 2012 would be. The attention to detail – from the meals we ate to our clothing fittings for the coming year – was a notch above even what I'd seen at HTC, where we'd always been ahead of the curve.

Team Sky had gained a reputation for professionalism at the expense of enjoyment, but that weekend in Milan suggested that there could be hard play as well as hard work. On the first night, after a formal dinner with team sponsors, we all headed out *en masse* for a few drinks and ended up in the Just Cavalli nightclub, most of us a little worse for wear. Team-building exercises have become fashionable in cycling in recent years, from survival camps in the forests of Scandinavia to go-karting, but to my mind there aren't many things better for creating camaraderie than a few drinks, a boogie and a taxi home in the small hours.

Before the year was out there was time for two more bits of good news. The first one, in truth, I'd known about for a few weeks, but could only now reveal: Peta and I were expecting our first child together. She – because I was already sure that it was a girl – had been conceived during the Tour de France and was due in mid-April, in the week of Milan–San Remo.

If the green jersey, the world championship and Peta's pregnancy hadn't already made 2011 special enough, more was to follow. A fortnight before Christmas I was voted the BBC Sports Personality of the Year. As much as recognition of my achievement, it was an eloquent statement about how far the sport had come in the UK, bearing in mind that, four years earlier, four Tour stages hadn't even earned me a nomination. It felt like a culmination but also the start of something even bigger; the plans Team Sky had outlined in Milan went beyond the goal of winning the Tour de France with a clean, British rider by 2014, and beyond almost anything ever achieved by a professional cycling team. I was looking forward to going for the yellow jersey, the green jersey and world domination. 'Believe in better' was the BSkyB corporate slogan. I believed that we could be better than anyone imagined.

The almost robotic professionalism that I'd seen only in fleeting glimpses in Milan was more evident at Team Sky's training camps that winter, not that I was complaining. At HTC the first of our two training camps per winter, in particular, had served mainly just to get us back on our bikes and clocking up some kilometres. At Team Sky there were drills and specific exercises every day. I'd trained well all winter, partly because I only needed to glance down at the rainbow stripes across my chest to feel an extra kick of motivation, but also because I thrived on the more regimented style of the Team Sky camps.

This single-minded focus on performance was hard to argue with, since the results were there for rival teams to see and envy, even if they were unable to muster the discipline to emulate them. At the same time, such a Spartan existence took some getting used to, having come from a much more relaxed, convivial ambience at HTC. When training was over every day, there was very little socialising and hardly anyone venturing outside the confines of their room: just about the only extra-curricular activity to look forward to was the odd game of pool. Light relief at Team Sky came in brief snatches – Brad's impersonations, Jez Hunt walking out of one massage, straight across the corridor and into a another one, lying to the second masseur that he still hadn't been seen.

The first races on my 2012 programme would be the Tours of Qatar and Oman in February. At our camps in Majorca, former HTC teammates had all agreed that I looked stronger and leaner than in any winter since 2008–9, and my form was matched by my excitement. On the plane to Qatar, though, I began to feel ill. I ended up spending 40 of the 48 hours immediately before stage one in bed. Antibiotics seemed to have cured me – I went on to win stages three and five after some incredible work by Bernie Eisel and the Spaniard, Juan Antonio Flecha – but lethargy kicked in between Qatar and Oman, and continued to affect me for the next few weeks. It was always the same with me and antibiotics: the short-term benefits came with long- or at least mid-term costs.

Oman was a much hillier race than Qatar but under normal circumstances at least four of the six stages lent themselves to sprint finishes. I vaguely contended in only two of them, with our sprint-train as rickety and erratic in Oman as it had been smooth and rapid in Qatar. My assigned lead-out man was the Australian Chris Sutton, who was a decent sprinter in his own right: with him as my last man, though, we just didn't gel. This early in the year, the lack of any outstanding candidate for this role wasn't yet a major worry, although I was still disappointed that Mark Renshaw had signed elsewhere. Of the riders on the Team Sky roster, the only one I could envisage doing a comparable job to Renshaw was Geraint Thomas, but his year and road programme revolved around the London Olympics and winning a gold in the team pursuit on the track.

I came home from Oman feeling completely drained. It wasn't only the lingering effects of the antibiotics but something that had nothing to do with racing: my first child was due in a month's time and I was scared. The anxiety was making me irritable, the pregnancy was making Peta ratty – especially when I was away at races – and we were starting to get at each other. In Qatar and Oman we'd argued on the phone on a couple of occasions, and although everything quickly returned to normal this only added to my apprehension. I wanted the baby to have a perfect life, a perfect family and perfect parents right from the first day, but we were both trying too hard. Together with after-effects of the antibiotics, the mental strain had started to wear me down and manifest itself in physical pain, specifically in my stomach.

As I had done the year before at San Remo, stress had left me vomiting a brown, bilious liquid that my HTC team doctor had then explained was stomach acid, and which he had treated with antacid medication. Twelve months on I recognised the same symptoms and so made my way to Manchester to see one of the British Cycling doctors, get it checked out and get some of the same tablets.

When I arrived at the velodrome that day and asked which of the doctors was around, I was told there was no one … except the psychiatrist, Steve Peters. Steve and I had known each other for years and got on OK, but our different takes on sports psychology meant that, unlike Vicky Pendleton or Chris Hoy, I was never going to be banging down his door for advice. My views were slightly more nuanced now than in the early part of my career – I no longer just needed 'sunshine blown up my arse', as I wrote in *Boy Racer*, because I got too much of that now and sometimes needed the opposite. Fundamentally, though, I still held the opinion that a lot of what I imagined Steve did wasn't for me.

These opinions, of course, had no bearing on me seeing Steve quickly to get a prescription for some basic antacid pills. Or so I assumed. Two hours of what felt to me like intensive psychoanalysis later, I was no longer sure of anything.

It had started with what was, for me, an utterly baffling discussion about the exact colour of the vomit that I was trying to describe. The conversation progressed from there, eventually, into a full inventory of everything in my life and how it made me feel. At one point, he asked me about Milan–San Remo: we got on to talking about failure there, and suddenly he was questioning whether I should even be taking part. At first my reaction was that he was talking rubbish, but before long he had me doubting San Remo, doubting my ability, doubting everything in my life. At one point I was almost reduced to tears and felt like a basket case.

I've seen Steve work wonders with others but the work he does is just not for me.

My sensations on the bike, like my mood, continued to fluctuate quite wildly in that period. I won the Belgian semi-Classic, Kuurne–Brussels–Kuurne, at the end of February after a textbook display by the team, and took stage two of Tirreno–Adriatico in the second week of March before abandoning the race early, confident of my form ahead of Milan–San Remo later that week. Rod and the Team Sky nutritionist Nigel Mitchell had me experimenting with what was known as a 'low residue diet', the purpose of which was to completely clear your intestines of food residue and its surplus weight. The diet lasted about a week and in my case consisted mainly of egg and rice. Some of the other Team Sky riders, like Brad Wiggins and Edvald Boasson Hagen, had tried the diet and swore by it. We now hoped and thought that it would give me a decisive advantage on the short climbs that pepper the last 100 kilometres of Milan–San Remo. However, the main effect that it seemed to have was to deprive me of energy; I was dropped on the Le Manie climb with 90 kilometres to go and never really recovered. Nigel would do some fantastic work with me in my year at Team Sky, but this wasn't an experiment that we'd be repeating.

I left Italy distraught, but two better performances without sparkling results at Dwars door Vlaanderen and Gent–Wevelgem brought much-needed reassurance. In my private life, too, things also felt a little calmer: as Peta's due date had drawn closer, the excitement of becoming a father had also overcome my trepidation about the baby's arrival. Peta finally went into labour on 3 April, and at five in the morning we headed to the Portland Hospital in central London. The greatest day of my life was about to begin. Over the next 17 hours Peta put my pain threshold to shame and made me glow with pride. At 10.30pm we finally had our beautiful baby girl: Delilah Grace Cavendish.

Everyone had told me that having a kid changes you and changes your life, but I hadn't expected the transformation to happen so quickly. Now for every decision I took, from what I ate for breakfast to when I trained and went to bed, how it would affect Delilah would be the first thought that entered my head.

It was a lot to take on board. For a few days I oscillated between boundless joy and terrible anxiety that I wasn't up to the challenges of parenthood. I remember one day a week or so after Delilah's birth, in particular, when the weight of it all completely overwhelmed me. I was up at Rob Hayles's place in the Peak District, training on the roads familiar from my gruelling first weeks at the Academy in 2003. The weather was gorgeous, and to Rob who was pacing me on the moped there was nothing obviously wrong as we came to a hill and started climbing. I'd made it a few hundred metres before the tarmac under the wheels started to feel like treacle, I could no longer feel the warmth from Rob's exhaust, and I pulled over onto the grass verge. My bike fell to the ground as tears started falling from my eyes.

Above: Greeting the crowds at the 2011 Tour de France team presentation, flanked by two of my best mates, Brian Holm on my right, and Bernie Eisel on my left.

Right: From l-r, 2010 Tour of California winner Mick Rogers, our then-team owner Bob Stapleton and Tony Martin.

Elder statesmen. **Below:** A photo opportunity with Eddy Merckx and Taylor Phinney of the USA at the start of stage six of the 2013 Tour of Qatar. **Below right:** Congratulations in Paris on the final day of the 2010 Tour from Bernard Hinault.

Left and below: Peta and me in the spotlight. The incredible night I won BBC Sports Personality of the Year in 2011 and collecting my MBE at Buckingham Palace in November 2011.

Above: Signing autographs at the 2013 Giro d'Italia in Verona. Not until you're on the bus with the door closed can you finally relax and start to gather yourself for the next day.

Below: A Team Sky press call. After hours in the saddle, another hour with the press can seriously drain your batteries, but it's all part of the game.

The smooth at City
Left: A joke with Brad
on the bus before stage
15. **Below:** Winning once
again on the Tour's final
prestige stage in 2012.

And the rough. **Above:** Outside my hotel room on stage 19 between Bonneval and Chartres. **Below:** Another hotel reception with Chris Froome ahead of stage16. If I look frustrated on this occassion appearances aren't deceiving.

I had to find other ways to enjoy the London Olympics, having been deprived the road race gold medal by bad luck, rival teams' lack of cooperation and some bloody good performances by other riders. **Left:** A friendly kiss in the velodrome from my co-commentator Jake Humphrey. **Below:** Ian Stannard, Chris Froome, Bradley Wiggins, David Millar and myself all smiles at the start line.

Above: Winning ways with OPQS at stage one of the Giro in 2013. On the podium with my daughter Delilah and great friend and sometime cycling jersey designer Paul Smith.

Below: I started the 2013 Giro in rosa and ended in rosso in Brescia with five stage wins, how could it get any better?

Above: Winning stage 13 of the 2013 Tour after my team provided a masterclass in the fine art of the echelon.

Above: Peta, Delilah and Finn. Having a family means that my career is as important as ever, but now because of what my success means to them.

When Rob looked over his shoulder to check that I was still there, he saw me not bobbing up the slope but weeping back down the slope on the grass. He turned around, parked the moped, and came to put his arm around me. He didn't need to ask what was wrong. Over several weeks he'd seen me growing more and more anxious, less and less confident of my ability to deal with fatherhood. They were natural, normal feelings, but at the time it took a lot of advice and support from true friends like Rob to make me realise that.

This period of readjustment – which really was all it was – lasted for a few weeks. As an athlete, you're used to being – almost encouraged to be – self-absorbed, and Delilah and fatherhood released me from that inward-looking, self-obsessed spiral. In almost every interview I did that spring I was asked whether being a parent wouldn't make me ride a little more conservatively, maybe to the detriment of my sprinting. I knew that wouldn't be the case and why that was: a certain fearlessness was in my nature, and having Delilah was an incentive to work even harder and if anything take even more calculated risks to continue winning.

I returned to racing at the end of April in the Tour of Romandy, where I spent four days riding as a *domestique* for Brad Wiggins before pulling out on the penultimate stage. Brad's determination and his physical condition had been impressive even at the training camps in the winter, and suddenly in races he could do no wrong. I'd always considered Brad the single most talented rider in the world, but for a long time doubted whether he had the application to win a Tour de France. But as he added victory in Romandy to the overall title that he'd taken at Paris–Nice in March, I already sensed that he was in process of proving me wrong.

As I prepared for the start of the Giro d'Italia – beginning in, of all places, Denmark – I still had no real complaints about the team. Yes, I was light on support at the Giro, with the Colombian climbers Sergio Henao and Rigoberto Urán also pursuing their own ambitious goals, but I'd known this would be the case since January and had fully approved. There was no point in devoting too many resources to helping me at the Giro when we'd be pursuing such lofty goals later in the year.

The lack of a bona fide lead-out train at the Giro initially concerned me less than Urán and Henao's very individual – and I thought individualistic – style of racing. After my friend Taylor Phinney won the first stage for BMC, Geraint Thomas showed me exactly what I'd been missing with some brilliant work in the finale to set me up for victory on stage two. Gee had been as brilliant and selfless as the Colombians had been (and would continue to be) frustrating. In the first two or three hours of stages, the rest of the team would surround me in the peloton like bubble-wrap, and I'd be moving serenely along, only to notice that there were two riders missing: Henao and Urán. If we were lucky, they'd be skulking and nattering at the back of the peloton; if we weren't, they'd lost a wheel through not paying attention and needed someone, usually Ian Stannard, to go and pace them back into the bunch.

Eventually I snapped at them: 'You're being asked to concentrate for four, maybe five, maybe six hours a day, you're being paid very well, and yet you still can't do it! If you were working in an office, you'd be there for eight, nine hours and you'd be sacked if you got distracted this easily!' If they didn't understand the words, because, with all due respect, neither spoke or understood English particularly well, they would certainly have known from my tone and gestures that I wasn't showering them with compliments.

My tirade led to the management deploying Juan Antonio Flecha as the Colombians' 'guide-dog'. That, at least, was the term they used.

Flecha was outraged … or pretended to be.

'Oh, I'm a dog now, am I?!' he trilled, trying not to join in the laughter.

In fairness to Urán and Henao, by the end of the three weeks they had taken some of my 'advice' on board and we were getting on OK. They also rode pretty well: Henao would end up ninth on general classification and Urán seventh overall and first in the young riders competition.

For me, stage three should have been win number two, but a kamikaze manoeuvre from the Italian Roberto Ferrari put me on the deck 100 metres from the finish line and turned one side of my body into a *smörgåsbord* of road rash. I was fortunate that a rest-day – or at least a travel one – awaited us before the race resumed in northern Italy. Two days later, with the cuts and wounds still weeping and screaming at me like teenage girls at a One Direction concert, I won again at the end of a gruelling stage to Fano on the Adriatic coast. It was the 11th Giro stage victory of my career and by far the most important. The reason? Peta was waiting with Delilah at the finish and to see me win for the first time.

When I won another stage, in Cervere in the second week, I promptly abandoned my plan to leave the race that day. With only a week of the race to go I was leading the points competition, snug in the red jersey that was equivalent to the Tour's *maillot vert*: there was no question of me pulling out as long as I still had a chance of winning that competition. Sadly, it wasn't to be, as I lost out by a single point to the Spanish climber, Joaquim Rodríguez. Who knows, had I worn one of Team Sky's own, high-tech skin-suits instead of the red all-in-one provided by the organisers, I might have been able to sneak inside the top 15 to gain the single point I needed to draw level with Rodríguez. With him leading the race on general classification and hence wearing the more prestigious *maglia rosa*, the red was passed to the rider in second place in the points competition, i.e. me. I tempered my bitterness, I should add, by conceding that Rodríguez was perhaps the more deserving winner, having cruelly lost out to Ryder Hesjedal for overall glory in those last 28 kilometres against the clock.

With the Giro over, all roads now led to the Tour de France. While Brad was underlining his credentials as a possible first British winner of the event by successfully defending his Dauphiné title, my last competitive outing before the Grand Départ would be at the ZLM Toer. This was a four-day stage race based in Holland that also took in some of the famous climbs of the Belgian Ardennes. It was a race usually dominated by sprinters, and this one lived up to that reputation, only perhaps not in the way that I or anyone else expected. I was beaten three times in bunch sprints, twice by the young German Marcel Kittel, and once by André Greipel, but despite this I pulled off a huge upset by winning the general classification. It was my first overall title in a professional stage race and one of the most remarkable results of my career.

The decisive stage took place on the third day, with the race going over one of the steepest and most notorious climbs in professional cycling: La Redoute in the Belgian Ardennes. At one point, surprised at how comfortably I was spinning my gear, I had looked around to see an array of grimacing climbers, all appalled that I was making it look so easy. I had then even *attacked* at the top of the climb to bridge a 50-metre gap to the lead group. Bernie wasn't particularly impressed, saying later that I shouldn't have been wasting so much energy so close to the Tour, but I was delighted.

At one point on the stage I had urged Juan Antonio Flecha to attack and thereby, in all likelihood, take the overall victory that his efforts deserved. He had declined the invitation in favour of protecting me, and in doing so I felt he'd more than earned his place in Team Sky's starting line-up for the Tour de France. This, with hindsight, was where the fault-line with Team Sky began – the crack that soon became an unbridgeable crevice in my relationship with the team.

The week after the ZLM Toer, I discovered that only Bernie, and not Flecha, had made the cut. This took me by surprise as I had presumed that at least two riders would be dedicated to me and my green jersey charge. The message that it clearly sent was that the team had now decided to play it safe. I understood and would never have disputed that yellow should be our priority, but I'd been under the impression that 'believing in better' as per the BSkyB motto, was going to be about big ambitions, pursuing nearly impossible dreams, defying history and conventional wisdom. I felt sad and disappointed that we were already accepting compromises even before arriving in Liège for the Grand Départ.

I got the feeling that it was going to be a very long three weeks. How long, though, and how different my professional future was going to look in Paris, I could never have envisaged.

The difference between riding a Tour de France in a team whose primary motivation is the yellow jersey and one with more diverse aims, like HTC's had been, was summed up neatly on the first morning in Liège. At least, that was how I came to look back on an apparently trivial incident at breakfast in the team hotel.

I'm the first to admit – and have done already in this book – that I have fastidious, you might even say anal, tendencies. I also take my coffee very seriously, like a lot of cyclists do. So I was pleased, then, when I came down to breakfast on that morning in Liège to see a Nespresso automatic coffee maker. I was less amused, however, when I opened up the flap under which you insert your coffee capsule to find one that had already been used by whichever of my teammates had served himself before me.

An, ahem, short speech followed, after which I was sure the same thing wouldn't happen again. Except it did, both the next day and again the day after that, until my morning diatribes were a feature of daily life – at least for the time that we were in Liège. Instead of the desired effect, though, all my speeches were producing was hilarity – so much so that the team produced a warning poster on my behalf and stuck it above the machine.

That was probably the most the team laughed in the entire three weeks – which in itself was telling – but the story of the coffee capsules became a kind of parable for me. For all that I loved Brad, Chris Froome, Richie Porte and the other guys, they were totally wrapped up in their own world – or their own coffee capsules, as it were. They had approached the business of making coffee the same way that they dealt with riding their bikes – with tunnel vision. The staff at Team Sky, I had noticed and would see even more clearly at the Tour, were there to execute their designated task and think of nothing else. It was efficient, it was professional, it put other teams to shame – but it also wasn't a lot of fun.

With every passing hour in the days leading up to the Grand Départ, it became more and more obvious to me that, in the management's eyes, going for green as well as yellow was simply too risky. When we talked about how I should approach the intermediate sprints, which my victory in the competition in

2011 had shown to be vital, I gathered that the team didn't feel it would always be able to justify the efforts needed to get me into a point-scoring position. Out of sympathy or solidarity, Bernie said privately that he would try to give me a hand

Our head *directeur* at the Tour was Sean Yates. One of only four British riders up to that point to have worn the yellow jersey at the Tour, Sean was revered as a legend of the sport in the UK. A superb time-triallist and *domestique* to Lance Armstrong, among other stars, in the 1980s and 1990s, Sean had known and been respected by Brad for years. Before the Tour I had done only one race with Sean, the Tour of Romandy, and quickly got the sense that he didn't particularly rate or admire me. I assumed that it wasn't personal and that he was one of those former bike riders with preconceptions about sprinters, namely that they were lazy and prima donnas. Sean's man management also just didn't suit me: I found him cold, uninspiring and miserly in praise. At Romandy I had buried myself for Brad yet couldn't remember getting even a 'well done' from Sean.

I didn't count on getting much support from Sean at the Tour, but even these low expectations were dashed. In our briefing on the bus before stage two to Tournai, I waited for him to talk about our plan for what was surely going to be a sprint ... and waited. Sean didn't even mention it; instead his instructions for the last 50 kilometres were all to do with Brad. Again, I think one or two teammates felt sorry for me; Edvald Boasson Hagen had a job to do for Brad, but he very kindly asked me whether he could somehow help. Eddy and Bernie did what they could, but two men were never going to be enough to set me up for the sprint, especially when Michael Rogers, Brad's in-race 'bodyguard', tried to budge me off Bernie's wheel. I ended up improvising, hopping from one opponent's wheel to the next in the final two kilometres – 'surfing', as we call it in track racing. Finally, I came out of André Greipel's shadow to take an improbable stage win, and one unlike any of my others in previous Tours. On the bus after the finish I wasn't particularly jubilant or even vocal in thanking my teammates; frankly, it would have embarrassed them, because only Bernie and Edvald had helped me.

In Tournai I'd somehow muddled through, winged it to win, but I knew that wouldn't work every day. With no team to surround, protect, escort him, a sprinter is left sailing in troubled waters, in the danger zone behind the arrow-head of the peloton, where the big sprinters and their flotillas cruise towards the finish line relatively unimpeded. This is where the real risks are being taken, where guys have to gamble, and consequently where the majority of crashes happen. In Rouen on stage four this was where I was, and the pile-up that duly ensued was a beauty. I wasn't too badly hurt, fortunately, but it was abundantly clear to me not only that it could have been much worse but that it had happened because I'd been left with only Bernie to pilot and look after me. On the bus that afternoon the most shell-shocked of us all was Brad: 12 months earlier he'd seen months of hard graft jeopardised by one innocuous crash in the first week of the Tour, and the pile-up in Rouen had clearly brought back a nasty memory.

By this point, five days into the race, team staff and other riders were beginning to notice and remark on how quiet I was. In Rouen the management asked me why it was, and I responded that there wasn't a lot for me to say about how we raced, since I wasn't the leader. This was slightly disingenuous, because I did have *very* strong views not only on how I was being left exposed, but also how tentative the other guys were in the closing kilometres of stages. Urged to speak up at our briefing the next day, I said that it was in everyone's interest to at least *commit* more, perhaps even just riding a couple of hundred metres on the front each: that would keep them out of trouble while also doing me a favour. Tim Kerrison, the team coach, also thought that one big effort like this at the end of stages would ultimately help our general classification riders to maintain and sharpen their form. Everyone agreed to give it a go, and the improvement was huge that day into Saint-Quentin. We still didn't have quite enough firepower to put me in a winning position, but the team had looked far more decisive and far less vulnerable. The contrast between Brad's mood that afternoon and his reaction the previous day was stark: 'That's how we fucking do it!' he roared as he climbed onto the bus.

My optimism that night, unfortunately, didn't even last 24 hours. On stage six, another sprinter-friendly one to Metz, a huge crash 26 kilometres from the finish left dozens of riders injured and even more delayed behind the pile-up ruled out of contention for the win. I had made it around the wreckage but to do so had skidded on my rear wheel, causing the tyre to explode. I immediately reached for my radio and announced that I'd punctured. I heard nothing so I repeated what I'd just said, all the time trying to cling on to the back of the lead group while riding on a flat. For a few hundred metres I was hanging in there, until the road began to descend and I could no longer stand the pace with no air in my tyre.

Finally, having remained silent in the radio the whole time, Sean Yates arrived in our first team car, waited while the mechanic swapped my wheel, then drove immediately off without even giving me a push, as is standard practice for the *directeur sportif* after a mechanical. Bernie had heard a muffled message in his ear a minute or two after my puncture, asked Sean to repeat it, but heard nothing back. Understandably, he had carried on, and I was left to claw my way back to the bunch alone. It's normal – officially illegal but roundly tolerated – for riders to draft in their team cars' slipstream after a mechanical, but Yates hadn't stuck around to allow me this luxury. Needless to say, I finished in a group of stragglers, some six minutes behind the stage winner, Peter Sagan, and I was not in good spirits when I arrived back at the bus. I had never been left stranded like that after a mechanical, not even as a 22-year-old neo-pro in a tiny one-day race in France. Here we were at the Tour de France, on a stage that I was the favourite to win, and I was the world champion. I was heartbroken.

My manager, Simon Bayliff, had been following the Tour in his camping car, and came to see me after the finish that afternoon. I sat on the steps of the bus, out of earshot of my teammates and *directeurs* a few metres above me, and told Simon what had happened.

'Sean fucking ignored me,' I said. 'He just left me. It was horrible.'

It was 6 July. This was the date when I realised this could be my first and last Tour de France with Team Sky. It was also the date of my last conversation with Sean Yates.

While I'd continue to do my best, offering Brad as much assistance as I could both on and off the bike, from Metz onward it was sometimes hard to reconcile my own frustration with the team's rampant success. First Chris Froome won the first big mountain stage in the Vosges, with Brad taking the yellow jersey on the same day. Then that pair finished first and second in the next big general classification showdown – a time trial in Besançon.

After the first big Alpine stage to La Toussuire, the media would forget the murmurs about my dissatisfaction, forget even that a Briton had a realistic chance of winning the biggest race on earth for the first time, and shift their attention instead to a perceived rift between Brad and Chris. Chris had been selected for the Tour as Brad's *domestique de luxe* in the mountains, yet had briefly accelerated away from his leader on the climb to

La Toussuire, embarrassing and briefly isolating Brad, and also sparking debate about who should be leading Team Sky.

My own view from inside the team was that Chris had acted in good faith, just a little clumsily. If he'd wanted to betray Brad, he would have attacked on the penultimate climb that day, not the final one, and he wouldn't have waited when he got the order to stop his effort over the radio. It was easy to see it as evidence of Chris's naivety, which could make you either laugh or wince at times, both on and off the bike. It may also, however, have been that Chris, like me, felt that we had gone from having the opportunity to aim for the moon *and* the stars to a risk-averse strategy with just one aim: securing the yellow jersey for Brad. To my way of thinking, we could have been leaving Paris ten days later with yellow, green and nine of the cuddly lions given to the stage winner every day.

Brad didn't say a lot that night, but it was obvious that he was upset or angry. Usually, when he was the next in line after me for a massage, he'd swagger into the room cracking jokes or taking the piss. That evening he sat on the adjacent bed waiting for me to finish without saying a word. I could see that he probably wasn't in the mood for talking, but as I got up to go I told him that I just had one thing to say – that in my opinion Chris hadn't meant any harm and that, if he had, he wouldn't have waited on the climb. I'm still not certain what was weighing more heavily on Brad's mind – the idea that Chris was out to flick him or the fact that Brad had shown a chink in his armour for the first time since the start of the season.

There was no doubt that the story of a 'civil war' was being blown out of proportion in the press, and Chris continued to do a sterling job on the road. I helped the team where I could in the Alps, hopeful that stage 15 to Pau, at least, would give me another shot at a stage win. Although classed as a 'flat stage', the course that day was anything but, with incessant short climbs and the race taking two hours to settle into the usual format of a break gaining time then slowly being reeled in. I had fire in my legs, so when Greipel's Lotto teammates asked Bernie whether we would help them to bring it back together for a sprint, and Bernie asked me over the radio whether I was up for it, I didn't hesitate.

'Do I want a sprint? Fucking right I want a sprint.'

And so Bernie and Lotto rode. The guys in the breakaway were quality riders and specialists in this kind of exercise, so it was tough going, but we began to eat inexorably into the gap. Or we did for a while. It was a hot day, Mick Rogers was on bottle-duty, and with around 50 kilometres to go he went back to the team car to fetch drinks. A few minutes later, when Mick reappeared close to us, we heard Sean's voice in the radio: 'Guys, stop riding. We're not going for a sprint. We'll just control it today.'

It didn't take a genius to work out what had happened: Mick was knackered and, even in the last stage before a rest-day, wasn't required to exert himself for the sake of me possibly winning a second stage. Once again I was disgusted, and once again I reacted by remaining silent and doing what was required of me to help Brad for the remainder of the stage.

There had been hints in the press throughout the Tour – and they would continue in the final week – that I was unhappy about not being the centre of attention in the team. In fact, the opposite was true – that was one of the few things that I was enjoying. In Pau on that second rest-day the whole team was herded onto a sun-blasted hotel terrace for a press conference attended by hundreds of journalists and dozens of TV crews, but nearly all of the questions were for or about Brad and Chris. When the end of the conference degenerated into the usual free-for-all, Brad and Chris struggled to extricate themselves, while I slipped back to my room almost unnoticed.

By now, my manager Simon and I were clear in our minds that I could never race another Tour like this one. This would clearly hold implications for Team Sky, but, for the moment, they had much more pressing matters to deal with. Brad and Chris continued to dominate in the Pyrenees, with Chris flexing his muscles and pulling away from Brad again on the climb to Peyragudes. Brad manifestly wasn't impressed, but reacted in much the same way as I did to my frustrations: he kept his emotions to himself. He was closing in on Tour victory, the dream for any cyclist. That, surely, was the most important thing.

I perhaps didn't always show it, but in those last few days I felt immense pride at what we were in the process of achieving, even if we could have been doing much more. Two days from the end, in Brive-la-Gaillarde, I listened, open-mouthed, as Sean outlined his plan for the day in our pre-stage briefing on the bus: we'd let the break go and have a quiet day. Fortunately, the other *directeur*, Servais Knaven, queried this, then Brad also chipped in that, in his opinion, we should ride for a sprint. Dave Brailsford had the final say.

'Cav's been fantastic for Brad, he's been patient, and he deserves a chance today,' Dave said.

Six hours later, after a superbly committed performance from the whole team, Brad even led me and the peloton into the final kilometre, with a break still a few seconds ahead of us. It was going to take a very long sprint and a remarkable comeback to catch them, but my form was now superb and there were riders all over the road, whose wheels I could 'surf'. It turned out to be one of the most spectacular and emphatic stage wins of my Tour career.

After a penultimate-day time trial won by Brad, sealing his overall victory, it was on to the formality of a final-day stage win for me, given that I'd never lost on the Champs Elysées. For a few hours I was able to put the disappointments and regrets of the previous three weeks and concerns about my future to one side and revel in the moment. Brad, in the yellow jersey, led me down the Rue de Rivoli, under the kilometre kite: Edvald came next, then I bolted as we swung out of the Place de la Concorde and was never seriously challenged.

Throughout the stage I had beamed with pride at the guys' dedication right to the end. It's common for most of the riders at the Tour to, if not completely let their hair down, at least treat themselves to, say, a beer and a pizza on the penultimate evening, but Brad, in particular, had insisted on us remaining fully focused. He had done it for me, not himself, and the guys responded with a performance that compelled me to thank them all individually in e-mails the following week.

All wasn't quite well that ended well, at least not as far as I was concerned, but I was delighted for Brad and thrilled to have contributed to such a historic moment for British cycling. It had been a very long journey, one that like Project Rainbow Jersey had started years earlier, with a vision that through hard work had been moulded into a plan. This had then come to fruition only thanks to some hugely talented and dedicated individuals. Everyone at Team Sky deserved immense credit for that.

At the same time, I knew that I deserved better. Prioritising yellow over green was of course logical, of course the right thing to do. Ignoring the points competition and near enough ignoring me altogether, though, was not something I could accept.

chapter nine

Throughout the 2012 Tour de France, two things had kept me going amid all of the angst: my family and the Olympics. Whenever I felt snubbed, wounded or sorry for myself, an image of Peta, Delilah and Finn would blink into my thoughts and suddenly I had some perspective. Every time that I had to hold back on the bike, every day that I felt I was wasting some of the best form of my life, I only needed to tell myself that it would all be worth it when I stood on top of a podium with an Olympic gold medal around my neck and 'God Save the Queen' ringing out over the Mall.

The Olympic road race in London had been an integral part of Project Rainbow Jersey: the last and probably hardest of its aims to achieve. In Copenhagen we had controlled, dominated and monopolised the race with eight riders, but in London we'd only have five to attempt the same job. Not only that, but Copenhagen had fired a warning shot that no one would forget; if the other countries had previously thought that it was impossible for a single team to dictate terms as we had in Denmark, they knew now that it was not, at least not for us. They would come to London knowing our winning formula and determined this time round to put a fly in the ointment. Moreover, although the course had been relocated and tweaked to potentially lend itself to a sprint finish, a 250-kilometre route that included nine climbs of Surrey's Box Hill was an intimidating challenge.

As had been the case in Copenhagen, we at least knew that no one would be better prepared than the British team. Rod and I had made several trips to Box Hill, in addition to the Olympic test event on a watered-down version of the same course that I'd won in 2011. By professional road race standards Box Hill wasn't difficult when taken in isolation: it was 2.5 kilometres long with an average gradient of just 4.9 per cent. The repetition of the nine laps, however, followed by what would no doubt be a breakneck 25-kilometre run-in to the finish on the Mall, would demand one of my best ever rides in a one-day race to take gold.

On seeing and riding the course for the first time, we had known that unless I was climbing as well as I'd ever done, then victory would be out of the question. Ending only a week before the Olympic road race, the Tour would take care of my form, but I needed even more than just good legs. I needed a specific regime starting months earlier, one designed to get my weight down and raise my capacity for suffering on repeat ascents of a climb like Box Hill. That was why Rod and Sky's head of performance science, a 40-year-old former swimming coach from Queensland called Tim

Kerrison, had put their heads together at the start of the year to come up with a plan.

Given the precedents, most people would have expected Tim Kerrison and me to go together like oil and water. Tim had only been in the sport since 2010, but in his two and a half years with Team Sky had forged a reputation as one of the brightest brains in cycling. He was a scientist, an academic, a physiologist – and this was what theoretically put us on a collision course. During my time at the Academy, one of the coaches, Simon Jones, had driven me round the bend with his sniffy insistence that I 'wasn't hitting the numbers' and would therefore never make it as a pro rider. I had proved him wrong and established myself in possibly the strongest team in the sport, T-Mobile, where I'd immediately locked horns with another physiologist, Sebastian Weber, who had similar ideas about my aptitude for elite cycling. After my first tests in my first winter, Weber had also suggested that I was out of my depth. We continued to clash until I started winning races and a mutual understanding set in: I had a hunger and a race-craft in a competitive context that made me unrecognisable from the bastard sibling who flapped and floundered aboard a stationary bike in an exercise lab; Sebastian was a great coach – just one who didn't really speak my language in cycling terms.

Tim Kerrison was, in the nicest possible way, even more of an egghead than Simon and Sebastian. A meeting of minds seem fairly improbable, but right from our first conversations I was pleasantly surprised. Not only could I see that Tim was both incredibly knowledgeable and innovative, he did something that no physiologist that I'd come across had ever managed before: he bridged the divide between the theoretical and the practical, taking numbers out of their abstract context and applying them to what was really happening on the bike and on the road. It's become fashionable among amateur and professional cyclists over the past few years to obsess over power output – the number of watts generated by each pedal stroke – which can now quite easily be measured and displayed on a handlebar-mounted device. For some, monitoring and comparing these figures is a sport unto itself, but Tim could relate the numbers directly to what really mattered – who crossed the line first.

Instead of saying to me, 'Cav, you're at 430 watts, that's much better than last week,' or, 'Cav, 410 isn't enough,' Tim laid out in detail exactly what would be required to win the Olympic road race, and therefore what was required in training.

'This is how much you'll weigh on the day of the Olympic road race,' Tim explained, 'and this is the number of watts that you'll have to produce over this many minutes on Box Hill to win.'

The words that resonated with me were the last two: to win. Rather than just dismiss me as a physiological ugly duckling, Tim was intelligent enough to frame the science within something that, he knew, was impossible to quantify: my ability to suffer. Even in his work in rowing and swimming before he joined Team Sky, Tim said, he'd rarely seen an athlete who could squeeze as much out of his or her innate capabilities. He said that it astounded him that I could even finish the Tour de France.

I'm not the greatest trainer, not when it's training for training's sake. Whereas other riders can pick out a circuit and do lap after lap, or work through prescribed, specific exercises focusing only on their heart rate or power output, I need different and much more varied stimuli. If I have to train alone, I'll never take the same road twice on the same ride, even if it means exploring new terrain and potentially getting lost. The idea, then, of simulating the Olympic road race course and the laps of Box Hill by finding an equivalent climb and repeating it seven, eight, nine times would normally have horrified me. Tim, though, made it bearable by planting a vision, a conviction in my mind: I wasn't training to improve, I wasn't training to hit a number, I was training to win the Olympic road race. Thus, a Tuscan climb known locally as La Riola became a slice of Surrey transplanted to Italy for an intensive block of training after the Giro in June. With Rod pacing me, baiting me, torturing me on the moped, the sessions were brutal. They exhausted but also, somehow, invigorated me. I could feel myself improving by the day, by the hour, or even with every repetition of the climb. Weight, of course, was a vital part of the equation, and I was helped hugely in this regard by the British Cycling and Team Sky nutritionist, Nigel Mitchell, who was sent to live with and cook for me in key training phases in both Italy and the UK.

The Olympics, then, had been at the forefront of my mind throughout the year and throughout the Tour. They became my sole preoccupation from the moment I crossed the line in

Paris as a stage winner and a member of the first team to guide a British rider to victory in the Tour de France.

That evening we attended a short reception hosted by our sponsors before being whisked off to the airport and a plane that would take us directly back to London. Our 'holding camp' was at Foxhills hotel and golf course in Surrey, where we spent five days resting, and recovering with a couple of fairly intensive training sessions on Box Hill on the Wednesday and Thursday. Brad had gone home for a couple of days, which left the other four members of the team – me, Dave Millar, Chris Froome and Ian Stannard – to enjoy some downtime with our families. When Brad joined us on the Wednesday he was relaxed, funny and an altogether different beast from the tense, introverted, hyper-focused rider that we'd seen at the Tour. He and Chris seemed to be getting on fine and the atmosphere was, on the whole, a lot more jovial than it had been in France. I was much happier, too, having been able to spend some time with my family, and also having opened up to Dave Brailsford about my intention to leave Team Sky. In fairness to Dave, he understood and the conversation was amicable.

The night before the road race, Brad left us for a couple of hours to go into the Olympic Village and officially open the Games, no less. When he arrived back at the hotel, we all sat down for our final meeting to go over what were, in truth, fairly simple tactics. As we had in Copenhagen, we would ride together throughout and look to bring the race back together, ready for a bunch sprint, in the final 20 kilometres.

All week I had had that special feeling – a magic in my legs and an unswerving belief that gold was my destiny. On the morning of the race, right up until the starter's flag going down, the five of us joked and laughed in a way that suggested we all shared the same confidence. We were all kitted out with aero helmets, high-tech skin suits and were quite an intimidating unit – at least when we started riding. The guys were absolutely flying. At one point, after around 50 kilometres, the Italian rider Luca Paolini rode off the front of the bunch and up to a TV motorbike to berate the pilot for riding too close and sucking us along. The motorbike had actually been nowhere near us. We were just going that fast.

One of my teammates would lead into Box Hill on every lap and I'd be safely tucked in behind, just floating up the slope. The road was so narrow that we could almost block it to prevent attacks, although one large group had already broken away early in the stage and there would be sporadic counter-attacks throughout.

As we came to the bottom of Box Hill for the last time, though, we were still very satisfied with how the race was panning out. One more ascent, another 2.5 kilometres of climbing, then we'd be over the top and, if not quite home and dry, then certainly very difficult to escape on the fast, mainly downhill roads into London.

We expected a flurry of last-ditch efforts from riders who would have no chance in a sprint, and they duly came. Fabian Cancellara's acceleration, in particular, set my alarm bells ringing, but I resisted the urge coming from my legs that seemed to want nothing more than to jump across to Cancellara's wheel. The night before, we'd accurately predicted and discussed precisely this scenario – a blizzard of attacks on the last lap of Box Hill – and finally agreed with Dave Millar that we were strongest as a unit and should stick to our own pace. As we crested Box Hill, I shouted to Brad to go faster, to suffocate a large group now opening clear airspace between themselves and us at the front of the peloton, but Brad couldn't hear me over the din of the crowd. It was in these moments that our race unravelled: the guys had already butchered themselves to get me here and the tiredness now started to tell, especially as teams that had been expected to help us were showing no interest in collaborating. The Aussies had Stuart O'Grady down the road in what was in danger of being the winning break, but where were the Germans? With 15 kilometres to go and our chances still alive but hanging by a thread, one German rider, John Degenkolb, moved onto my shoulder to find out what I knew about the time gap, since race radios weren't allowed at the Olympics and information was scarce.

'So is it still a minute, eh? Fuck, it's gonna be tough ...'

'Yeah,' I said, 'it is, so you guys had better start riding.'

Degenkolb replied that he couldn't: he was André Greipel's lead-out man, and if he worked now he'd have nothing left for the last kilometre.

'Lead-out man?' I said. 'There's not even going to be a sprint if you don't hurry up and start helping, so I don't know why you're worried about that.'

Degenkolb either didn't listen, didn't care, or his hands were tied. Germany didn't work, we were on our last legs and, sure enough, the break stayed away. Alexandre Vinokourov took gold, my Sky teammate Rigoberto Urán silver, and the Norwegian Alexander Kristoff bronze. Having punctured two kilometres from the finish, I was third rider from a large second group to cross the line, in 29th position, 40 seconds adrift of Vinokourov.

I'd be lying if I said the reaction to my second 'failure' at an Olympics didn't irk me, and it started to get under my skin as soon as I made my way through the mixed zone to do my first post-race interviews. The BBC's Sports Editor, David Bond, asked whether I'd paid for and was still weary after my exertions at the Tour de France.

'Don't ask stupid questions,' I snapped, without hanging around to give him an answer.

The press coverage the next morning reflected the same lack of understanding. The *Sun*'s headline was FROM BRAD TO WORST. It was clearly too much to expect the press to understand the irony of hailing Brad and denigrating me: it could be argued, could it not, that Brad hadn't fulfilled his brief if the bunch hadn't come back together for a sprint, whereas I hadn't even been given the opportunity to do my job. I would never have made this argument, because the guys had been fantastic, but it was no more ridiculous than any attempt to pin the blame on me.

While cycling in Britain has grown rapidly and my public profile has followed the same curve, the casual viewer still had a fairly loose grasp on the intricacies of the sport and didn't understand how a rider could be the favourite for a race, perform admirably, yet still 'only' finish 29th. In 2008 I'd started to earn some recognition in the UK for my four Tour de France stage wins but was equally well known as the single British cyclist who hadn't come home from the Beijing Olympics with a medal. I'd even had to borrow the track sprinter Jason Kenny's silver medal and pretend that it was mine to get an upgrade to first class on my flight back! In the autumn of that year, when I'd told Bernie Eisel that I wasn't among the ten nominees for the BBC Sports Personality of the Year, Bernie had thought it was some kind of joke – either mine or on the part of whoever had drawn up the shortlist.

Four years on, I was doomed, once again, to be the 'forgotten man'. Well, perhaps not completely 'forgotten', given that I was due to make my debut as an in-studio pundit for the BBC in the velodrome, and most TV viewers would probably be sick of the sight and sound of me within a few days. Even so, I was still somehow the runt of the British cycling litter. In the BBC studio, I would happily play along with and even encourage any reference to my Olympic jinx, but certain comments and questions, like the one from the BBC guy after the road race, still made me shudder.

My own disappointment didn't stop me revelling in the so-called British 'gold rush' on the track, or in my new gig as the BBC's track-cycling oracle. I'd done similar things before, but in previous TV appearances found that the presenter's ego sometimes got in the way of whatever insight you were trying to deliver. Fortunately, this wasn't the case with Jake Humphrey, and I thoroughly enjoyed myself. The hardest part was purging my speech of all swear-words.

After Brad's Tour win and then yet more success, it was wonderful to see Britain suddenly gripped by cycling fever, as much as I thought there were some riders who had sacrificed too much to be competing in London. I was fairly blunt about Geraint Thomas and what I perceived as his misplaced priorities in *Boy Racer.* Typically, though, Gee didn't hold it against me: one, because he's not the kind to bear grudges; and two, because he already knew exactly where I was coming from. I felt the same as I had done after Beijing and Gee reacted similarly when we spoke at the Tour of Denmark a month after the London Olympics. I was aware that it sounded disrespectful and like sour grapes, but I firmly believed what I was saying: the gold medal that Geraint had won in London in the team pursuit, to go with the one he already had from Beijing, would change nothing for him.

'What, so I should have just concentrated on helping you win the road race? Is that it?' he replied.

I explained that, no, what I meant was that he had sacrificed too much for the track, and got what out of it? Your average Joe in the street didn't even know who was in the team pursuit team. Which was fine – it wasn't that kind of recognition that interested me, either – but Gee had put his road career on hold for *years* for those medals. In the peloton he is rightly considered to be one of *the* most powerful and talented riders around, yet at the time of writing he would acknowledge himself that he has won very little, and certainly not an amount commensurate with his ability. With my business head on, and based on my experience over the previous few years, I could also hazard a guess at how much money it had cost him to prioritise the track over the road. Even having gone down the track route and won that second medal, I thought Gee and some of the other guys, like Pete Kennaugh, or whoever represented them, weren't doing enough to boost their profile. I told Pete that he should be doing *Attitude* magazine cover shoots ... and was only half taking the piss.

Perhaps I had another, more fundamental conviction – you could even call it a prejudice – about the comfort zone that they had found at British Cycling and Team Sky. From their point of view, with their objectives, I could see how Sky was the perfect team. No other team would have allowed them to put their road careers on the back-burner in the same way as Sky, certainly not on their salaries. This brought both advantages and disadvantages for them personally and for cycling in the UK.

While Team Sky might have been the perfect team for someone like Gee, the same wasn't true for me. I was different and so were my feelings about where would be the best place to pursue my career. Having informed Brailsford a few days before the Olympics that I wanted out, I gathered that he was also open to an amicable separation. The negotiations had dragged on but finally reached a satisfactory resolution at the beginning of the autumn.

A year and a week after I was unveiled as Team Sky's new star signing, another announcement was made to confirm that I would ride for Omega Pharma–Quick-Step in 2013.

chapter ten

O n 17 January 2013, in a hotel in Argentina, I found a position on the floor as close as possible to the television set, turned the volume low so as not disturb my sleeping roommate, and watched a man I used to know tell the world that he was the biggest cheat in sport.

My instinctive reaction to Lance Armstrong on Oprah Winfrey? Too many adverts.

Lance and I had met at the Interbike trade show in Las Vegas in September 2008. Introduced by George Hincapie, once Lance's *domestique de luxe* and then mine, we had instantly struck up a rapport. There was something mesmeric about Lance. That's something that people often say about so-called 'celebrities', but not until I spent an hour or two with Lance did I really fully appreciate what it meant. I think it's best summed up by saying that if Lance was in a crowded restaurant or bar, you could somehow sense or feel his presence. There was a buzz, an electricity that seemed to take hold of the room. The energy that he radiated seemed to hang everywhere, yet when Lance spoke the space suddenly emptied to leave just you and him. His eyes were like strobe lights, burning through you. He inserted your name into every sentence, paid attention to everything you did, remembered everything that you said. It was hard, as a 23-year-old who had watched him win seven Tours de France, goggle-eyed, not to be impressed or at least intrigued. My teammates that year, George Hincapie and Michael Barry, would continually tell stories about him – sometimes more appalled than amused, yet Lance clearly fascinated them.

That first encounter in Vegas had coincided, within the space of a few days, with the announcement that Lance was making a comeback to the sport. A couple of nights out in Las Vegas hadn't suddenly made us close friends and we had no contact until a congratulatory text message after my victory in Milan–San Remo in March 2009. For the next couple of months after this George would tell Lance that I'd bought an expensive watch, or a sports car, and I'd get a text from Lance: 'Cav! Don't waste your money on watches! What did I tell you? Save it. Be smart with it.' And so he had told me; in fact, in Vegas he never tired of repeating it. Perhaps I was under his spell, but when it came to giving me advice he appeared both genuine and generous.

For all that he was the same man – brash, charismatic, uncompromising – I think that Lance could see as soon as he came back in 2009 that a lot had changed in the four years since his infamous farewell speech on the Champs Elysées in 2005, in which he told the 'cynics and sceptics' that he was 'sorry they can't believe'. The signs were there at the Tour of California in February 2009, where the Irish journalist, Paul Kimmage, tackled him in the pre-race press conference. Kimmage thought, and had written, that Lance had cheated his way to those seven Tour titles, and likened his comeback to the recurrence of a cancer, and this led to a fairly feisty exchange that, of course, Kimmage's colleagues in the media lapped up.

Like everyone else, I was well aware of the doping rumours that had swirled around Lance and his career, but never dwelled on them too much: firstly because I hadn't been competing against him between 1999 and 2005; and, secondly, I had gathered from riders who had competed in that era that doping had been widespread if not endemic. Rolf Aldag, my *directeur sportif* at T-Mobile and later HTC, had made this very clear in a presentation to the team at the beginning of my 2007 debut season: in his era, Rolf said, the sport had been so poorly policed that it had degenerated into anarchy, which in turn had made drug use a near necessity for most. That, at least, was how they saw it. Rolf was telling us this, he said, because he wanted us to understand that cycling had changed beyond recognition and that excuse – 'everyone did it' – no longer washed. You could compete and win races completely clean. Having heard murmurs about the grim reality of professional cycling and for years been told by fellow junior and amateur riders that doping was *de rigueur*, Rolf's words came as a massive relief. They were also confirmation of what I'd already seen in the handful of races that I'd done as a T-Mobile *stagiaire* (triallist) at the end of 2006: I could hold my own with nothing more in my medicine cabinet than a normal multi-vitamin.

So, no, I wasn't completely naïve about Lance, but neither was all the speculation going to prejudice my relationship with him. The same went for Kimmage after that press conference in California in February 2009: when he requested an interview a few months later for his newspaper, the *Sunday Times*, I happily obliged and went in with a completely open mind. Just because a friend or acquaintance doesn't get on with someone, I'm not going to allow that to colour my judgement before meeting the person. That's just not my style.

For Lance, though, I can imagine the face-off with Kimmage was an early hint that he wouldn't inspire the same kind of deference the second time around. I saw him again at Milan–San Remo in March, then again at the Giro in May. We talked a fair bit at the Giro, but one thing really struck me: if he had been a *capo* or *patron* once – the unelected but also uncontested spokesman and overlord of the peloton, who ruled by intimidation – he wasn't that guy any more. You can usually spot a *capo* – when they take a toilet break, the peloton slows immediately until they've attended to nature's call and slotted back into the pack. One day at the 2009 Giro I was shocked, then, to see Lance pull over to the side of the road and the peloton swish by without batting an eyelid. I caught a glimpse of Lance's face as he realised, and his expression was one of fury and indignation, perhaps tinged with sadness. You could almost see the penny dropping – I was *that guy*, but they don't think that I'm *that guy* any more.

At the Tour that year Lance was extremely strong – too strong according to the United States Anti-Doping Agency (USADA) and the 202-page report in which they laid out their evidence against Armstrong just over a year later. Lance swore to Oprah Winfrey that he didn't dope for his comeback, but an expert quoted in the USADA report stated that the likelihood of certain anomalies in blood samples taken from Lance during the 2009 and 2010 Tours was 'less than one in a million'.

In 2009 and even on the eve of the 2010 Tour, when the *Wall Street Journal* published allegations aimed at Lance by his old teammate Floyd Landis, I'd paid very little attention to the low, slow drum-roll of controversy. Now, though, the idea that Lance had doped to ride that 2009 Tour in which I'd won six stages switched something in me. If the suffering that we sometimes endure in races is hard to convey to the ordinary punter, it's even more difficult to describe the bitterness of knowing the pain was made even worse by other riders cheating. I had felt the same anger after the 2008 Giro and Tour, where certain riders were lit up like fireworks, but were caught much too late for it to make any difference to those of us whom they had tortured on the road.

Even ignoring the immorality of it, the betrayal of the sport and the fans, it was very easy to condemn doping when you were its direct victim; the outrage came less spontaneously, less naturally when the crimes were committed years ago, when you'd been told, like I had, that back then that was the norm. It was also harder to demonise someone, like Lance, who had always treated you well and given you the impression that they liked and valued you. Having reason to believe that person had tried to cheat you out of a race and part of your livelihood – plus inflicted dire agony on you for five, six hours over giant Pyrenean or Alpine passes – immediately changed things. I can only imagine how someone like my old HTC teammate, Marco Pinotti, must have felt about Lance and the large number of other riders who had been doping in, for instance, the 1999 Tour. Or, for that matter, how Marco, who I know has always ridden clean, had even managed to finish that Tour in his first year as a pro.

As the allegations rumbled to a crescendo through and beyond Lance's comeback, up to the moment when he was forced to confess, being repeatedly asked to give my opinion on the matter became somewhat tiresome. Some won't believe me or will accuse me of being short-sighted or self-absorbed when I say that I, like the majority of clean pros now, simply don't feel that what happened 15 years ago bears any relevance to us. Or rather it does, but only really on two levels: on one hand we've all benefited from the slow, no doubt belated recognition of the problem and from the resulting, huge improvements in anti-doping; on the other hand, we're also now held accountable for an era and a poisonous culture that is alien to what we know. We're asked to comment on Armstrong and have our morals judged on the strength of what we say, when a lot of us are, rightly or wrongly, too preoccupied with the here and now to have an opinion.

Even though I was watching those Tours that Lance won, wide-eyed and innocent, I also can't pretend that I'm eaten up with resentment or feel betrayed now that I know that it was all a big charade. As unjust, as distressing as it may be, as hard as it is for us to accept, I'm sure that Lance still feels that no one and nothing can take away the emotions of those seven Tours *at the time,* and the same really goes for those of us who were watching. Whether Lance could ever have savoured the pure, unmitigated joy that comes with winning clean is another issue. That, together with the money and the dignity that he's lost, I'm pretty sure, have been the most effective punishments.

When the USADA report came out, I was at least *ready* to be angry with Lance, and so deliberately didn't contact him after its release. I also gave one or two interviews to the press from which he'll have gathered, I'm pretty sure, that I took a dim view of at least some of what he was alleged to have done. As of the time of writing, we haven't spoken for approximately a year.

If there's one aspect of the Armstrong saga that continues to baffle and anger me, in addition to those claims about the 2009 and 2010 Tours, it's the lack of consistency both in our sport, cycling, and across *all* sports.

Objectively, even Lance's biggest detractors will have to admit that the race to expose him at times resembled a witch-hunt. When you tot up all of the hours and all of the millions spent on exposing Lance and you set that against the total indifference to other riders and their doping, you can't ignore the double standards. I know that people say and will continue to argue that Lance was the key link in the chain, perhaps the only single rider who could not only influence but dictate the culture of the sport, and I'd agree in so far as he was bigger than professional cycling for many years. The role of *capo* wasn't one that he fulfilled only in races, but also in the broader realm of the sport. He *could* have led the revolution against doping – but equally, without doping, would he have been winning those Tours and would he have wielded the same power? I doubt it. The argument, then, that he deserved to be targeted so singularly, the sacrificial lamb on the altar of clean sport, doesn't quite hold water.

I will certainly never be persuaded that riders who confessed their own doping and gave evidence against Lance in return for meagre, six-month bans – in a lot of cases served in the off-season – were truly brought to justice. Among the riders who were offered and took these plea bargains, or 'sweetheart deals' as Lance called them, were good friends of mine like George Hincapie and Christian Vande Velde, but my relationship with those guys doesn't alter my opinion: they were as culpable as Lance.

The problem, of course, is and will remain getting people to open up about their past when there's no incentive. After the USADA verdict and amid the hysteria that it created, there was talk of a 'Truth and Reconciliation' commission which would enable riders to come forward, confess doping offences committed within a certain timeframe and be granted clemency in return for the information that they provided. I'm not familiar with the finer details, and it sounds like a nice idea … but it's not going to work. Why? One word: ego. Even now, when they've retired and there's no threat of sanctions or public humiliation, riders cling to their careers because that's what their identity has been constructed on, what they've dedicated their lives to, the reason they're admired. They're terrified of losing it all. It's also very difficult to convince people that the stigma of having cheated can be cleansed, or will magically disappear, as soon as everything is out in the open.

So what do we do with the skeletons in cycling's closet? Mine might not be a popular view, but sometimes I wonder why we insist on rattling them around and whether the time hasn't come to simply concentrate on the present. To me, it's gone far beyond the point where the soul-searching has become useful to the sport, and in fact it's counter-productive. What more are we going to learn about the period before I turned professional and the so-called 'EPO Generation' that we don't already know, haven't already heard about *ad nauseam*, and how will that help us now?

I think journalists get frustrated when riders of my age and peer group are hesitant to talk about doping – they assume this is us upholding the same law of silence, the *omertà*, that prevailed for so many years. I can't speak for other riders, but I imagine that a lot are like me: it's not that we're *nervous* about expressing our opinion, or have something to hide, it's that many of us feel that we don't know what we're talking about and therefore don't feel qualified to pontificate.

In 2008, my second year as a professional, the UCI introduced a much-trumpeted new weapon against doping: the biological passport. I still don't know and don't care how it works; I give my blood sample and forget about it. It's the same thing with people asking me about in-vogue doping products. What do I, whose 'medical regimen' consists of a multi-vitamin and a beta-alanine tablet (a legal amino-acid, before you look it up) know about EPO or blood transfusions? No more than I know about nuclear physics. Yet if I don't give a comprehensive, eloquent answer, I'm accused of harming the sport, not being a good role model, or being an Armstrong apologist. I could stand there bullshitting all day about anti-doping and how it should change or evolve, but it would be just that, bullshit, because someone who has never doped doesn't know the first thing about anti-doping. To me, dope-testing is part of the post-race routine when I win and something I'm asked about, continually, in interviews. No more.

Having said all of this, one thing does haunt me: the risk of forgetting to update or making innocent mistakes on my whereabouts form. Out of competition testing and the obligation to log your 'whereabouts' information – input an address where you can be located for one hour every day into a central database called ADAMS – have been necessary evils since even before I turned professional. Every three months we're asked to supply our information for the following quarter of the year, which we're then allowed to update and change by phone or email. The reality in my case, with the amount of travelling that I do even when I'm not racing, is that the three-month updates are often not much more than a guess. I have to make regular amendments, which clearly makes it a perilous exercise.

I'm lucky, in a way, that I got a nasty fright very early in my career with two missed tests at the end of 2005: one because I'd mixed up my 'racing location' and 'training location' on the form, and one because I'd been packed off to race in Germany at short notice and clean forgotten to update my whereabouts. Six years later, in 2011, the Mount Etna incident and then the near miss at the Tour of Britain – caused by me foolishly delegating responsibility for my whereabouts to another person – put me on one strike and nearly two. At the end of that season I was given a further incentive not to make the same mistake again when a story appeared in the Italian newspaper, *La Gazzetta dello Sport*: CAVENDISH SKIPS A DOPE TEST. Such are the complications of keeping your whereabouts updated that probably half of the athletes registered have at least one strike against their name at any one time, but of course that's lost in the media spin. 'CAVENDISH SKIPS A DOPE TEST' implies … well, you know.

The result of all this is that I've become hyper-vigilant, you could say even paranoid. I live in terror of making another slip, so much so that I'd happily carry a GPS chip or be electronically tagged, to enable the authorities to locate me at all times. In August 2013 I attended Bernie Eisel's wedding in Austria, and was chatting to Bernie and another Team Sky rider, Christian Knees, the evening before the ceremony when I was suddenly gripped by panic: I hadn't updated my whereabouts. I had to run inside to the hotel reception, get the address, find a spot in the grounds with mobile network coverage, then send my update via SMS. It doesn't come naturally to obsess about out-of-competition testing and your whereabouts if you're not doping and aren't worried about someone turning up to take a blood or urine sample. I can only imagine that it's more of a priority when you are trying to evade or fudge the tests.

Here again, in the whereabouts system, there are big inconsistencies: three missed tests, which might be caused by something as simple and stupid as your mobile phone running out of battery, or a surprise invitation to an awards ceremony, can result in a two-year ban. That's right, two years. This, when, as I've already mentioned, a former teammate of Lance Armstrong can confess and get six months, and other cheats see their suspensions reduced to a year provided that they supply some information about what they did and how.

The other persistent frustration is the discrepancy between our sport and others. Take tennis. Five years after the UCI, the International Tennis Federation finally got its biological passport up and running in 2013. In 2011 a grand total of 21 out-of-competition blood tests were carried out in tennis, as against the 4,613 in cycling. USADA, the agency which finally nailed Armstrong, performed 19 tests on tennis players in the first three months of 2013 ... and 35 on, well, I don't know you call people who do curling. You consider this, then you hear Andre Agassi saying that 'tennis has always led the way in anti-doping' or Marion Bartoli, the 2013 women's Wimbledon champion, insisting that 'doping doesn't exist in tennis'. I don't want to pick on one sport in the way that others have singled out cycling, but how can she be so confident when, over more than a decade, Lance *alone* sailed through *hundreds* of tests?

The problem with statements like Agassi's and Bartoli's is that they perpetuate the narrative that the public has been hearing for years – namely that cycling is riddled with doping and other sports are clean. Meanwhile, at times I've felt like launching into an impassioned defence of cycling using the same vocabulary that Lance employed famously on the Champs Elysées in 2005 – maligning the 'cynics and sceptics' – but had to stop myself firstly because these words have become synonymous with Lance's cheating, and secondly because it can sound like you're protesting too much. But the layman doesn't truly realise what disparity exists between the measures in place in cycling and other sports. For example, in 2011 the UCI became the first governing body in any sport to ban all injections of even legal products aiding recovery – vitamins, sugars, enzymes, amino acids and antioxidants. There was a feeling in cycling that a 'needle culture' had been allowed to develop over several decades and anecdotal evidence suggested that legal injections were often a precursor to more serious stuff.

Some people's bodies naturally recover well, and I'm one of the lucky ones; Rob Hayles says that you can see from how quickly my wounds heal after a crash that I'm blessed in this regard. Nonetheless, even I have noticed how much harder it is to recover, day after day, on a three-week tour, with no intravenous drips. Some doctors would argue that it's even *unhealthy* to deny us this option, since we reach a state of dehydration that puts severe pressure on our kidneys and liver. Again, I'm loath to pick on tennis, but the discrepancy was brought home to me again when I heard Tim Henman, in his pundit's role on the BBC, matter-of-factly answering a question about players recovering after five-set matches and explaining that they would just use an intravenous drip. Perfectly fine, perfectly legal in that sport, but strictly forbidden for us cyclists. Even so, I welcome the needle ban: anything to ensure that the doping plague that had taken a grip of cycling doesn't return; and anything to hopefully make people realise that we're light years ahead of other sports in the war on drugs.

I know that we won't change perceptions overnight. The suspicions and questions won't go away, and those skeletons in those closets will keep on rattling. At Team Sky we had a Belgian doctor, Geert Leinders, whose earlier work with the Dutch Rabobank team has become the subject of an investigation by Belgian prosecutors, although Leinders denies any wrong-doing. This I only discovered after I'd joined the team. Did it bother me? Well, it would have if there had been any reason to suspect that he was doping me and other riders then, but there was nothing. Zilch. I saw very little of Leinders, but the impression I formed was of a relaxed, quite cultured and humorous man, into music, whose most heinous crime during the few months that I knew him was the one he committed against fashion, with his slack-waisted jeans. The last I heard the investigation hadn't concluded and, after he stopped working for Team Sky towards the end of 2012, he was going to do a history of art degree. Brad Wiggins was hauled over the coals for his supposed 'association' with Leinders in 2012, but, again, in the team, it would never have occurred to us that Geert might have been implicated in doping scandals unless we'd read the press. This is the problem you have as a rider now. Am I supposed to demand that my team sack the doctor, or distance myself from guys like Rolf Aldag, Erik Zabel, Brian Holm and Bobby Julich – all former riders and confessed dopers, all of whom have treated me brilliantly, 100 per cent professionally, and all strongly believe that you can now compete clean?

Those guys all found a way back into professional cycling and, who knows, one day so might Lance. That night in Argentina, though, as the face of a man I used to know flickered on the TV screen, and tears welled in his eyes, the only sympathy I felt was for the sport I love – not Lance Armstrong.

chapter eleven

Over the course of my seven years as a professional cyclist I have being accused of many things. Bowing to convention, though, has not been one of them.

Take any journey with a team of professional cyclists, in a plane, a train or an automobile. Look around and you'll see a group of young men doing what young men generally do: you'll see headphones, glossy magazines full of gadgets and girls in bikinis, and perhaps if you're lucky the odd newspaper (turned to the sports pages, of course).

When you understand this, there can be few surprises – or so my new Omega Pharma–Quick-Step teammates thought. On our flight to Slovakia in December for our first gathering of the 2012–13 winter, I could feel their eyes on me. I looked up to see Matteo Trentin in the seat next to me craning his neck to get a better view of what I was doing; the expression on his face was one of utter bafflement.

'*Ma che cazzo fai?*'

My Italian may not be brilliant, but I knew what that meant. 'What the fuck?'

'It's a puzzle book,' I said. 'Logic puzzles. It's training for the mind. For decision making. Helps me in sprints.'

Matteo was bewildered at first, then curious, then before long he too was hooked. Soon there wouldn't be a copy of *GQ* in sight.

For me, Omega Pharma–Quick-Step had been a natural choice as soon as I knew that I could leave Team Sky. The Belgian team's manager, Patrick Lefevere, had declared and repeatedly reaffirmed his interest in signing me during my time at HTC, much to Bob Stapleton's annoyance. So when he knew that I'd be on the market at the end of the 2012 season he quickly made an offer. Other teams proposed bigger salaries, but there were several reasons, besides Patrick's long-standing admiration, that swung the balance in his favour. One was the chance to link back up with Brian Holm and Rolf Aldag, both of whom had joined Omega Pharma–Quick-Step after the collapse of HTC. Another was my relationship with Specialized, the bikes and the company, who had supplied us at HTC and would again here. Finally, I was attracted to the history of Patrick's team, which had existed in various forms with various names since the 1990s, and which had traditionally thrived in the races that I'd dreamt about as a kid – Paris–Roubaix, the Tour of Flanders. Races for real men, real bike riders.

For every incentive to choose Omega Pharma–Quick-Step, there were also regrets about leaving Team Sky. The main one, clearly, was that the starry-eyed hopes and expectations that

I'd had a year earlier hadn't been fulfilled, while other regrets concerned what and perhaps more to the point who I was leaving behind. I had been desperate for Bernie Eisel to come with me to Omega Pharma–Quick-Step, but Bernie had also signed a three-year contract with Sky at the end of 2011 and he, unlike me, was happy enough to stay. Having said goodbye to Mark Renshaw the previous year, I'd now lost my two most important and trusted teammates within the space of 12 months.

There were at least some familiar faces, old friends at my new home. As well as Brian and Rolf, there were also former HTC riders Tony Martin, Bert Grabsch, the Velits twins and Frantisek Rabon. My first impression of the other guys in Slovakia was also unreservedly positive. It had been billed by the management as a team-building exercise, taking the form of a military-style survival camp a bit like the ones that Bjarne Riis had introduced, amid much fanfare, at CSC a decade ago. Riis's were notoriously brutal, sleepless two- and three-day ordeals in the Scandinavian wilderness; they were all about pushing limits of endurance and fostering team spirit, or, as cynics said, being seen to by the press.

Our camp in Slovakia was somewhat tamer but no doubt considerably more enjoyable at the same time. A similar comparison could be made a month later between our first real, bike-riding, training camp of the winter and the one I had attended a year earlier with Sky – though here the contrast resided more in the atmosphere than the difficulty level. The format with Omega Pharma–Quick-Step was much more like it had been at HTC or, before that, T-Mobile: Sebastian Weber had tried to tailor highly specific training programmes and drills in my first training camps there in the 2006 and 2007, and most of us had ignored him.

Here, at the first camp in Majorca before Christmas and the second one on the Costa Blanca in January, we pretty much just rode our bikes. The team physiologist, a young Belgian named Koen Pelgrim, told me one day that I was on the list to do a rig test in the lab, to which I replied that there was absolutely no point: I'd be shit because I always was in these things and the tests said absolutely nothing about my ability to win races. At first he tried to insist and said that he understood but it was his job. Eventually he gave up. This more or less summed up the low-stress, commonsense approach to most things in the team. What we lost in science and po-faced seriousness we made up for by being relaxed and having fun both on our bikes and at the hotel in the evening. Peta said that, on the phone, it was the happiest that I'd ever sounded when I'd called from a camp.

I got the sense that a few people, riders and staff, had been apprehensive about me joining the team, because of my reputation for being hot-headed or demanding. Over the next few weeks and months many would tell me that I'd surprised them; yes, I could be short-tempered if people didn't live up to the standards that I expected, but if they did I went out of my way to express my gratitude. I was also never awkward for the sake of being awkward, unlike other riders who had been my teammates in the past.

It was about being professional and a perfectionist. So when, at my first race of the year, the Tour de San Luis in Argentina, I complained about my brakes feeling spongy, that wasn't just me being a diva, something I would prove by working every bit as hard as the mechanics to find the cause of the problem and solve it. In this case, having completely stripped the brake unit down and changed the cables, we were still scratching our heads, until finally we realised that the problem was something most people wouldn't even have noticed: a tiny piece of plastic threading the brake-cable into my frame. We solved it by gluing the piece of plastic to the frame, before making a short home video to send to Specialized and show them what we'd done. I gave my equipment suppliers this kind of feedback on a regular basis. With time the smart ones had realised that I was providing information that could and often did help them to improve their product, not just kicking up a fuss.

I had added the Tour de San Luis to my programme at the end of January as a spur to keep my training up and my weight down over Christmas and the New Year, and I arrived in Argentina in good form. Leaving Sky meant that, for the first time since my junior days, I wouldn't be coached by Rod, and was instead going to try a DIY approach using my own knowledge, intuition and some of the training programmes that Rod and Tim Kerrison had given me the previous year. It was very early days but it seemed to be working: I won the first stage in Argentina, the first time in my career that I had won my first race of the season, then I was part of a team that blew the opposition away at the Tour of Qatar. I won four stages and the general classification. Friends and family said that I was unrecognisable from the person and rider that I'd been at Sky a year earlier.

After a period of good, old-school training on the Isle of Man, then another productive week at Tirreno–Adriatico, where I reinvented myself as a mountain *domestique* for my teammate Michał Kwiatkowski, I arrived at Milan–San Remo confident but cagey. I'd said in the press that, my 2009 win notwithstanding, it was a race that I would always have a chance of winning, but only in particular circumstances that were beyond my control. In the build-up to the 2009 race I'd more or less written myself off, and journalists had taken every bluffed word at face value, but in the four years since then I'd learned the hard way that Milan–San Remo really was a cruel mistress. When I said now that I didn't consider myself a favourite, I really was telling the truth.

I did at least have the considerable advantage that day of excellent form and my team's multi-pronged attack. The plan was nothing revolutionary in tactical terms, but it had the potential to lure rival teams into a fatal trap: Sylvain Chavanel, our ace *baroudeur* or breakaway specialist, would try to pull away in a group on the penultimate climb, La Cipressa, whereupon we in the main group would stop working on the pretext that we had Chava down the road. Chava, meanwhile, would also 'sit on' the break, collaborate only half-heartedly if at all, his excuse being that I was back in the peloton and that we wanted a sprint finish.

In either eventuality – whether the break stayed away or was absorbed by the bunch – we would all have saved energy and given ourselves a clear edge.

What no one had banked on, not even having seen the forecast, was weather conditions that would have made an Eskimo think twice about venturing outdoors. What began as cold drizzle in Milan turned to sleet as we left town, and then a blizzard as we neared the coast. The first and highest climb on the route, the Passo del Turchino, was completely snowbound and therefore impassable. Unable to find a suitable deviation, the organisers announced – and our *directeurs* informed us over the radio – that the race would be suspended at the 117km mark and restarted 42 kilometres up the road, the Turchino and Le Manie climbs having been removed from the route.

The last half hour or so before the stoppage was more like something from Napoleon's Moscow campaign than Milan–San Remo. No one was changing gear, it being impossible to move the chain onto cogs cloaked in a thick layer of ice. You couldn't see through the sheath of snow that had settled on your glasses, yet you couldn't take those glasses off, either, because when you did your eyes would freeze over … It was absolutely brutal, some said barbaric. On the bus my teammates and I howled in agony. Michał Kwiatkowski was shaking like a pneumatic drill. We drove towards the restart and the weather improved considerably – it was now around five degrees and the snow had turned to rain again – but some riders either hadn't recovered or weren't prepared to risk the same ordeal again. Out of my team, Tom Boonen, Niki Terpstra and Stijn Vandenbergh all announced that they were pulling out. Which was fine – if a little hard to understand for someone who had grown up on the Isle of Man, with Isle of Man weather. I shrugged, slapped some embrocation oil on my calves and thighs and went outside for the second half.

In 2009 I'd known or could have guessed that it was my day almost as soon as I hit the Capi – the sequence of three short but steep promontories which act as the gateway to the San Remo finale. Four years on, in the same place, I had the same sensation not just of power but almost of a euphoria coursing through my leg muscles. After the Capi, Chavanel guided me expertly up the side of the peloton and onto the front at the foot of the Cipressa, where it was time to execute the plan. Chava accelerated, dragging a small group with him, while I hung back and cruised up the climb.

Chava had gone over the top and down the other side when, from my point of view, everything started to unravel. First, my brakes wouldn't grip on the wet, treacherous descent of the Cipressa, then I heard our *directeur sportif*, Wilfred Peeters, imploring Chava to go harder in the break. This would have been perfectly normal had we not agreed before the race that Chava wouldn't work. My conclusion later was that Peeters didn't have a lot of faith in me, which may also have explained why he didn't put more pressure on Boonen, Vandenbergh and Terpstra to stay in the race. I didn't hold it against those guys, and I know that everything's easy with hindsight, but I believe now that I could have won that day with their help, and that I'll never have a better opportunity to repeat my 2009 triumph.

Instead, neither Chava nor I could quite pull it off. The peloton came back together, Chava latched onto another small group that attacked over the final climb, the Poggio, while the same issues with my braking made it impossible for me to join them. Chava was always going to struggle in a sprint, especially after his earlier efforts, and could only manage fourth. My friend and former teammate, Gerald Ciolek, won an unexpected victory but that brought cold – very cold – comfort.

It would be over-dramatising things to say that my honeymoon period with the new team was over, but San Remo did mark the start of a very necessary but sometimes uncomfortable period of mutual adaptation. The problems, if you can call them that, in my opinion stemmed from a culture and cycling heritage that was also the team's strength and one of the reasons that I had plumped for Omega Pharma–Quick-Step over other outfits. Simply put, both the Belgian riders and staff lived for, built their world around and couldn't see beyond the ten weeks of racing stretching from late February to the end of April: the Spring Classics. Within this period was one week that they elevated to an even higher, positively astronomical plane of importance and prestige – the eight days of what they called the 'Holy Week', book-ended by the Tour of Flanders and Paris–Roubaix.

I shared the Belgian obsession with these races, even if I was unlikely to win one, but I also quickly found out that this fixation could have a damaging effect on mentalities within the team. The young Belgian riders, I noticed in two Belgian stage races that I rode in March and April, the Three Days of West Flanders and the Three Days of De Panne, seemed to focus on the Classics (and Flanders and Roubaix in particular) almost to the exclusion of anything else. Either that or they suffered indirectly from the hysteria around these races in Belgium, which lasted for weeks and generated kilometres and kilometres of newsprint in dailies like *Het Nieuwsblad* and *Het Laaste Nieuws*. Any race that was seen to have any bearing on what would happen in Flanders or Roubaix would be dissected and discussed over pages and pages, meaning that any decent performance by a young Belgian rider would receive inordinate amounts of coverage.

None of this would have bothered me – if it hadn't affected me. Those same young Belgians who fantasised day and night about Flanders and Roubaix, desperate to see their name in *Het Nieuwsblad*, weren't fully committing in their roles as *domestiques*. Sometimes I was getting the impression that they would rather finish in 20th place, in the second group, than bury themselves to bring that group back to the front and therefore give me a chance in a sprint finish. Or, in the lead-out train, they would back off and refuse to take the necessary, calculated risks because they were afraid of crashing and jeopardising their Classics season. They were two different types of egotism – the former more to do with naked ambition, the latter with self-preservation – and, without naming names, I'd seen a version of the former at Tirreno–Adriatico and

Gent–Wevelgem, and examples of the latter at Scheldeprijs. Such a singular preoccupation with one period of the year and two races, in particular, was completely alien to me, having spent most of my career in a team, HTC, where we approached every race as if it was our last.

Matters weren't helped by what I still perceived as Wilfred Peeters' lack of confidence in me. He would invariably work to make a break succeed rather than try to bring it back in the expectation of me winning a bunch sprint. I made these points to Patrick Lefevere, to Brian and to other members of the management, and was told things would improve as soon as the Classics were out of the way. To the Belgians the end of April might as well have been the end of the season, but these guys had so much they could offer outside of the Classics. For example, when we arrived in Naples for the Giro d'Italia start in the first week of May, Julien Vermote was a 23-year-old in his third pro season that the team didn't seem to know what to do with. He would leave three weeks later having discovered – and shown me – that he could look after a sprinter in a stage race like few other riders in the peloton, and hence suddenly having found his identity as a rider.

The team as a whole in Italy brought back memories of our very best groups at HTC. Brian, who claimed to hate Italy as much as he loved Great Britain, but would change his mind after this, his first full Giro, was one of our *directeurs*; a former Italian pro named Davide Bramati or just 'Brama' was the other. If Rolf Aldag and Brian had formerly been one of the best comedy double acts in cycling, Brian and Brama, or as Davide called himself, 'cycling's Mourinho', ran them close. From the first day, when Brian came up to my room to tell me that Team Sky's Head of Technical Operations, Carsten Jeppesen, had called me 'fat', thinking that it would fire me up, the whole team just clicked. In the best, most sociable teams, riders will stay at the dinner table shooting the breeze for an hour, maybe even two after their meal. Here, not only would we do that, but instead of trotting off to bed we'd then all cram in one room to continue the conversation.

Camaraderie off the road translated into cohesion on it. I would win five stages – every sprint that I contested, including one that I had completely ruled out on the morning of the stage. That particular victory came at the end of the second week, on a beautiful but unforgiving route through the Langhe hills in Piedmont. I'd put it to Brian in the morning that the guys had ridden too hard to set up my stage win the previous day and therefore deserved a rest, and besides, there was no guarantee that I'd get over the climbs in the finale. Brian agreed, and off we went on what was going to be longest stage of the Giro at 242 kilometres. Two hours in, the break had gone and gained 13 minutes and we were happily cruising along in the bunch. Then Brian buzzed in on the radio.

'Right, guys, to the front. We're riding for a sprint today ...'

I could have throttled him but, now that he'd said it, I also couldn't opt out. The guys duly went to the front, rode like dervishes, the gap came down, and it was left to me to apply the *coup de grâce* on one of the hardest, hilliest finishes that I've ever even attempted to win on. I finished half-dead, on my hands and knees – but victorious. When Brian tried to congratulate me later, I gave him the shoulder. I was still furious at him for what he'd made me do.

That was my fourth stage win of the five and my last before a final week jammed with mountains and blighted by more bad Italian weather. The sensible decision at this point might have been to pull out and rest up for the Tour, but I never really considered that option. It wasn't only the fact that I was leading the points competition and had the chance to add the Giro's red jersey to the Tour de France *maillot vert* that I'd won in 2011 and the Vuelta a España *maillot verde* that I'd taken in 2010. I also couldn't bring myself to desert a team of riders who had already sacrificed half of their race for me, in some cases compromising the personal objectives that they'd come to Italy to pursue.

I wouldn't deny that more of the kind of weather that we'd seen at San Remo made the last week slightly less arduous than may otherwise have been the case. Climbs were airbrushed from the route or neutralised, and one entire mountain stage was cancelled entirely, depriving my main rivals of vital points. It still took something quite special on the last day – first place in two intermediate sprints and the stage win – to overhaul an 11-point deficit from Vincenzo Nibali and become the first Briton to win the points competition at the Giro d'Italia. I now also joined an even more elite group – riders who had completed a grand slam of points jerseys in all three major tours. Only Eddy Merckx, Laurent Jalabert, Alessandro Petacchi and Djamolidine Abdoujaparov had previously achieved this feat. The list perhaps would have been longer, but the Giro's excessively mountainous routes and its points scale opened the competition to a much broader range of riders than the Tour's *maillot vert,* in particular. That was why, in 2012, I'd been pipped by a climber, Joaquim Rodríguez, whereas here I'd edged out the overall Giro winner Nibali.

I had ticked another box in my checklist of lifetime ambitions, my form was fantastic, and my team at the Giro had neared perfection. The outlook had rarely if ever been brighter as I readied myself for another Tour de France … and yet that Tour was about to leave me wondering whether, at 28, my best days might have already come and gone.

Juan Antonio Flecha's omission from the Sky team had been the first hint that my 2012 Tour de France might not turn out quite the way I wanted. This time, the line-up for my first *Grande Boucle* with Omega Pharma–Quick-Step filled me with optimism. It wasn't a team of one-dimensional *rouleurs* picked solely for their ability in a lead-out train, but a collection of multi-talented riders as adept at helping me in the closing kilometres as they would be at sniffing out chances for stage wins of their own. Tony Martin exemplified that versatility: Tony was the world time trial champion yet also loved getting his hands dirty for me in a bunch sprint. The *'Panzerwagen'* – the tank – as Brian had christened him, had ridden the Tour with me three times at HTC and was the prototype of what you wanted a Tour de France teammate to be: a Terminator on the bike, a gentleman who never whinged off it. Then we had Jérôme Pineau, who I suspect had been a bit of a scally in his youth (or whatever they call a scally in Nantes) and who had confessed to thinking that I was a bit of a prat before we became teammates. A lot of French riders held that view – and Jérôme explained what it was: in races, all they ever heard me say, or the only word they could consistently make out, was 'fucking'. Or so Jérôme reckoned. He and I were joined in the team by another Frenchman, Sylvain Chavanel, Jérôme's great mate and one of the most powerful, classiest riders in the world; if ever Chavanel was in a break, the whole peloton knew that it was in for a tough day. Sylvain, like Pineau, was always smiling, always upbeat and fulfilled the same anti-depressant role that had always been Bernie Eisel's in my previous teams.

Like Jérôme, another of my teammates, the Dutchman Niki Terpstra, also had some fairly negative preconceptions about me before the start of the year – and this time the feeling was mutual. Niki was one of those guys who didn't care who he pissed off in a race, just as long as he was doing his job for his leader. This made him an absolute menace if you were riding against him, or a precious ally if he was your teammate. Peter Velits, a Slovakian who had finished third overall in the 2010 Vuelta, was far too amiable to divide opinion in the same way, but equally valuable to my sprint train. Our young Pole Michał

Kwiatkowski was similarly low-maintenance. He was one of the biggest prospects in cycling, and right from our first training camp in Slovakia Michał and I had gelled, and I'd quickly asked Patrick to change Michał's race programme and pencil him in on the shortlist for the Tour.

The last two members of the team were also the last two components of my lead-out train: Matteo Trentin and Gert Steegmans. Matteo would be the penultimate man to peel off in the last kilometre, and had also been entrusted with an even more onerous role: he was my roommate. Matteo was 23 years old, blond, drove a Fiat Punto and hailed from high in the mountains of northern Italy, where his training options were limited to left and right into the same valley, or two different ways up a huge Dolomite climb. Matteo, like Michał, hadn't been due to ride the Tour, but was finally included on my recommendation.

In the train, Matteo would precede Gert Steegmans: a giant, veteran Belgian with an enigmatic reputation. My first memory of Gert as a rider was from Scheldeprijs in 2007, where he'd been the Quick-Step team's sprinter and I'd beaten him to take my first professional race win. Nearly six years on, when I signed for the team, Gert was probably the single rider that I was most looking forward to working with. He could be loud in the bunch, he could be a clown, but he was also one of the more deep-thinking riders around. As the last man and therefore most prominent member of the train, Gert was a convenient scapegoat when things went wrong and the criticism started coming from the public, the press and even the management. Gert, though, had a quality that I needed to learn: he could take it all on the chin.

The National Road Race Championship in Glasgow the week before the Grand Départ gave me a rare opportunity and obligation to race without the support of a full-size team. This handicap, together with the tight marking to which I was also subjected at the Nationals, meant that it would take something both unusual and special to win. Four laps from the end, I supplied it by moving clear with Pete Kennaugh and Ian Stannard, both of Team Sky, and Dave Millar of Garmin, then agreeing with Dave that we would work together against the Sky riders to ensure that one of us two prevailed. The way that I finally took the win, burning off Stannard after Dave had effectively taken care of Pete Kennaugh, suggested that I was in fantastic shape for the Tour, which I would have been, had I not started to notice the first symptoms of a chest infection the day before the Nationals. It got worse over the next few days, and one of the team doctors, Helge, told me that I needed to start a course of antibiotics immediately. I replied that antibiotics always ruined form, to which he replied that it was better to ruin my form than ruin my lungs. So I started the antibiotics and prepared to fly to Corsica, where the race would begin three days later.

In the airport and on the plane, my legs and back ached, and my whole body tingled with fever. I went straight to bed on arriving at the hotel that afternoon, but was then kept up most of the night with cramps. I trained the next day and waited for the antibiotics to kick in. That night, the Thursday, was even worse. I told Helge in the morning that I might not be able to start. We talked about stopping the antibiotics, but agreed to wait another day and see how I felt on Saturday, on the morning of the first stage. Twenty-four hours later, it wasn't good: my muscles were still strangled by cramp and I was overcome with lethargy. We decided that I should start anyway and that three things might save me: the adrenaline, the simplicity of the course on that first day and the fact that I'd been careful not to talk about being ill in the press or even to anyone outside a small circle of people within the team. The Tour is a three-week game of poker, and to admit any sort of weakness or ailment is to invite your opponents to exploit it.

In the event, the most troublesome obstacle on that first stage would be not illness, not other riders, but … a bus wedged under the finish line. The story was classic fodder for TV quiz shows, but for those who didn't see it: the Orica-GreenEDGE team bus and its driver were running late, having arrived at the finish-line just half an hour or so before the race was due to arrive, and – depending on who you believed – had either been waved underneath the bridge-like structure overhanging the line or been told to stop and ignored the advice. What no one could dispute was the outcome – a bus blocking the road and panic in the road.

It had all been going so smoothly, so easily. A benign-looking course doesn't necessarily translate to a benign race, but this had been the least hairy first stage of a Tour that I could remember. With 25 kilometres to go we had taken control, with 10 to go we were building like a wave, with six to go we came to a chicane and a wall of noise from crowds banked on either side. It was at exactly that moment that I heard a voice, Brian Holm's, in my earpiece: 'Finish … three kilometres to go.' That was about all I could make out. Brian repeated, '… three kilometres to go.'

'Gert! Did you hear that?! Did he just say the finish has been moved to three kilometres to go?!' I shouted to Steegmans.

Gert said he didn't know. I got the same response from other riders from other teams. Total panic reigned for a few seconds, until Brian chimed in on the radio again, the message clearly audible this time: 'The finish-line has moved. It's at three kilometres to go now.'

Three kilometres? I looked down at my computer and saw six to go. Fu—

We had dropped back and now needed to quickly move forward as the peloton swarmed. One of the guys – might have been Tony, might have been Niki, might have been Peter – spotted an opening through the middle and tried to drag us through. Everyone made it, except me. I probed for another gap, and had finally drifted left towards the barriers and clear air when André Greipel brought down Tony Martin four positions ahead of me, causing a domino rally. In the run-up to the Tour I had been testing hydraulic brakes recently developed by the team's component supplier, SRAM, and had liked them so much that I'd decided to use them on the first stage (hence becoming the first rider ever to use hydraulic brakes at the Tour de France). Now, behind the cascade of flesh and metal, I slammed them hard and came almost to a dead stop, while those around me skidded and sprawled. The only way around the bodies was left, off the route and into a slip-road. By the time I'd finished the detour, only five or six seconds later, the peloton was disappearing over the brow of a small rise. At this exact moment there was another crackle in my ear: 'GUYS,' Brian shouted, 'the finish has been changed back. Normal finish now!'

Fu—

I tried but, as I feared, it was too late to rejoin the bunch and move into a sprinting position. Marcel Kittel, the young German who had beaten me once at the ZLM Toer in June, took the win in what turned out to be a heavily diluted sprint finish, in terms of both numbers and quality.

Even when I'd lost out in circumstances beyond my control, the frustration, the self-flagellation, the regret would usually have kicked in within a minute or two of me climbing onto the bus. In Bastia there was a further reason to rue what the press would describe the next day as a 'débâcle', a 'fiasco', even 'a farce' of a finale: with no prologue on the Tour route this year, it had been a very rare opportunity for a sprinter to take the yellow jersey. Reminding myself of this would usually have been an exercise in pure masochism, and yet here, as I sat down, unbuckled my helmet and silently stared into space, the anguish had subsided as soon as I glanced out of the window. Standing there, with Delilah in her arms, was Peta, and that was enough for everything else to fade into insignificance. Minutes later, what was now the familiar post-race commotion of Velcro shoe-straps being unfastened and the race relived through my teammates' breathless post-mortems was interrupted by the shocking appearance of Tony Martin at the top of the steps. You would have said that he'd spent the last hours wrestling sharks, not riding a bike. For a few minutes he seemed woozy but OK, then Helge went to start cleaning his wounds and Tony simply passed out. Soon Helge and the Tour doctor would be unloading him into a stretcher and taking him to hospital. That night it was already being reported – because most right-minded people had assumed – that Tony had been taken back home to Germany and was out of the Tour. In fact, when he'd woken up in the hospital, more or less the first thing he'd said to Helge was, 'I can ride tomorrow, right?' Sure enough, the next day in Bastia he'd be on the start line, wrapped like a mummy in bandages, swathed in pain. It was nuts when you thought about it: the Tour de France was probably the only sporting event on earth where you could sustain injuries like that and have completely healed by the end.

I'd finished my course of antibiotics and thought that I was improving, but even a small, easy, uncategorised climb as the route turned inland on stage two gave me a very abrupt reality-check. It was Jérôme Pineau's job throughout the Tour to keep things ticking over at the front and ensure any breakaway was within a safe, catchable distance – which was what he was doing, only I couldn't stand the pace.

'Jérôme! Slow!'

It was an instruction that Jérôme would hear a few times that day. I looked down at the digital display of my power meter and noticed to my dismay that I was barely nudging above 300 watts, the sort of power I'd usually put out without breaking sweat, yet here I was labouring. I didn't so much fear as expect the worst on the Col de Vizzavona, the first 1,000-metre climb of the Tour, and the worst was pretty bad. As I sunk through and out of the peloton like a lead weight, other riders glanced across and gawped, almost quizzically, as if to say, 'Are you taking the piss?' If only! My team stuck with me, but even sitting up and pootling along taking sips from their bottles, they were nearly leaving me behind. We finally caught and finished with a large *gruppetto*, 17 minutes behind the stage winner, Jan Bakelants.

The next day was another hilly, sinuous one along the cliffs on the west coast of Corsica, and even fully fit it would have been a push for to me contend. The good news was that I had started to feel better and that we were about to leave Corsica for the French mainland. The island had never hosted the Tour, so it had made a highly symbolic venue for the Grand Départ, and its beauty had also taken my breath away. At the same time, between the flights to get onto and off the island and the yacht that we took from the finish on day two to our hotel, it all felt a bit gimmicky. I'll always be the biggest advocate of both the Tour de France and the Giro d'Italia ... which is why I don't think the Tour needs any bells and whistles: the history, the reputation, the difficulty and the riders are enough.

Three stages in, despite the missed opportunity of taking yellow on the first day, I wasn't alarmed. I was inching back towards full health and, I had no reason to doubt, the first of several stage wins. On the morning of stage four, the team time trial, I ribbed Tony Martin, who still looked as though he'd spent our time in Corsica swimming with Jaws, about my brilliant record in team time trials in the Giro d'Italia, pointing out that I'd done two with him at Tour and never won. I don't know whether this galvanised him, or for that matter how he was still managing to ride through the pain of his injuries, but when we did practice laps that morning Tony did a passable and out-of-character impersonation of Mark Cavendish; while I stayed fairly quiet, silently purring at the smoothness of our riding and our rotations, Tony barked instructions and encouragement. I loved watching him in that mood. I also knew that, in spite of the *Panzerwagen*'s injuries, we'd blitz it and either win or get very close. We went out and set the fastest time, 25 minutes and 57 seconds, then spent a tense hour and a half in the 'hot seat' beside the finish line, watching 17 teams fail to beat our mark. At ten to four, still glued to the TV monitor, we held our breath as Orica-GreenEDGE whipped around the last corner into the finishing straight, came over the line and stopped the clock on … 25 minutes and 56 seconds. They had beaten us by 75 hundredths of a second – or the difference between me being fully recovered or only 90 per cent, Tony having one less nasty wound, or one of us nailing a corner or going wide. And people wonder why 'marginal gains' are so important.

Most riders would agree that you can do as many Tours de France as you like, but it's not necessarily going to qualify you as an authority on major French tourist attractions or areas of outstanding natural beauty. The stages become numbers, or days of the week, and the 27 regions and 96 *départements* get lumped either into one of the main mountain ranges or the paradise, at least in my mind, that is any landscape without a major mountain. Years later you realise that your memory retains a full, pin-sharp film reel of certain stages and their setting, but has discarded others to the cutting-room floor.

It's the same with all races. We remember what's marked us, marked our career, perhaps even changed its course. Stage five, rolling west out of Cagnes-sur-Mer towards Marseille 228 kilometres away, appeared to represent nothing more complicated or nostalgia-inducing than an opportunity to win my stage. Instead, it turned into a odd sort of journey down memory lane. First, after 140 kilometres we bowled into a town whose name I vaguely recognised, through streets that were also vaguely familiar. Then I finally twigged: we were approaching and about to ride through what had been the finish line of stage two in 2009, the first of the six stages that I'd won that year. As we did, a broad grin spread across my face as I announced to everyone within earshot: '2009 Tour de France. Stage two. I won here.' Good job that it was a hot day and everyone was wearing shades so that I couldn't see the rolling eyes.

The next attack of *déjà vu* came a bit later and was more significant. I'd seen the name of the last climb of the day, the

Col de la Gineste, on the route-book, and thought nothing of it, even when Jérôme Pineau talked about how it was a travesty that it wasn't classified, how it was much harder than the preceding fourth-category climb. As we saw the road swirling up the cliffs above us, like smoke out of a chimney, it all came back: I'd done this climb on my very first day as a fully fledged pro, in GP La Marseillaise in 2007. Not only that, but I could remember being absolutely mystified as to how one of the Brits in the race, Jez Hunt, was up the road, on the attack, on such rugged terrain. I'd put this to another British rider, my teammate at the time, Roger Hammond.

'Cav,' he'd chuckled, 'this is nothing. Not for professional racing, anyway.'

I think at that point, in 2007, I started to panic. Six years on, my team swarmed around me, as per our plan, and practically carried me over and down the other side, until the break was absorbed and we bombed down into the boulevards of Marseille. Trentin went early, so early that I thought we'd blown it, but he held on into the last corner where Gert took over. Gert is a huge hulk of a man, very fast and very explosive, the combination of which had provided some spectacular lead-outs but also posed me a fair few problems since the start of the year. Here, with 200 to go, he was moving so fast that it was tricky to even move around and kick past him. Finally, my nose was in front, I'd unglued everyone from my wheel and taken a relatively easy win, despite not having brilliant legs.

So far, so good. One sprint, one win. Two more back-to-back opportunities now awaited us, but, unbeknownst to me at the time, so did one of my hardest weeks to date as a Tour de France rider. By the end of it *L'Équipe* would be running a sort of obituary of my sprint domination with the headline CAVENDISH NO LONGER REIGNS. The worst of it was that, deep down, without even really admitting it myself, and maybe for the first time in my career, I'd started to wonder whether they might be right.

I don't like excuses and have never had much time for people or bike riders who make them. Yet as that hardest week unfolded I could find and point to factors that in some way mitigated the near misses that, it being me, were now invariably described as 'failures'.

In Montpellier on stage six there were undoubtedly a couple of issues. One was my bike – or 'that fucking bike!' as I referred to it on the bus after the stage, my booming voice easily audible to the scores of fans and journalists huddled around the bus. I had four or five bikes at the Tour, and I'd sensed that something might be wrong with this one on the second day in Corsica. Yes, my legs had felt heavy, listless, but that still didn't seem to fully explain why I was struggling so badly. I'd wondered whether someone had shunted me on the first day and slightly damaged the bike, cracking the frame or a wheel and making them feel spongy. I'd asked the mechanics to strip it down and check it out. Meanwhile I had ridden stages three, five and was 40 kilometres from the end of stage six on a spare when I came down at a roundabout.

The team car stopped, the mechanic handed me a new machine ... or so I thought until, our radios having let us down and left me chasing without any teammates, I realised to my horror that I'd been given the same, spongy bike from stage two. It either hadn't been changed or hadn't been fixed, hence the 'that fucking bike!' diatribe.

My mood wasn't helped by the fact that we had also gone too early again, duped by the stampede of general classification contenders and their teams that was now a daily occurrence. The conventional wisdom was that by staying at the front they would avoid crashes. In reality, it was more dangerous than ever up there, with more and better sprint teams sniffing around than in all of my previous Tours. Our problem was getting sucked into the frantic, stop–start chaos of it, losing patience and confidence in the timings we'd discussed before the stages. If one guy went too early or too hard, that could compromise everything. I wouldn't ever criticise the guys if I felt that they were committed, and they had certainly been that in Montpellier. At the same time, I could also tell myself that the combination of the damaged bike, the chase after my crash and the imperfect lead-out had contributed as much to my defeat as the bloke who had beaten me – in this instance, André Greipel.

It's rare for me to be beaten in a sprint and not immediately atone the next day. In Albi, on stage seven, I didn't even get the opportunity: Peter Sagan and Cannondale unleashed hell on a second-category climb midway through another blisteringly hot and fast stage and that was me kaput. Sagan duly won the stage and left me looking at an already daunting 105-point deficit on the points classification.

Two days in the Pyrenees took my mind off my sprinting and onto the fight for survival. And on stage nine to Bagnères-de-Bigorre it was quite literally a fight. Early in the stage an Euskaltel rider swerved in front of me, I locked on the brakes, stalled, and shunted Geraint Thomas. I apologised and Gee didn't make any fuss but from over my shoulder I could hear, even with my limited Spanish, what I knew was an expletive-laden tirade. I looked around. It was Ruben Lobato, another Euskaltel rider. Further angry words were exchanged, his again in Spanish, then Lobato decided to communicate in a more universal language: physical violence. He slapped me, sending my glasses flying off my face, and I swung back. All this was going on while we were still on our bikes, still moving: we were a couple more lusty blows away from having a punch-up in the middle of the peloton. Luckily, there were no *commissaires* watching and no TV cameras. We were probably fortunate, too, that one of the elder statesmen in the peloton, Stuart O'Grady, stepped in to break us up.

That night, after the stage, buses were waiting to take the riders to Tarbes airport, where we'd catch a plane to Nantes for the first rest-day of the race. And which team was sharing our bus? Euskaltel, of course. I took the chance to explain to their *directeur sportif*, Igor González de Galdeano, who said Lobato was young and naïve but that he'd have a word. He also mumbled something about how it was in everyone's interests to get on, because we'd be in trouble if the *commissaires* saw us fighting.

'Hang on, you're forgetting something,' I said. '*He* punched me, totally unprovoked.' Usually when I'm in the wrong I'm the first to admit it, even if hours and days might have to pass before I do, but I wasn't going to apologise for retaliating when someone slapped me in the face at 40 kilometres per hour.

The first rest-day, and the chance to spend time with Peta, Finn and Delilah, was the best possible distraction for 24 all-too-short hours. Then we were straight into some of the most challenging days of my Tour de France career. When the route had been unveiled nine months earlier my eyes had lit up on seeing the second week, with three probable sprint finishes in four days.

But while I got the sprint finishes I had hoped for, I couldn't say the same for the results.

On stage ten into Saint-Malo my defeat to Kittel would have been headline-worthy enough, had the finish not been notable for other reasons. Kittel's teammate, the Dutch rider Tom Veelers, had let his head droop and stopped looking where he was going as he finished his lead-out, veered right into my line and into my body with 300 metres to go. In the impact I stayed upright but lost momentum, while Veelers had crashed spectacularly in the middle of the road. Immediately fingers were pointed at me, mainly because, having concentrated on the frames immediately before and during the collision, the TV analysts generally neglected to mention that the road veered left *after* Veelers' fall at exactly the same angle that I had taken.

I had then, admittedly, compounded the damage by getting shirty with a journalist who shouted above the scrum outside our bus: 'Mark, are you to blame?'

How shirty? Enough to pull the voice recorder out of his hand – confiscate it, if you like – and only hand it back a couple of seconds later, after the realisation of how this would play in the morning papers had rushed to my head.

It didn't look great, I'll admit. There were better ways of diverting attention away from me, the crash and another missed opportunity to win a stage. Any journalists who hadn't rushed to our team bus at the finish had waited for Veelers, and their questions had the effect of stoking his anger. I got hold of his number that night and called him with the intention of apologising and defusing things, despite not believing that I'd been in the wrong, but Veelers was having none of it.

'You can come and apologise to my face,' he said. To me, this was him starting to milk it.

If Veelers' aim was to get people on his side and turn them against me, the boos that greeted me as I rolled onto the time trial course the next day confirmed that it had worked. Fans were still jeering – and had been since the start of my ride – when, approximately halfway around the course, a shower of warm liquid flew horizontally across my path, dousing my skin suit, helmet and sunglasses, and, worst of all, splashing my tongue and lips. On the Tour you're sprinkled or soaked with water or beer at some point every day, but having urine thrown at me was a shocking, repulsive first.

Really, I just wanted to cry. Or stop. Back in 2009, in a Tour time trial in Annecy, a British fan had heckled me on a climb – something along the lines of 'Cavendish, get up off your arse.' I'd turned and shouted something back at him, and there, too, had been tempted to get off. Here I was too despondent, too upset to be angry. In the hour or two after I'd crossed the line, got back to the bus and told the team and some journalists what had happened, members of the team staff, Peta and my manager had all talked about taking some kind of action, getting the race organisers involved, maybe even the police.

I told them that we should just forget it; I didn't want sympathy or justice, I just wanted the whole thing to end. It was the feeling that I'd had in 2010, when I sat on the bus in Reims, towel over my head, stomach churning like a washing machine, the world seemingly collapsing around me. What had troubled me most was that it hadn't been just that one idiot, which I often got somewhere along the course at the Tour, but so many people along the route booing that the noise had accompanied me from the start ramp to the finish line.

That afternoon, back at a nearly empty team hotel on an industrial state outside Saint-Malo, the whole experience had left me exhausted, sickened and shell-shocked. The news that Tony Martin had won the time trial brought some solace, but in quiet moments that evening the sights, sounds and, worst of all, rancid taste of that afternoon flooded my thoughts. Every rider that I had seen that day, and every rider that I would discuss it with over the next two or three days, would agree that Veelers' crash the previous day had not been my fault. The *commissaires* had also exonerated me. Without wanting to sound egotistical, I could see that the press had been all over it because the 'Bad Boy Cavendish' storyline was one of their favourites. Veelers might have been under the misapprehension that they were genuinely outraged, genuinely sympathised with him, which perhaps they did a bit … but they were mainly preoccupied with what it said about me and my Tour. Was this not, they had asked, yet more evidence of me slowing down and resorting to unfair tactics to compensate? Then there had been the incident with the journalist's Dictaphone, a massive media-relations own goal on my part, although admittedly not quite as dramatic as the papers and TV reports had made out. This all explained the public's reaction but didn't lessen the blow. Popularity wasn't something that I'd ever necessarily craved – but unpopularity wasn't something that I enjoyed, either.

The next day something unprecedented happened: led out perfectly by Gert Steegmans, I was outgunned, out-sprinted and outclassed by Marcel Kittel on the finishing straight in Tours. I had always said that the day when I had good form, a decent lead-out, no physical or mechanical problems and yet was still beaten – that would be the time to start attaching some credence to the hysterical inquests that the press conducted after every one of my defeats. I had said it while never really believing that the day would come, not for a few years anyway, and yet here it apparently was.

I was racking my brains for a reason, an excuse, an alibi, but this time could find none that was sufficient to explain the loss. Yes, I had been ill early in the race, yes, I had felt 'twisted' on the bike ever since my crash in the first week, and, no, my condition wasn't exceptional, but even this aggregation of marginal losses shouldn't have put me behind Kittel. Unless, that was, the press were right, and the German Dolph Lundgren lookalike and sound-alike really was now the Master of the Universe when it came to sprinting.

The only way to put things right was to restore what I still hoped was the natural order and do it immediately, the next afternoon on the stage to Saint-Amand-Montrond. This was a stage that had had me licking my lips for reasons beyond the relatively flat route profile: we, like other teams, knew that we would be racing on roads that were exposed, windy and therefore ripe for echelons – the game of cycling snakes and ladders that could be used to split the peloton by strong riders or teams who knew how to use those gusts to their advantage. In the crudest, most simplistic possible terms, echelons happened when a team or group of strong riders attacked with the wind gusting hard from one side; by fanning diagonally across the road towards the wind direction and rotating quickly and cohesively, they could condemn the riders at the bottom of the line to a place in the gutter, in the wind, and in imminent danger of losing contact. Once one of those riders lost the wheel – or was deliberately shut out by a 'ticket collector' placed at the back of the line to decide who was allowed into the echelon – there was no way back. It was a fine art that demanded strength, timing, nous and balls; at Omega Pharma–Quick-Step we were considered experts.

In the days that followed what became a famous stage, there would be all sorts of fanciful, verging on folkloric stories about code words devised by Wilfred Peeters and plans concocted the night before by our team and the Dutch squad, Belkin. In reality, our attack was a spur-of-the-moment decision, naturally informed by our prior knowledge of the course. Gert Steegmans had wanted to go even before we dropped the bomb, inside the first 50 kilometres of the stage; Gert had even started pulling away when Tony Martin shouted that it was too early and we should wait. Not long later, though, we plunged the detonator and blew the race apart. Kittel was among the many, many riders – over half of the peloton – left grovelling in the gutter. They would either have to ride faster than our group or wait for a change in the wind to repair the damage. Neither was going to happen.

For 70 kilometres we pounded the pedals and the gap kept growing. Then, with around 30 kilometres to go, the message from the team car was that the winds were about to get even stronger. All day, Alberto Contador's Saxo Bank team had been freeloading on our work, telling us that they didn't want to help with the pace-making, yet it was they who now suddenly stepped on the gas to whittle the group down even further and distance the race leader, Chris Froome. As 13 riders started to pull away, I watched Michał Kwiatkowski in front of me try, try, try to be the 14th, and ultimately lose the wheel of the rider ahead of him. I now had a choice to make: to stick or twist, stay or go.

I went, performing my fastest, hardest sprint of the Tour to bridge the gap and join the front group.

Of the 14 now sure to contest the stage win, we had three – Sylvain Chavanel, Niki Terpstra and yours truly. The only rider even remotely likely to challenge me in a sprint was Peter Sagan of the Cannondale team, but Niki had an idea: he would attack with just over a kilometre to go, Sagan's sole teammate in the group would have to close the gap, whereupon Chavanel would come up behind with Sagan on his wheel and me on Sagan's. Chava would then peel off at 400 metres to go and leave Sagan in the wind, in the jaws of our trap. We executed the plan almost to the letter.

It was my 25th Tour stage win, which lifted me to joint third in the all-time league table, alongside André Leducq and behind only Bernard Hinault and Eddy Merckx. It was perhaps the first one of those 25, however, for which I'd had to race, *really* race. Maybe a successful rematch with Kittel would have comforted my ego, marked my territory once again, but that could wait for the Champs Elysées. A win was a win – and this one was pretty memorable.

Before Paris, the Arc de Triomphe, the Eiffel Tower and a thousand other Tour de France clichés slid into view, the final week of the race had consisted of huge Alpine climbs, oodles of suffering, one time trial and two bits of unexpected but welcome news.

The first very pleasant surprise came on stage 14, where we'd set out for a sprint and got one ... but for my roommate, Matteo Trentin, and not me. I was so proud that afternoon. Conventional wisdom stated that, at 24, one Grand Tour in 2013 was more than ample for Matteo, yet he'd finished the Giro in May and put his hand up to do the next less than two months later. His victory in Lyon was made even sweeter by the advice that I'd asked Bramati to pass on as he drove past the peloton and up to Matteo. I reminded Brama that it was one of those rare, very long finishing straights where you could see the line from two kilometres, and this created an optical illusion which would dupe the other guys in the break and make them sprint too early; Matteo was to ignore them at all costs, look only at the distance markers and launch his sprint at exactly 250 metres to go. Brama had passed it on and Matteo had listened, as he always did. He had made huge contributions to many of my victories in 2013, so I was now delighted to have had some input in this, the most prestigious result of his career to date. What had I told him in the plane to Slovakia the previous November? Puzzle books. Decision making. Train the mind, not just the legs.

The second revelation as far as I was concerned in the Alps, after Matteo's win, was something that happened to catch my eye in Gap on the morning of stage 18. Ever since stage six to Montpellier, I'd felt somehow misaligned, wonky on the bike, and had attributed the discomfort to one or possibly both of two things: the after-effects of that fall and/or occasional, recurring biomechanical issues which I believed dated back to my dental surgery in the winter of 2009–10. My *soigneur*, Aldis, had been working hard throughout the Tour to loosen and massage out the twinge in my gluteal muscles, but I was still shifting and twisting in the saddle as I pedalled. Tony Martin sat behind me in the bunch one day and said I was riding as though I had ants in my shorts.

It wasn't that, and now, in Gap, I belatedly realised what the issue might have been: I'd been riding for days with one pedal crank longer than the other. On one side the crank was 170mm, like I always used, but on the other it was 172.5mm. I couldn't believe it. I was lucky that I wasn't going to finish the Tour with one leg 2½ centimetres longer than the other! There were no doubt other reasons for my legs lacking bite – elasticity, speed in the four true bunch gallops that I'd contested to date – but this certainly could not have been helping.

Matteo's victory, added to my two stages, and Tony Martin's time trial win nonetheless already made the team's Tour a success, but I had an unbeaten record to defend on the Champs, a score to settle and a reputation as the world's best sprinter to restore. I was nervous that day, but then I always am before the Champs. This year, the wait before the stage start would be particularly long and so even more tense, the race organiser, ASO, having decided to celebrate the conclusion of the 100th Tour by finishing at dusk.

We didn't leave from Versailles until nearly six in the evening, and wouldn't arrive on the Champs for the first of our ten laps until nearly eight.

Barring accident, the Tour was going to be won overall by Chris Froome. I was delighted for Chris: I felt that he'd been unfairly criticised in 2012 for what were portrayed in some quarters as treacherous tactics, namely 'attacking' Brad in the Alps and Pyrenees, but which were in fact nothing more than evidence of Chris's naivety. Chris had grown up in Kenya and South Africa, been educated at a Johannesburg boarding school, and had a life story that most of us at Team Sky couldn't vaguely relate to, and yet it was hard to imagine how anyone could dislike him. My first memory of racing with Chris was from the 2006 Commonwealth Games, where he hadn't particularly stood out, and then we had both also competed in the Under 23 world championship road race that year in Salzburg. With one big difference: whereas I had just rocked up in my Team GB tracksuit and got on the plane, Chris – riding for Kenya – had had to pose as a representative of their federation in emails to the UCI, and then as a *directeur sportif* in the organisers' briefing on the eve of the race. That summed up Chris: he seemed incredibly innocent but also had a determination that, ultimately, I think, he used to channel whatever frustration lingered after the 2012 Tour into 2013.

Without the pressure of one must-win last sprint, Chris would no doubt enjoy the Champs more than I could. The first nine of the ten laps, as always, were witheringly fast but relatively uneventful, despite me puncturing on circuit number two and stopping for a wheel-change under the Arc de Triomphe. Alas, that wasn't the omen that I'd hoped; having deliberately moved off Steegmans' wheel and onto Greipel's as we came through the Place de la Concorde with 400 metres to go, I thought about going for a long one, hesitated, then couldn't pick up enough momentum on the bumpy right side of the road to overhaul Kittel *or* Greipel. The three of us all finished within centimetres of each other, but the photo-finish spoke unequivocally: I had lost, yet again, to Kittel, had even lost out for second place to Greipel, and in the process lost my 100 per cent Champs Elysées record and a little faith in myself. Never before had I experienced this sense of anticlimax, the weird juxtaposition of relief and elation at finishing the Tour, coupled with the despair of failing to win the last stage. Never before had I ridden past the gap in the barriers through which the winner was ushered towards the podium. Never before had I come across the line and glimpsed the Arc de Triomphe through the gloomy tint of defeat.

At that moment I would gladly have been teleported to anywhere else in the world: anywhere but the Champs, any place where I didn't feel compelled to smile and be happy because, you know, I'd just finished the Tour de France and everyone else was grinning. Despite it having gone ten at night, and despite only having finished third, I still had the obligatory dope-test to complete before I could go anywhere. I duly put my bike down, trudged though the door of the mobile dope-control booth and provided the urine sample. I was all done up and ready to leave when the testing official informed me that I'd only given them 75 millilitres and they needed 90. I would now have wait until I could supply the missing 15 millilitres. It took an hour, drinking enough water to sink a small ship.

I finally stepped back out into darkness at nearly midnight. Immediately I felt all despondency lift not because acceptance or comprehension had set in, but because my family was there to greet me. Little Delilah, in her mum's arms, didn't know about the Tour de France, didn't care – she just wanted to see her daddy.

She stretched out an arm, let out a gurgle, and at that moment her daddy didn't care about the Tour de France, either.

epilogue

If you live on the Isle of Man and have been sentenced to jail, the building that you'll inevitably call home is a grey, star-shaped structure beside an RAF airbase in the north of the island.

It was a place that I'd occasionally passed on bike rides but, needless to say, never expected to see from the inside. That, though, changed one day in the spring of 2010.

A few months earlier, I'd got the news as I waited at Frankfurt airport for a connecting flight to the Tour of Missouri: Andy, the younger brother who had once also been my training partner, but in recent years had gradually become a stranger, had been arrested on drugs offences and was facing time in prison. In April 2010 he stood in a courtroom and waited for a judge to deliver his verdict. The judge spoke: the defendant was guilty on four charges and sentenced to six years in prison.

When I'd heard about the arrest, my predominant emotion had been anger, but that had soon passed and been replaced by concern. In the same period, my friend Jonny Bellis had almost lost his life in a motorcycle accident, and the ordeal that his parents endured in the days, weeks and months that followed had given me a wake-up call: as my cycling career had progressed, I'd become more and more self-absorbed and less and less attuned to what was happening in my family's life. Andy going to jail was painful for all of us, but it was also an opportunity for me to help bring us closer together.

As soon as his prison sentence began, Andy had started writing me letters and we'd spoken on the phone. It took a couple of months, but we then arranged my first visit. I was nervous, naturally I suppose, when I pulled up that day in the car park, walked over to the gatehouse, gave my name and who I was there to see. When I was finally shown into the visiting area, Andy was waiting for me with arms spread wide. It was like the last few years hadn't happened.

We talked that day like we'd never talked before. About everything. Like brothers should. The hour flew by. A few weeks later I was back again, and Andy was doing great: every time I visited, in fact, he'd learned a new skill, got a new qualification, in some way moved forward. He finally did his GCSEs, taught himself to play the piano, then the guitar, then he was writing songs. I started to think, and still believe now, that it was the best thing that could have happened to him. He was finally released after three years, not six, on good behaviour.

Andy was anxious about getting out, not least because he'd got married young and had a wife waiting for him. He'd been a joiner before going in and was lucky when he was released to find a guy who had also done time and could offer him the same kind of work, to help put him back on track. That's one advantage of living on a small island like the Isle of Man – people tend to look out for each other. Andy seems determined to take his second chance and is applying himself much more now than he ever did before. It's nice, for me, to see that he no longer takes his life for granted, just like I no longer take my brother and my parents for granted.

Obtuse though it may seem, this all helps to explain why Delilah's tiny outstretched hand wiped away all of my disappointment on the Champs Elysées. Cycling and my career were, *are* more important than ever – but they're important because of what they mean to my family. Every time I climb on to my bike now, I do it for them and their future. While I had always known that I was emotional, a big softy double-wrapped in alpha male, I would also never have believed how becoming a parent and discovering the real meaning of unconditional love would transform me and the way I view the world.

Of course this doesn't mean that losing a sprint won't still eat me alive and make my insides crawl. That was exactly how I felt on the Champs until the second I stepped out of that doping control to be greeted by Peta, Finn and Delilah. That night we and the whole team went with the sponsor for a plush, end-of-Tour celebration dinner, had a laugh and a joke and a drink like everyone else, but I still couldn't pretend that I was satisfied with my two stage wins. On the journey home the next day and for the next few weeks, in fact, the memory of the sprints that I'd lost would prod, pursue and preoccupy me. Even after finding out in Gap that my cranks had been uneven and piecing together everything else that could possibly have hindered me in those sprints, I still couldn't, wouldn't rest until I knew for sure this was how it was going to be now – I would be fast, sometimes still the fastest, but no longer emphatically faster than all the rest.

The only way to test the theory was to get back on my bike and back to racing. The Tour of Denmark started ten days after the Tour de France and gave me the answer I needed, the answer I was hoping for, but the answer that I was too afraid to expect: all week I felt like a distant, far superior relation of the rider that I'd been in that Tour, with a different level of zest in my legs, a different speed and a different fitness. On the traditional, race-ending stage to Frederiksberg in the suburbs of Copenhagen, I felt quicker, stronger, more agile than I had even when winning on the same finish line 12 months earlier, and before that in 2007. Maybe there *was* life in the old, 28-year-old dog yet.

Over the course of the week in Denmark, in fact, I had finally realised what the problem at the Tour had been. It was the antibiotics that I'd been taking at the start – they always knackered me, but only after I'd stopped taking them and for a week, in some cases a fortnight, after that. It had happened in the spring of 2012, and it had happened now in the summer of 2013. At the Tour I simply hadn't been myself. It had been the first time in my career that I had not found form somewhere on the route of the Tour de France.

This, then, was all very reassuring, but as I write a few weeks later, I'm not kidding myself, either: my best years as a sprinter are more likely to be behind than in front of me. This, at least, is in terms of what my God-given speed will allow me to do, even if, over the next few years, I discover and develop ways to eke even more out of that innate ability. After the 2013 Tour, even accounting for the antibiotics and their effects, I had already decided that 2014 may be the year when, for the first time, I have to dedicate substantial time and energy to working on my sprint in training. I'm not old yet, and it'll be a few years before natural decay robs me of my speed, but the more seasons you race as a professional cyclist, the more your body is being conditioned to ride at relatively low intensities over long periods of time, several hours a day. This is helpful in one sense, as sprinting is also a test of freshness, and as the years go by your body adapts itself to these drawn-out, multiple-hour efforts. Unfortunately, it also means that you're gradually losing brute velocity.

Another important consideration, of course, is your opponents. You can never legislate for the emergence of a once-in-a-generation talent, and it may be that, in the second half of my career, a nemesis comes along to ruin all of my plans and take my records. Could that rider be Marcel Kittel? Who knows? At the moment he's a very fast, above all very powerful rider against whom I'm still pretty confident in a head-to-head drag race. It's not for me to point out, but a few shrewd observers did remark after the Tour that I had won four stages out of 14, aged 23, in my second Tour, whereas this year he won four out of 21, at age 25. Whatever happens over the next few years, I do know that he's a lovely guy and a fantastic advert for sprinting and cycling. I just hope that, one day soon, the way he defends his sport and his transparency about anti-doping is rewarded with some positive coverage at home in Germany.

If it's not other riders, judging by the way professional cycling has evolved in recent years, it may be race organisers who end not only my reign but the opportunity for any sprinter to take his place among the crowned heads of the sport. Television rules, we know, and these days so do social networks. The message being sent from armchair viewers to race organisers on Twitter, in particular, is that sprints are boring and more climbs are what is required. The Vuelta a España now finishes up a mountain every other day, the Giro d'Italia is similar; even the Tour de France has cut down on the number of stages likely to yield bunch gallops. Sprints and sprinters are being phased out, or at least marginalised, and it's because when people say they're 'boring', what they really mean is that they don't understand them. There's also a huge misconception, a blatant failure to acknowledge the evidence lurking behind those calls for more mountains, more summit finishes; *they* are more boring because the Riccardo Riccòs, the Leonardo Piepolis, the Lances – riders who would attack at the bottom of an Alpine climb and solo to the finish – those riders are gone and we all know why.

What we're left with is a cleaner sport, but one that's much more conservative, with riders making moves much later in stages because they're not physically capable of mimicking their doped-up predecessors. Hence, races peppered with climbs and major tours laden with summit finishes will generally end in disappointment … for the fans, as well as for exponents of what I still consider to be my noble art, sprinting.

One day, who knows, I might be able to influence these things in a different capacity. I'd love to run my own team, or perhaps poacher will turn gamekeeper and I, the 'Bad Boy' sprinter, the supposed scourge of the cycling establishment, will end up behind a desk drawing up plans for cycling's future. Before you run for cover, that's still a long way off, and there are still plenty of boxes left to tick on that list of things to do, races to win and records to break before I retire. One thing my experience at Team Sky in 2012 certainly taught me, and will remain as a guiding principle as long as I'm still riding at the top level: the Tour de France is my *raison d'être* as a cyclist, the fulcrum of everything that I do, and something that I shouldn't and won't sacrifice ever again.

'Legacies' are for old legs whose days of winning sprint finishes are long gone, but I can at least begin to think about how I'd like to be remembered. A few words on a mucky stone, maybe draped with some old cycling jerseys, should say it all: Mark Cavendish, cyclist, Tour de France lover and fighter, former world champion and, above all, family man.

acknowledgements

Mark would like to express his gratitude to the following people, invaluable contributors either to the execution of this book or to the story at its heart:

Delilah, my angel and the centre of my universe.

Peta, the woman who changed my life and continues to make it better every day with her love and support.

Finnbar, my step-son, who embraced and accepted me to the point of getting interested in cycling!

The family whose love has been unfaltering, even if its target has sometimes been hard to reach.

Simon Bayliff, who changed my life professionally, and everyone else at Wasserman.

Rod, who at times has been caught in a tug o' war, but whose loyalty has remained unwavering and inspirational.

Patrick Lefevere for giving me the opportunity to ride for a fantastic Omega Pharma–Quick-Step team.

Andrew Goodfellow and Liz Marvin at Ebury, and David Luxton at David Luxton Associates.

Daniel Friebe, without whose patience and persistence this book could never have come into being.

Rob Hayles, for his professionalism, his humour and his inability or unwillingness to break a partnership born on that incredible 2005 day in Los Angeles.

Finally, the national and trade teammates who have earned the victories, the records and the accolades every bit as much as the cocky Manxman who was first across the line.